WITHDRAWN

RADICAL E

RADICAL E

FROM GE TO ENRON—
LESSONS ON HOW TO RULE THE WEB

JOEL KURTZMAN AND GLENN RIFKIN

3/02

John Wiley & Sons, Inc.
New York • Chichester • Weinheim • Brisbane • Singapore • Toronto

ISBN 0-471-41047-0

Printed in the United States of America.

10 9 8 7 6 5 4 3 2 1

To my wise and thoughtful sweetheart, Karen
JOEL KURTZMAN

To my Janie, sweet inspiration
GLENN RIFKIN

ACKNOWLEDGMENTS

A book such as this one could never reach completion without the extraordinary efforts of a lot of people. The authors wish to express deepest gratitude to all of them. In particular, we want to thank George Harrar for his wisdom and input, and without whom this book would not have been completed. We would also like to thank our partners and colleagues at PricewaterhouseCoopers for their specific comments, knowledge, and experience, particularly William G. Dauphinais, Roger Lipsey, Saul Berman, and Dan Lyle.

We would also like to thank Lawrence Alexander and Airie´ Dekidjiev of John Wiley & Sons for their faith and generous support. Thanks also to Jessica Noyes at Wiley for guiding the information flow back and forth.

Thanks as well to the many executives and managers in our case study companies who generously gave their time and insights forming the foundation of Radical E. In addition, we would like to acknowledge the following people for their input along the way: Sam Hill, Laureen Rowland, Amiel Kornel, David Lavin, Tom Nutile, Cathy Levendoski, Eric Thode, Tiffany Freeman, Angelika McClelland, Ryndee Carney,

Patrick Morrissey, Kathleen Colan, Jeff DeMarrais, James Pomeroy, and Linda Rutherford.

We would also like to express heartfelt thanks to Helen Rees for helping to bring this book together and for her staunch support all along the way.

Glenn Rifkin would like to thank Benjamin, Laura, Cameron, and his incredible family for their love and support. Joel Kurtzman would like to thank Karen, Katie, and Eli for their strong and enduring support.

CONTENTS

Acknowledgments   vii

INTRODUCTION
A Radical Start   1

CHAPTER 1
The New Rules   5

CHAPTER 2
GE Plastics—Making the Internet Part of the Culture   25

CHAPTER 3
Enron—Redefining Yourself through New Markets   47

CHAPTER 4
Victoria's Secret—It's the Brand, Offline and Online   63

CHAPTER 5
Nortel—Agility, Not Speed, Fuels Success   81

CHAPTER 6
David Bowie—An Interactive Community That Rocks   99

CHAPTER 7
GM—Finding a Catalyst for Shaking Tradition   115

CHAPTER 8
Southwest Airlines—Simplicity Wins, Complexity Confuses   139

CHAPTER 9
Progressive—Innovation Driven by Pragmatism   157

CHAPTER 10
Staples—Multiple Channels Mean Repeat Customers   175

CHAPTER 11
Get Radical Now   195

Index   201

INTRODUCTION

A Radical Start

Sitting in Leslie Wexner's office at corporate headquarters in Columbus, Ohio, we asked him what he thought about the Internet and its impact on Victoria's Secret. At 63, Wexner is chairman of The Limited, Inc., and Intimate Brands, Inc. He is a legendary merchant who built an empire of retail brands from a single Limited store in 1963.

Victoria's Secret has made a major commitment to e-business, so Wexner's response was surprising. "I think the technology and innovation are important," Wexner said in a quiet voice. "But I like to think about things in a historic sense because it balances me out. People interested in Internet technology tend to see it as the only invention the world has ever seen. My response is, 'The invention of the steam engine was really more important because in the history of man, no one could move faster than a man or horse could move. But the steam engine made locomotives and ships go ten times faster than a horse, and they could run endlessly without getting tired. That really changed the world.'"

Wexner was not being coy. He talked about the transformation in retailing that resulted from the jet airplane, the credit card, and even air conditioning. "A global economy and globalization arguably are more influenced by jet planes than they are by e-commerce," he said. "Imagine the interconnection the Internet allows; but if we were still moving on sailing ships and horses, it wouldn't matter much."

As you will see, Wexner's perspective on business history played a vital role in his company's e-business strategy. To us, Wexner's insight did not seem stodgy and dated. Just the opposite. It is the embodiment of why we called this book Radical E, not just E. And while, as you will read, there are many characteristics that make a company radical, the ability to maintain perspective during the past few tumultuous years is a key to Radical E. In a medium like the Internet, which is inextricably tied to speed, it is the counterintuitive outlook of a radical like Wexner to refuse to get caught up in the hype. Victoria's Secret moved quickly but didn't career wildly into the e-business morass.

In fact, few innovations in recent business history have promised more but delivered less than e-business. Big-company executives have scuffed their brogues on the Internet more than on anything else. For a great many companies, the Internet has been little more than a cost laid on top of an embarrassment laid on top of a loss.

Like most business trends, e-business set off a flurry of lemming-like responses from big companies reacting more to the publicity than to the reality. Fearful of missing a business revolution, traditional companies raced to get on the Web and create the impression that they were enterprises of the future, not the past.

In the first several years of Internet mania, tens of billions of dollars were spent on Website designs and aggressive marketing campaigns. Most of these efforts by the bricks-and-mortar companies were given short shrift by the business media, which was excited by the instant-riches stories in the dot.com world. The "real" story was about start-ups and 20-something billionaires and market valuations exceeding those of the biggest traditional corporations. How could one argue with the wisdom and insights of an 18-month-old start-up worth more than General Motors?

We talked to many corporate executives who admitted to bemusement or bafflement or flat-out disbelief at what was raging around them. The business world had suddenly become *Alice through the Looking Glass,* and all the long-held tenets about commerce and customers and profits had become inverted, seemingly overnight. With little first-hand knowledge of the Web, these executives couldn't help but feel like Gertrude Stein when she commented on Oakland: "There's no there there," they felt in their collective hearts.

Thus, most corporate Internet initiatives got banished to the classic black hole of popular business trends. Committees were formed, consultants were hired, reports were written, and strategic business plans were formulated. Many CEOs had the uneasy feeling that they and their companies required Nobel Prize–level thinkers along with a cadre of young, irreverent, body-pierced technologists to understand the Internet and its chaotic machinations truly.

In many cases, because they were related to technology, the plans drifted into the hands of the information technology department, and alienating layers formed between the CEO and the e-business battle-front. Though no one admitted it, the bravado stance that nearly every big company took regarding its commitment to e-commerce was more posturing than reality.

Except at a few extraordinary places.

Some big, traditional companies saw e-business as a huge competitive opportunity, even as the dot.com excitement roared around them. And at a time when most bricks-and-mortar organizations raced to and fro trying to figure out how to emulate the fast-moving start-ups, these traditional companies did something radical: They turned left when everyone around them was turning right. They did not ignore the e-business tidal wave, but they refused to panic and succumb to the hype surrounding them.

In fact, they made big bets along with big commitments, and they moved fast but not just for the sake of speed. They created a new way to embrace the Internet—a combination of traditional business methods and innovative online offerings, which we call Radical E—and in so doing began to have dramatic impact not only on their own organizations but on entire industries as well.

In this book, you will meet nine of these organizations—eight big companies and one radical individual—and get a detailed look at how they've transformed themselves into e-businesses. You will read about how their e-business initiatives got underway and about the type of thinking and planning that happened as these initiatives became reality. You will read about measurable results and metrics for success—profits, lower costs, new product introductions, exciting new connections to customers, and new ways to do business that actually shake a company to its soul.

What we discovered as we dove into our search for radicals was that the perception that traditional companies were late to the e-business game was flat-out false. Indeed, there is an argument to be made that those who stood on the sidelines may actually have had a slight advantage. Rather than rushing down the wrong rabbit hole and being forced to backtrack or even begin again, they had a chance to learn from winning strategies that emerged from the chaotic past five years. It is not too late to learn from these innovators. In fact, for those companies that have not yet devised an integrated e-business strategy, it may be a matter of survival to learn from the innovators. There is time, but not much, to get in the game.

In Chapter One, we present the definition and characteristics of Radical E. Though we have purposefully avoided making this a how-to guide to e-business, we do provide a list of the ten crucial lessons that we gleaned from the organizations in our case studies. In choosing which companies to profile, we sought to represent a variety of industries. Though some lessons are inextricably tied to a specific industry, we believe that most of the insights in the case study chapters are adaptable to any big or small company that is seeking e-business success.

And as you read on, these central questions should remain: What does the Internet really do for my business? What makes it radical? To paraphrase Clausewitz's famous statement on war and diplomacy, "The Internet is simply an extension of business, *by other means.*" This book is about those *other means.* And how to profit from them.

Joel Kurtzman
Glenn Rifkin
Concord, Massachusetts

The New Rules

Here's a safe bet. Five years ago, Jack Welch was not about to harness the future of General Electric to e-business. Nor was Jeff Skilling at Enron, Leslie Wexner at Victoria's Secret, John Roth at Nortel, Rick Wagoner at General Motors, Herb Kelleher at Southwest Airlines, Peter Lewis at Progressive Insurance, or Tom Stemberg at Staples.

These top executives—many of whom are certified visionaries in their respective industries, and all of whom have crafted notable success stories during their stellar careers—were on the sidelines when the cyber-revolution began. Few, if any of them, had ever touched a computer keyboard or surfed around the World Wide Web. They, like legions of fellow industry leaders, moved into a humbling stretch of business history in which the biggest companies seemed the farthest away from the arc of the New Economy. Something huge was happening. An unstoppable wave of new companies was seemingly changing the world, and these captains of industry were suddenly lost at sea.

And as it turned out, it was the best thing that could have happened to all of them.

Why? Because the frenzied race to the Internet over the past five years was a modern-day Gold Rush, where the promise of unimaginable riches touched off a chaotic and often incomprehensible charge into uncharted territory. A few found the gold, but most were left with empty pockets, glazed eyes, and heartache. It wasn't the cyberspace 49ers who changed the world; it was those who followed and built the virtual railroads, cities, telegraph lines, and industries in the aftermath.

In other words, now that the dot.com mania has faded into obscurity, it is time to get down to real e-business.

Despite the disappointments many companies now associate with the Internet, no one doubts that the Internet is cataclysmic in its own right. The implications of this burgeoning channel of communications and commerce are huge. But after five tumultuous years of hype and hysteria, the real advent of the Web and of e-business is *now*. What we have seen so far is only prologue. Most important, the winners on the Web will not be start-ups, but big businesses. Unlike the doomsayers of the late 1990s, we believe big businesses have the advantage in e-business, if they understand how to exploit and leverage the virtues of *big*.

Business legends like Jack Welch and Leslie Wexner don't pretend that they understood the implications before, but they do understand them now. There is opportunity amid the chaos. Forrester Research predicts that by 2004, $2.7 trillion worth of goods and services will be transacted on the Web. An Internet strategy built on speed and agility is the bridge to the real New Economy. Companies that have been paralyzed by uncertainty and fear of the Internet find that they still have time to get into the game. In many ways, the clock has only just started.

Though it would be difficult to find a company, big or small, that has yet to launch a Website, we believe that most organizations are still wrestling with the Internet rather than embracing it. A recent survey of CEOs by PricewaterhouseCoopers found that 69 percent of these CEOs worry that they didn't think things through before embarking on their e-business initiatives. And 34 percent worry that their efforts could fail. As David Kenney and John F. Marshall wrote in a recent *Harvard Business Review* article, "The Internet has been a letdown for most companies." Though the Internet remains a high priority and tens of billions of dollars have been spent on Website development, the payoff for most companies has been painfully small, both in generating revenues and in gathering strategic customer data.

But after looking deeply into the Internet fortunes of dozens of big companies, we believe it simply doesn't have to be that way. Big businesses can learn the dance, and quickly, too. Though it continues to be a work in progress, the Internet is producing winning strategies. Because this is new, unexplored territory, it is tough to predict long-term success. But the early returns are more than promising.

Enron Corporation, for example, did not launch its e-business initiative until November 1999. A year later, Enron handled $336 billion worth of transactions online! General Electric Plastics didn't create its own e-business unit until June 1999, when it was doing $100 million in annual revenues online. A year later, GE Plastics did more than $1.3 billion in sales online. In February 2000 General Motors initiated Covisint, an online supplier marketplace, along with Ford and Daimler-Chrysler, and the automakers expect to handle more than $60 billion worth of transactions in 2001. Nortel Networks made its Internet debut in 1999 and in 2000 did $10 billion worth of business online. The company estimates that 87 percent of its revenues can now be traced back one way or another to its Website.

In truth, as Jack Welch told the *New York Times* at the end of 2000, "The Internet was made for big companies. With the Web, every day you wake up and laugh at how little you knew the day before. It's like peeling back an onion. Every day we uncover hundreds of millions of dollars in efficiencies."

What is most impressive about these online success stories is that they emanate from very big organizations—places, as New Age business thinkers have often told us, where ideas go to die. Instead, what we've found in our research and in hundreds of interviews with executives is that these companies are thinking and acting in a surprising way. They are, in fact, being *radical* at a time that calls for radical behavior. And most illuminating is that these companies are using the Internet to alter significantly the way they do business. Marcia Stepanek, writing in *Business Week*, says, "What distinguishes many of the most Web-savvy companies is not their technical prowess but their imagination. Everyone has access to Net technology. The crucial question is, Who has the brains, guts, and creativity to take full advantage of it?"

What a growing cadre of business leaders has learned as the dot.com dust has settled is that it is *not* business as usual on the Internet. It is also not a completely revolutionary field of enterprise. Instead, it is an intriguing mix of solid, long-held business tenets coupled with radical ideas about reaching customers in ways heretofore impossible to imagine. It is about instilling into the very heart and culture of the organization that the rules have both changed *and* stayed the same. That apparent paradox is at the heart of being radical and is an intensely difficult concept for big companies to grasp and an even finer line to walk. But the winners are emerging from among those who grasp it and execute it the best and the fastest. Being radical doesn't guarantee success or even survival, but it undoubtedly provides a huge advantage.

And even though it is probably premature to declare winners in a game that has just gotten underway, we have identified a group of players who, by any measure, are well ahead of the competition or, at the very least, are demonstrating extraordinary results when it comes to e-business. Our list is hardly exclusive. New, impressive candidates for case studies already offer enough inspiration for a second book. But having spent countless hours researching these cases and speaking with the principals involved, we believe there are great e-business lessons to be learned from these radicals:

General Electric Plastics

Enron Corporation

Victoria's Secret

Nortel Networks

David Bowie

General Motors

Southwest Airlines

Progressive Insurance

Staples, Inc.

Getting to Radical

Success on the Internet will require a new kind of excellence, which we call *Radical E*. It will require the right approach, the right strategy, and the right tactics. Further, it will require something intangible: the right spirit. For companies prepared to radicalize themselves for the Web, we are quite optimistic.

E-business, to the radical thinkers, is no longer a separate concept. It is an element that will continue to be integrated into nearly every aspect of the way we conduct commerce. In fact, we believe that e-business *is* business. We also believe that established, brand-owning companies have the best chance of winning the e-business battle. Big businesses' vast distribution channels, global marketing prowess, networks of partnerships, supply chains, financial stability, and existing customer bases provide the foundation and scale that dot.com startups could never replicate.

But e-business is no monolith. It will have multiple futures and multiple forms. As in most areas of life, success will go to those with the most innovative ideas. Companies establishing winning e-business strategies are making long-term commitments to this new and explosive channel. They are deftly integrating the Internet into existing channels and building cross-channel foundations that strengthen the entire enterprise. The Internet doesn't *replace;* it reinforces excellence, rejects the old and outmoded, and rekindles excitement. Big companies find that being out front generates positive energy throughout the organization.

Major players—like the ones featured in this book—see the Internet as a powerful agent of change, but they also see it as something short of *cataclysmic* change, at least so far. Radicals are good at keeping things in perspective.

The Internet *eventually* will work its magic on every level of business and in every aspect of society. It might do so a little more gradually than the early masters of hype suggested it would. And when it does, it will do so in ways that will be advantageous for large companies with large resources. Today, according to PricewaterhouseCoopers, some industries can more easily use the Internet to enhance their bottom lines than can others. Industries with highly standardized products that suppliers can easily compare, or those that deal in frequently traded, low-cost wares, will benefit greatly from the transaction efficiencies that the Internet provides. The evidence is already clear that big retailers with big brand names are more successful on the Web than are dot.com start-ups. And perhaps more revealing, the most successful players in the coveted business-to-business segment of e-business are all large, established companies with winning Internet strategies.

What is happening today with regard to e-business is what has always happened in business, but more rapidly and with higher stakes. Failure, perhaps not as volatile and widespread as the dot.com conflagration, is instructive not because it is unique, but because it is normal. Companies do not have a right to prosper—they must earn it every day, new companies and mature companies alike.

The winners win by doing things differently. They do it by having different business strategies and different business models. And when they do it *right,* it takes a long time for their rivals to catch on and catch up.

Southwest Airlines, Dell Computer, Whole Foods, Snap-on Tools, Home Depot, and others have survived and thrived in mature markets by solving basic business problems differently—*radically.* Other companies have tried to emulate their approaches but have, for the most part, failed. Companies that adopt radical approaches can retain their leadership roles for years, and sometimes for decades, despite competition. The companies featured in this book have solved their e-business problems in ways that are no less radical.

What do we mean by radical? Simply put, radical companies have embraced the Internet with two key ingredients: passion and focus. If they were late to the game, measured in Internet time, they turned that tardiness to their advantage. When they joined the fray, they did so in bold, steady strokes, refusing to panic when the dot.com frenzy was at its height. Innovation is a corporate anthem; taking risks, a mantra.

For some of our case studies, like Progressive Insurance or GE, risk taking and innovation are long-held cultural imperatives. For others, like GM and Nortel, getting radical has meant overcoming entrenched and moribund internal hierarchies and traditions. Radicals, whether newly converted or old hands, put tools into the hands of bright people with bright business ideas who question the status quo. And then, most important, they hold those bright people accountable, and if they succeed, they reward them well.

The case studies we present are a diverse and eclectic group. Not every characteristic is shared, not every experience taken in the same manner. But in exploring these organizations, we found several radical elements that most shared in their approach to the Internet:

- They don't "dabble" in the Internet. They do it right or not at all. They have embraced the idea that they must adapt and change and that failure is not an option.

- The people leading the e-business initiatives are not technologists by background and are not burdened by careers in information technology (IT). In effect, they don't know what they don't know, and that is incredibly liberating. They bring a fresh view and a solid understanding of the core business to the Internet.

- In that light, they don't allow the IT organization to hijack the e-business initiative and turn it into another long-term, low-payoff project whose seriousness is then undermined in the eyes of the rest of the organization.

- They have created the excitement of a dot.com start-up (the original, precollapse excitement, that is) within the company but have done so with the stability of a big company with deep pockets, global reach, and a chance to change the world.

- They share best practices across the entire organization; plagiarism of good ideas is encouraged, and turf wars are virtually nonexistent.

- They realized early on that multichannel customers are the best customers, so they are not afraid to promote the Web across all channels. They've seen the evidence that offline buying is heavily influenced by online shopping. At the same time, they've taken advantage of the Web's ability to gather crucial customer data to strengthen their marketing efforts.

Out of the Dot.com Haze

As you will see in the forthcoming case studies, the road to Radical E is paved with clear-sighted leadership, solid execution, and a healthy dose of serendipity. The leaders of the organizations in our case studies had a mix of reactions to the dot.com tidal wave that washed over the second half of the 1990s. David Bowie, as a legendary rock star with roots deep in the traditional bricks-and-mortar recording industry, saw the vast potential of the Internet early on and rushed to embrace it. His digital philosophy cut against the grain of the music business, and in his fifties, at a time when most rock legends are launching retro tours and playing to nostalgic baby boomers, Bowie was reinventing himself on the Internet.

Jeff Skilling at Enron, on the other hand, had grown deeply suspicious of the Web propaganda and had made clear to Enron employees his disdain for traditional bulletin-board Websites. He thought there was little value in spending time and money on information sites when Enron was in a transaction-intense business. It took an enterprising 30-year-old gas trader in Enron's London office to initiate the company's move to e-business, and Skilling was kept out of the loop until just before the initiative was about to launch. He has since become Enron's e-business champion.

Wherever they stood on the issue, the e-business leaders in this book plainly felt the impact of the dot.com frenzy. What characterizes all these radicals is that they didn't rush to respond for the sake of responding. They felt the pressure and took the time to make decisions that made sense for their organizations. And when they moved, they moved decisively. John Roth at Nortel Networks, for example, penned a now-legendary memo to all employees in 1998 about the need for a right-angle turn toward the Internet. In January 1999 Jack Welch signaled to 300 GE executives that the Internet era had begun and that laggards would not be tolerated. Rick Wagoner, upon becoming president and chief operating officer (COO) of General Motors in 1998, told his senior managers that he didn't want GM merely to keep pace online—he was betting the company's future on the Internet.

Of course, radical enlightenment can only come with a solid understanding of what went wrong. The dot.com start-up frenzy of 1998 and 1999 proved to be a classic white elephant for Wall Street and millions of disappointed investors. But if it did nothing else, the rush to the Internet got the attention of big business. And what became clear is that it is far easier for a large company, with its attendant infrastructure and resources, to learn e-business than for a start-up to gain the scale and leverage of an established company.

What wasn't so clear was how to turn the Internet into a positive business opportunity. When it comes to the three most basic imperatives of business—revenue, profit, and share-price growth—for most companies, established and new, e-business has been a disappointment. A big disappointment! E-business has often been a tangle of conflicting aims mixed with wild-eyed and sometimes oversold expectations. It is, in some ways, business's problem child.

More troubling still, for many companies e-business has so far produced no indicators that would suggest that today's big buildup of Web-enabling capabilities—along with its appetite for capital—will result in tomorrow's growth in profit and revenue performance. Just consider three indicators usually associated with profit and growth:

Building strong brands. Although many powerful brands have successfully migrated to the Web, few new, Web-only brands have been created on the Internet, Amazon, eBay, and Priceline notwithstanding. Given the sheer number of Internet start-ups, shouldn't there be more new e-brands by now?

Customer loyalty. Research suggests that customers are *less* loyal on the Internet than in the world of bricks and mortar. Poor service, slow downloads, confusing navigation, and unfulfilled expectations trigger a quick click away, usually forever. As a result, customer acquisition costs are often very high—sometimes even higher—than offline. Further research suggests that profits elude many Internet companies, especially Internet retailers, because high customer acquisition costs can only be justified if there is long-term customer loyalty. Without brands, what you have are commodities. And as every beginning business school student knows, sales of commodities are driven almost exclusively by price.

Pricing power. Without strong brands and customer loyalty, prices are what drive sales. But so far, to get those sales, prices have been moving the wrong way: down! Selling-off surplus inventories at a discount—the Priceline model—is the icing on the cake; it is not the cake itself. But few Internet businesses, whether start-ups or spin-offs, have figured out how to bake a premium-priced, high-quality Internet cake. Very few businesses have developed ways to make their online business offerings exclusive.

No wonder executives have lost sleep. The Internet, for many executives, has assumed the punch line of an old joke: You can't live with it and you can't live without it.

At his CEO summit in 2000, Microsoft Chairman Bill Gates spoke about the dilemma that he and other industry leaders face. Gates believes that American business has so far captured less than 10 percent of the benefits to be had from digital commerce. "Part of the goal here is to take all the transactions, all the business understanding we have today, and get those into digital form," he said. "You could say it's a transition from a still largely offline economy to a real-time, digital, online economy."

Gates characterized the Internet era in three phases, each defined by "a little different kind of mania." In phase one, the mania was to get a Website up and running; it had to be "neat," and the measure of success in this phase was hits on the site. He said that this phase lasted from 1995 to 1998, and concepts such as the notion of how many unique users there were and what the reach and scope of the site were "had not really developed."

The next phase had its transaction mania. Companies bragged about the percentage of revenue they got on the Internet or spun off that portion of the company to try to get a separate valuation for that piece of the organization. "Gross sales were what people worshipped, even in many cases at the expense of developing a long-term profitability model," Gates said.

Now, he added, we are at the very beginning of what he calls the rational phase of the Internet. In the rational phase, people ask, "What does it have to do with profits?" Though big vestiges of second-phase thinkers are still out there, Gates believes that the rational phase will allow traditional companies to ask the question, "How can we take the things we've done and do them differently?"

If nothing else, Gates' view, which is widely shared, gives comfort to big companies that continue to struggle with their e-business initiatives. The cornerstone of the rational phase will be radical action. Radicals will find great opportunity moving forward if they push their organizations to think and act differently. In this book you will see how radicals think about the daunting chaos of the Internet. At Enron, for example, if you want to see the eyes of executives like Jeff Skilling get wide with excitement, just tell him that the analysts and industry experts are nay-saying an idea. That is when Enron knows the opportunity is the greatest.

Lessons for Radicals

In order for any book on e-business to be of value, there must be lessons to take away. We believe that the case study method, as taught at vaunted business schools such as Harvard, offers the best illustrations of radical thinking. Rather than laying out academic platitudes that may or may not apply, a hands-on case study provides the details that often fall through the cracks in broad discussions.

We have visited the companies in the case studies and have talked to countless executives about their e-business experience and enlightenment. We pushed for an understanding of where they were, what they were thinking, and how their e-business strategies were born, evolved, and came to fruition online. We talked to the business leaders as well as the technology leaders to get their insights and philosophies about the company behind the Website, where they started and where they hoped to go.

Without question, each of these case studies is unique. Citing David Bowie and General Motors in the same sentence will likely raise some eyebrows. What can giant automakers learn from rock stars? What can those selling sexy lingerie learn from those selling optical networking equipment? How does an auto insurance giant dance to the same online tune as an airline selling discounted airfares?

Prospective radicals will understand. Nontraditional thinking is more vital today than ever before. Radicals embrace failure, learn from it, and move on. As Enron's Skilling likes to say, "No shots, no ducks."

And while the industries might differ dramatically, what we did find is that the labor of passion, especially as applied to this new world of the Internet, bears very similar fruit. Commonalities across strange borders caught our attention as we put together this book. We concluded that while there are many lessons to be learned from these radicals, ten demand special attention:

1. The CEO Must Lead the Way to E-Business.

If there is one trait common to all successful e-businesses, it is the presence of a CEO who has not only made the commitment but also is personally involved in the effort. From Jack Welch at General Electric to John Roth at Nortel, the leaders of our case study companies have made the transformation of their organizations into e-businesses a personal mission. Speak with the executives and employees and you quickly understand the impact the CEO has on any corporate iniati-tive.

"One of the beautiful things about GE is that when Jack makes something important, everybody understands very quickly that it is important," says Peter Foss, president of GE Polymerland in Huntersville, North Carolina. By making e-business a corporate prior-ity, Welch has turned GE into a veritable template for e-business trans-formation. He not only sent the message but also initiated an Internet mentoring program for himself and the company's other top execu-tives so that they could be hands-on participants in the makeover.

At Southwest Airlines, founder and CEO Herb Kelleher used to fumble just turning on a computer, but his imprint is all over the com-pany's Website, nevertheless. No executive surpasses the Southwest CEO when it comes to keeping things simple, and this operating phi-losophy is embodied in the Website.

Not only did David Bowie personally help design the BowieNet Website, but he is also an active participant in its chatrooms and mes-sage boards. "Post an intelligent question on the BowieNet message boards, and you may well get a response from Bowie himself," says Chris Mitchell, an Internet journalist and editor of *Spike* magazine. "How many CEOs can say that about their Website? For that matter, how many CEOs have the faintest idea how their own Websites work? BowieNet works because Bowie gets the Web."

CEOs who hand off the e-business initiative do so at their peril. Without their personal support, e-business runs the risk of becoming another program du jour or getting usurped by the IT department and ending up as a long-term technology project that never quite reaches fruition.

2. Launch and Learn.

Time is of the essence in the transformation to e-business. While we believe the real battle has just begun, we don't believe that old, hierarchical management styles will win this battle. Big companies must shed their bureaucratic hackles and get into the game. Those who want to take endless meetings, do e-business studies, and seek perfection in their e-business initiatives are more likely to fail.

General Motors, with its reputation as a stodgy, slow-moving leviathan, decided to "launch and learn" when it came to the Internet. Get the core pieces in place, GM says, and you can add, subtract, and adjust as you go. By launching its OnStar program in the mid-1990s, for example, GM had the beginnings of new, breakthrough technology that would transform cars into rolling Internet portals. Much of what OnStar has evolved into has come in recent years, but by starting early, GM gained a huge competitive advantage in that space. As the noted consultant and author Gary Hamel says, "The risk of forging ahead is much lower than the risk associated with doing too little."

3. Reward the Nuts and Dissidents.

Radicals create a culture where offbeat ideas and entrepreneurial freethinkers are sought out and rewarded. Start an e-business unit inside a big, traditional, bricks-and-mortar organization and the lunatic fringe usually shows up immediately looking for jobs. E-business gurus say to hire them and let them shake things up.

Enron's Jeff Skilling, for example, is a former McKinsey consultant who learned early on that nontraditional businesses require nontraditional thinkers. At Enron, he has long encouraged such behavior, and it has paid off in a raft of new business opportunities built around the Internet. "In every company, you've got the radicals, the nuts. We searched them out," Skilling says, "because they needed to be in these new businesses."

4. Use the Web to Build a Community around Your Brand.

The Internet is first and foremost about making and keeping human *connections,* not about moving bits or bytes or conducting online transactions or even about creating frictionless markets. It is about people. Radicals understand that in this way online is not a far reach from offline and that building a community around a company's brand is critical to long-term success. The best and most radical e-businesses realize that they constitute a single interactive community with their customers. They further realize that they must create strong bonds to hold that community together and that they can never take those bonds for granted. To that end, radical companies realize that when it comes to e-business, it's not the Internet, stupid—it's the *access* to people that the Internet provides that is important.

According to Carl Steidtmann, chief retail economist for PricewaterhouseCoopers, "Everyone will be a retailer because virtually all businesses will be just one click away from interacting directly with their customers. All companies must think like retailers. That is, they must develop their key asset: their relationship with their customers. Time Warner and AOL are merging because AOL has 20 million relationships. Customer relationships are paramount to success."

After all, the Web is a crowded place—far more crowded than any main street or shopping mall. It is cluttered with billions of unique pages, millions of addresses, and tens of thousands of businesses. So how do you cut through the clutter? The old-fashioned way. The most effective way to cut through the electronic debris of the Internet is by using a name that everyone already knows. Having a powerful brand is even more important on the Web than it is in the mall.

Victoria's Secret, for example, is so attuned to its brand and the community around that brand that it has designed features into its Website specifically to enhance that relationship. Buying sexy lingerie is an extremely personal endeavor, and to that end Victoria's Secret created a Wish List option on its site so that women can trigger personal e-mails to specific people (i.e., husbands, boyfriends) explaining exactly which bra or panties or silky teddies they desire, along with size and color. Acknowledging intimacy makes its customers feel part of the community.

5. The Internet Gives You the Power to Control the Customer Experience.

Most pundits praise the Internet because it shifts the power from the seller to the buyer. While we agree wholeheartedly with this assessment, we have seen radicals flip this to their advantage. Radicals know that bricks-and-mortar experiences for customers can vary all over the lot in terms of quality, customer service, and interactions that they simply can't control, with suppliers or intermediaries of one sort or another. On the Internet, a company using superior technology and an innovative game plan can produce a Website that redefines the customer experience in a positive way.

David Bowie has embraced the Internet for just this reason. While music industry executives and artists flail about trying to fight the Internet tide, Bowie has seen a future that flourishes online. Rather than be constrained by middlemen such as record companies or promoters, the Internet allows Bowie and his customers to decide what they want, how they want it, and when they want it.

Staples, Inc., the giant office products company, has done the same thing by empowering its customers on the Internet. Staples has empowered purchasing managers inside client companies. Purchasing managers are the very same individuals that the Internet was supposed to replace. However, Staples turned purchasing managers into staunch allies by creating a rule-based purchasing software module and placing it on everyone's desk. When people need a pencil or copying machine, they click on the item on the Website and add it to their shopping cart.

The Staples system requires a purchasing manager to approve each order before it is actually entered into the Staples order system. When it asks for approval, it provides the manager with data on all purchases and purchasing trends and on each client's Staples account. The overall aim is to give power and information to the purchasing manager. Another aim is to save time for the manager and enable the manager to see what each employee needs. Those data, in the hands of the purchasing manager, become strategy. They can be used to negotiate better deals, forecast purchases, and see what is well utilized and what is wasted. It also allows both Staples and its customers to feel in control of the buying experience.

6. The Business Use of the Internet Is to Increase Profits.

Big business is interested in profits, and that is what the Internet must be about. Too many companies have rushed online without a plan for profitability and have ended up with sinkholes rather than positive additions to the bottom line. Ask Leslie Wexner what his metrics for success online are and he will respond, "Show me the money!"

Radicals see the Internet's power to increase earnings, often as quickly as the Website is launched. By keeping its Website transactions as simple as its offline ticket sales, Southwest Airlines has reaped added profits from ticket sales. Enron has what Jeffrey Skilling calls a loose/tight organization—an organization that has sharply focused goals, tightly managed financial controls, and the right rewards system, all inside a loosely structured, nonhierarchical organization. The point of having a loose/tight organization is that anyone with a bright idea can pursue it. The point of having sharply defined controls is to make people understand that they should only pursue opportunities that will truly make money.

Companies are not research universities, and they are not places for techies to play with new technologies. The purpose of businesses—e-businesses or otherwise—is to create products and services in the pursuit of profits. Enron's secret has been to hire smart, motivated people and give them the wherewithal to pursue those profits.

7. Seek Agility over Speed.

Though we believe there is still time for big companies to build a strong Internet presence, speed helps. The road to Radical E is an expressway, not a two-lane country road, and companies must implement and move fast. Like any other new business opportunity, first-movers do have significant advantages, but while there is time to get in, there is not time to make mistakes.

Thus, radicals understand that agility is more important than pure speed. As John Roth of Nortel Networks points out, speed alone can send you careening over a cliff. Being agile means you can move fast but change directions when necessary. And with the volatility of the New Economy, changing directions is a way of life.

8. Expectations Are Higher on the Web, so Failure to Deliver Is More Destructive to Your Business.

Radicals understand Internet time and Internet space. Surveys have shown that customers are far less tolerant of failure online than offline, so the best e-businesses have made the commitment to underpromise and overdeliver. They understand that a customer who is disappointed once or twice is unlikely to return to the Website again.

GE Plastics has used Six Sigma, a quality management measurement tool, to shrink its order-to-delivery time on the Web dramatically. Rather than ignore customers' desired delivery dates and ship materials when they were ready, GE Plastics is now meeting or exceeding request dates. Whereas orders were regularly a week or more late, GE Plastics is now delivering 85 percent of its orders the next day. "Six Sigma fits like a glove with e-business because it allows us to produce and deliver just what customers need when they want it," Jack Welch says.

At Victoria's Secret, chief information officer Jon Ricker knew that the company would need an industrial-strength Website to handle the expected traffic. He and his team specifically avoided the technology hype and designed a site that would maximize the experience for home PC users with 28.8K modems and 200 megahertz computers. And despite the very visual brand, they carefully adhered to the unspoken eight-second rule for Websites. If Web pages don't download in eight seconds or less, a visitor is likely to log off. In a recent study by Keynote Systems, an Internet performance tracking service, Victoria's Secret had the fastest download time of any retail site in the survey: 1.16 seconds. Wal-Mart.com took the full eight seconds.

9. It Doesn't Matter Whether You Develop or Acquire the Needed Technology as Long as You Have It.

Too many big companies, especially in the high-tech arena, get hopelessly stuck on the not-invented-here (NIH) syndrome. Engineers want to develop new technology in-house regardless of how long it takes. Radicals know that there is no time anymore for this type of thinking. Some of the most successful e-businesses, such as Cisco Systems, have grabbed substantial market share through acquisitions and mergers.

Nortel, which was an old-line engineering company with an entrenched NIH philosophy and culture, began its march to e-business success by spending $7 billion to acquire Bay Networks in 1998. Since then, it has made 16 strategic acquisitions and has become a leader in the optical networking arena. More significantly, the Bay Networks acquisition was the key ingredient in turning Nortel into a Radical E company. It was a classic case of the tail wagging the dog as Nortel's

Roth decided to spread Bay's Silicon Valley culture all over Nortel rather than swallowing up the smaller company without a trace. Thus, Nortel got not only needed technology to sell, but also the leadership and vision to build Nortel's own Internet presence.

10. Seek Disruptive Customers Who Lead You to Needed Change and Advancement.

Radicals turn to their customers as partners in designing their e-businesses, and really smart radicals seek out leading-edge customers who will push them and the business to the limit. Nortel's Roth has coined the term *disruptive customer* to describe such customers (playing off the term *disruptive technology*, coined by Clayton Christensen, a Harvard Business School professor and author of *The Innovator's Dilemma*).

What are disruptive customers? Simply put, they are your fastest-moving customers. If you stay with them and cater to their needs, they will keep you ahead of the pack. But—and this is a powerful caveat—they will continually require you to change. As a result, Roth says, to play defense and protect your assets is the surest way to *e-xtinction*. Rather than defend assets, you should trash them, Roth says, and keep moving. By selling off assets and buying new ones when the need arises, you can keep your company focused around the customer.

How to Use This Book

The next nine chapters present a lineup of remarkable organizations and their varied reactions to the advent of the Internet. While we have purposely subtitled this book "From GE to Enron—Lessons on How to Rule the Web," we acknowledge that it is extremely difficult to declare rulers in a game that is clearly still in progress.

However, if one or two or even all of these companies fall into economic difficulties—and business cycles almost guarantee that some will—it will not be because they sat back and let the e-business tidal wave pass them by. As we have heard time and again from our radicals, the risk of sitting back and waiting is far higher than that of taking decisive action to get your company into the e-business fray. These are winning strategies not because they guarantee victory, but because they are serving as catalysts for these organizations to move forward quickly and deftly into the online world.

As you read these case studies, you will see our list of ten key lessons in action and will hopefully find countless other lessons that emerge and may not be common to each case study but are valuable to you. It is enlightening to see the range of reactions to e-business just among these nine organizations. While there are many commonalities, there are also glaring philosophical differences. GM, for example, is a staunch believer in the power of the online exchange with its Covisint venture. GE Plastics, conversely, refuses to participate in online exchanges, believing that its brand will only get diluted by cooperating with competitors in such a venture. One shared view: Even the most radical don't see the Internet as a panacea or as a solution to all their offline woes.

For companies like GM, the present-day business realities of a slowing economy, sluggish vehicle sales, bloated inventories, supplier pricing issues, and product design cycles add up to what would be insurmountable problems for most corporations. Facing high-pressure quarterly earnings demands and anxious shareholders must take precedence over long-term strategic business solutions. Integrating the Internet while all this is happening might be more than most companies could handle. Yet what is instructive is that GM executives believe that the Internet will not only change the entire automotive industry but may also be the company's last best hope to fuel the return of the golden shine to its vaunted name.

For others, like Southwest Airlines, the Internet came along at exactly the right time to solve a potentially disastrous problem—that is, how to sell tickets to customers when the usual distribution systems were disrupted, and in a way that keeps the airline economically viable.

In all, we have purposely chosen a group of industries—insurance, office supplies, automotive, plastics, airlines, entertainment, energy, high technology, and retail—that provide a variety of e-business challenges. In this way, we address both the business-to-consumer and business-to-business concerns that have thus far characterized the e-business debate.

But more than that, by offering a range of industries, company sizes, and competitive situations, we hope that you will begin to think differently—radically—about your own product, service, or brand. Whatever stage of e-business your company may be in, we hope the lessons from these radicals will be inspiring and invaluable to you as you push ahead.

2

GE Plastics
Making the Internet Part
of the Culture

There is no time for lengthy evaluations of Internet opportunities.
We have to pounce—every day!

CEO Jack Welch, General Electric

At General Electric's annual meeting in April 2000 in Richmond, Virginia, John F. Welch, GE's legendary chief executive officer, spoke to shareholders about one of the company's key tenets: the principle of reality, or seeing the world as it is, "not the way we hope it will be."

"Seeing reality today means accepting the fact that e-business is here," Welch said. "It's not coming. It's not a thing of the future. It's here. Reality today means 'go on offense.' One cannot be tentative about this. Excuses like channel conflict, or 'marketing and sales aren't ready,' or 'the customers aren't prepared' cannot be allowed to divert or paralyze the offensive. Moving aggressively raises some thorny issues with no clear and immediate solutions, but the challenge is to resolve these issues on the fly in the context of the new Internet reality. Tentativeness in action can mean being cut out of the markets, perhaps not by traditional competitors but by companies never heard of 24 months ago. Reality in the Internet world means moving at a fanatical, maniacal pace everywhere in GE!"

Welch focused on the need for "speed and more speed" and boasted that GE was in the process of going to "levels of speed, agility, and performance we could only dream of just a few years ago. There is no time for lengthy evaluations of Internet opportunities. We have to pounce—every day!"

GE executives knew that this was not just a public pep talk for shareholders. Jack Welch, on the doorstep of retirement after a remarkably successful 21-year reign as GE's CEO and the world's most admired business leader, had never been prone to hyperbole. When Welch makes a pronouncement, it reverberates throughout every corner of the $130 billion company to every one of the 350,000 employees. People listen and act quickly.

Like other big companies, GE was relatively late in making a corporate commitment to the Internet. But if any corporate giant could recover and make a rush to Internet leadership, it was GE. Radicals like GE don't downplay first-mover advantage, but they understand that an organization can only achieve online success when it is ready, both culturally and organizationally, to make the transition. The Internet advantage will ultimately go to the best execution, not simply the earliest.

In truth, back in January 1999 at his annual executive meeting in Boca Raton, Florida, Welch had issued a corporate mandate that e-business would be the company's top agenda item. There, he told the company's top 300 executives that he expected each of the company's 20 business units to be the e-business leader in its industry, extending his 1980s mandate that every GE business must be number one or two in its global market or else fixed, sold, or closed.

He further mandated that an e-business leader would be appointed in each unit and that that person would report directly to the business unit's CEO. Many big organizations trying to make the e-business transition were channeling the Internet effort through the information technology (IT) organization and the chief information officer (CIO). Welch understood that this was a business initiative, not a technology play, and that such a reporting structure would never allow for the kind of rocket-like launch he was seeking for GE's Internet assault. In addition, a dedicated e-business staff would be hired to drive the initiative and push GE into high Internet gear. When the executives returned from Boca Raton, the word spread fast, and by summer GE was well on its way to transforming itself.

GE has earned plaudits for its swift transition to e-business. Every GE business unit is now doing thriving commerce on the Web. The company bought more than $6 billion worth of goods through the Web in 2000. "We'll save hundreds of millions of dollars," Welch told the *New York Times* at the end of the year. "Nothing else would give you that type of quantum change."

In early 2001, GE began making significant structural changes by moving vast amounts of administrative work online. According to *Businessweek*, GE expected to cut thousands of jobs and save $1.6 billion in 2001 by digitizing many tasks.

Gary Reiner, GE's CIO, says there are four keys to GE's success thus far:

- There must be a total focus on productivity, both GE's and its customers'.

- GE follows the paper and then eliminates it.

- People, unexpectedly, are enjoying the transformation to doing business online.

- Six Sigma, the company's quality management initiative, has turned out to be the perfect platform upon which to build GE's e-business.

One business unit in particular used Welch's Boca Raton message to accelerate an Internet effort that had, in fact, begun years earlier. GE Plastics, one of the company's most successful and, to the outside world, most prosaic businesses, had embraced the Internet before nearly all of GE's other more flamboyant organizations. As early as 1994, GE Plastics had launched a Website featuring brochureware or product information for its customers. By 1997, GE Plastics, through its Polymerland distribution business, had become the first unit in GE to allow customers to do business transactions on the Web. Customers had been reluctant to buy and conduct business on the site, and by the end of 1998, Polymerland was doing just $10,000 worth of transactions per week over its Website.

However, under Peter Foss, president of GE Polymerland in Huntersville, North Carolina, the unit pressed hard to enhance its customers' purchasing experience by using the Website. GE Polymerland came into existence in 1988, after GE purchased Borg-Warner Chemicals. The division had been established as a wholly owned subsidiary and renamed Polymerland, Inc. Through Polymerland, GE sold both its own and non-GE resins to customers around the world. The unit developed world-class distribution systems and customer service operations, and in 1999 the company changed the name to GE Polymerland to centralize all its distribution efforts, including the Internet.

Though it has a jazzy, magical-kingdom kind of name, GE Polymerland was anything but glitzy. Foss admits that he didn't have an Internet *vision,* nor did he view himself as leading edge. He just wanted to show off at a major plastics convention in 1997 and thought a Website with transaction capabilities would help make GE Plastics look innovative to the attendees. But sometimes timing is everything, and Foss had timed his efforts well to coincide with a burgeoning interest in business-to-business (B2B) e-commerce.

In 1999, after Welch's Internet edict, and with B2B e-commerce suddenly taking off in the United States, the Polymerland site began to flourish. Customers were attracted by the new levels of customer service available on the Web 24 hours a day, seven days a week. Like Staples.com and other radicals, GE Polymerland.com suddenly created a new access point into the company, and as more and more customers got their own businesses online, the stampede was on. By June GE Polymerland was doing more than $2 million a week in online orders. Welch invited Foss to corporate headquarters in Fairfield, Connecticut, to share best practices with other GE business leaders. A steady stream of GE executives made the pilgrimmage to Huntersville to learn more and take home a model for their own Websites. "One of the beautiful things about GE is that when Jack makes something important, everybody understands very quickly that it is important," Foss says.

GE Polymerland's online success drew the media. *Fast Company* magazine profiled the unit and reported, "Polymerland has become a definitive model within GE—a full-scale, fully operational instruction manual for bringing an old-line business into the online arena. At an organization that has arguably set the standard for big-company management, Polymerland represents a standard for Web-based transformation."

But GE Plastics was just getting started. For the $7 billion business and its 15,000 employees, the early innovation merely set the stage for an ambitious Internet effort that would raise the stakes and turn the decidedly Old Economy business into an Internet power and the online leader in its industry.

Grabbing the Reins

In the spring of 1999, Gerry P. Podesta, an engineer and 17-year GE veteran, was living in southeast Asia running GE Plastic's local business unit. He got a call to return to the United States to become the division's general manager for e-business. Characteristic of Podesta and all of GE's other e-business leaders was the distinct lack of a computer background. Podesta had no IT or Internet experience but knew how to run a business. And more important, he knew GE Plastics and understood its business model viscerally. At 41, he was the kind of young but seasoned GE talent who had gotten noticed at the top levels. With the Internet changing GE's entire business structure, rising stars like Podesta had the perfect profile to lead the effort.

When he took over the GE Plastics e-business initiative in June, he was surprised at the lack of structure written into his job description. There was, for example, no budget. The mandate: Whatever it takes! There was the clear message that "this is the right thing to do, so let's just do it . . . and let's do it fast," he says.

In his new role, Podesta became part of the parent company's command staff on e-business. The 20 new e-business general managers started meeting once a month with GE's CIO Gary Reiner to compare notes, share best practices, and push hard to make the elephant dance faster. Plagiarism was encouraged. "When someone has a good idea, everybody has it," Podesta said.

GE Plastics wouldn't seem to be a glamour spot for a young up-and-comer, but Podesta knew his history. Though the 45-year-old division is headquartered as far off the beaten path as possible, in Pittsfield, an old mill town in the Berkshires of western Massachusetts, it was the place where Jack Welch himself had spent 20 years as head of GE Plastics, building a powerhouse business and launching his own renowned GE career. When Welch named Jeffrey Immelt as his successor in November 2000, it was no surprise that Immelt had spent 15 years at GE Plastics as well.

And if the business itself seems mundane, that too can be misleading. Yes, GE Plastics makes and sells little colored pellets or resins that manufacturers turn into plastic goods, but there is more to it than mere commodity sales. GE Plastics is an innovator, and its research and development people work closely with customers designing and creating breakthrough products and ways to make them. The pellets from GE become a wide range of products—from Hoover vacuum cleaners to bumpers for Saturn cars to Sony CDs and radios to Tupperware containers to Ford headlights to Nokia cell phones to Motorola pagers. When Apple Computer unveiled its hugely popular and colorful iMac personal computers, the startling colors of the plastic Apple monitors were made possible by breakthroughs by GE Plastics' researchers.

Like other units in GE, GE Plastics divided its e-business initiative into three parts: the sell side, the make side, and the buy side. In this way, Podesta could focus his team on culling out the distinct advantages of the Internet for specific functions within the company. For example, on the sell side, Podesta quickly changed the compensation structure of the sales force so that it would be incentivized to get customers to order over the Web rather than by telephone or fax. In that same vein, GE Plastics quickly introduced innovative *wizards* or online tools such as color and materials selectors that allowed customers to do technical work on the GE Polymerland Web site.

On the make side, Podesta worked with GE Plastics' chief financial officer and CIO to set new finance policies on the Web. Senior managers of GE Plastics were polled to find the six key finance metrics they would each like to see every morning when they arrived at their desks. The team made clear that the metrics had to be common and identical—apples to apples—so that everyone was working from the same data. In addition, Podesta instituted a rule that no data could be manually inputted; they all had to come from another system so that it was clear that it was high-quality data. Once the metrics were identified, the project was handed over to the IT team, and a system was up and running in 90 days.

On the buy side, GE Plastics focused on how it negotiated and transacted deals and how that could be streamlined for the Internet. Like many other GE business units, Plastics began to embrace e-auctions for purchasing materials. At the same time, the unit focused on rolling out an e-transaction capability that would take paper out of the buying process. The average cost of a paper-based transaction is $70. Online, the same transaction costs about $5. With about 300,000 transactions a year, GE Plastics is saving nearly $20 million in costs already.

With the formalizing of GE's Internet initiative and Podesta in charge, Foss began to see a crucial shift in online business. "In 1997, we knew fulfillment would be important, but it wasn't until the middle of 1999 that we realized this could fundamentally change the business," Foss says. "We realized this was a lot more than order entry." Polymerland could take all the information on its business from its file cabinets and make it available online to customers on a 24/7 basis. "What a wonderful information democracy this created," Foss says. "We also knew there was no money in an information democracy."

But if some of the Website's versatility didn't initially translate into huge savings, it certainly became a powerful lure for customers. When Polymerland started offering transaction functionality on the site in 1997, only 15 percent of its customers had access to the Internet. By the middle of 1999, that number had surged to 90 percent. The audience was in place and ready.

And like other great radicals, GE Plastics knew that its customers were smart and worth listening to when it came to designing its Website. So rather than looking to the company's IT organization or outside consultants to drive the Website's development, Podesta and Foss turned to discussions with customers for insight. "How can we use the Internet to serve you better?" they asked. One customer pointed out that he couldn't start to mold a part until he received official notice from GE that the product was certified for specific properties. He always had to wait until someone from Polymerland could fax him a paper copy of the certification, which often delayed him for a day or more. So Podesta put the capability on the Website, and customers could pull their own certification, download it, and print it out. In a year, that function saved 30,000 phone calls to GE Polymerland. In all, Foss says, more than 200,000 calls were eliminated in one year due to functionality now online.

The result is not only more satisfied customers but also significant cost savings. Podesta estimates that online transactions save the company $3 million to $5 million each year, compared with purchases that go through traditional purchasing channels. The savings result from the fact that more than 90 percent of online orders require no human intervention and go directly to a warehouse.

Customers have become believers. Chris Groszcyk, a mechanical engineer in Motorola's personal communications sector, has molders who buy resins from GE Plastics to use in cellular telephones. There are occasions when Groszyck needs to interact with GE directly to discuss design issues and technical problems relating to the applications for products. Logging on to the GE Polymerland Website, Groszcyk found himself in a live online chat with a customer service representative. "I didn't have to do anything," he says. "I was sitting there and all of sudden someone came on and introduced herself. She asked if I had any questions, and I explained what I wanted. She pointed me to exactly where I needed to go and then answered my questions along the way. It was great. It was like having a personal assistant guiding me through the Polymerland Website."

It was the kind of experience that couldn't have happened over the telephone or by fax, and it solved Groszcyk's problem in 15 minutes. "It went quickly, efficiently, with no mistakes," he says. "The biggest problem with search on the Internet is that it will come up with 8,000 pages of useless information and one thing you need. You may hit it, you may not. Here they point you directly to the information you are looking for."

Scott Blaine is a commodity manager in the purchasing group for the BCG Division of ADC Inc., a $2 billion telecommunications equipment manufacturer in Minneapolis. He is working closely with GE Polymerland to create an e-commerce connection to the plastics maker for online ordering of resins. At the same time, he has worked with GE engineers on the Internet to do crucial product development.

In the rush to produce hardware for transferring fiber-optic cabling, a new customer requirement, Blaine asked if GE Plastics engineers could help develop this new product in half the normal development time. By working in a secure environment online and giving Blaine's product developers access to an online engineering room, they were able to complete the assignment in less than three months as opposed to the six months the same project would normally have taken. "Not only was there a cost reduction," Blaine says, "but this allowed us to be on the market first." Most impressive was the manner GE Plastics presented. "They acted more like a small company," Blaine says.

Building a Community

For Podesta, the Internet clearly represents far more than a faster and more efficient distribution channel for the company's 30,000 resins. Beyond its capabilities for real-time order tracking, pricing, and ordering, as well as access to crucial customer information, the Website has become the center of a growing community. As a true B2B transaction and development center, GE Polymerland.com is taking customer service to a new level. "We plan to offer everything a plastics industry person could want," Podesta says.

For example, the site is a plastics-industry America Online, replete with discussion groups, chatrooms, and jobs boards. Podesta set up a partnership with Monster.com, the online job-listing site, to create an exclusive job-listing service for the plastics industry on GE Polymerland.com.

In addition, customers can track not only current orders but also everything they've bought over the past six months. There is a real-time tracking system so that a customer can type in an order number and find out exactly when the order shipped or is going to ship. And if there are questions or problems, a customer can type in his or her phone number and click on a representative call button. A GE representative will call back within minutes. That person will be able to view exactly what the customer is seeing on his screen—a design specification, for example—and help solve the customer's problem in a joint online session.

Using the ColorXpress section of the Website, customers can match colors via their computers and order color chips online with a 48 hour turnaround, a process that used to take weeks.

Moving fast has already paid off. In just over a year under Podesta, GE Polymerland.com skyrocketed in popularity, surpassing all expectations within GE. From annual online revenues of $100 million in 1999, GE Plastics did more than $1.3 billion via the Website in 2000. Part of the success comes from the globalization of GE Polymerland.com over that span. Podesta estimates that the site reaped $10 million a week from business in Asia and Europe and another $2 million to $3 million per week in new online businesses such as silicones and diamonds. In the fourth quarter of 2000, GE

Plastics' profits surged to $430 million, up 21 percent from a year earlier.

Despite the upsurge, Podesta was not satisfied. The numbers, as strong as they were, represented just 30 percent of GE's customers in North America and just 13 percent globally. Podesta points out that the use of the Internet was astounding but admits that this business was mostly from customers GE Plastics already had. He says that it is difficult to tell whether customers are buying more because of the improved quality of service via the Internet.

"The plastics industry is a finite industry," Podesta explains. "There are 7,000 or 8,000 people out there in the United States alone who buy plastic resins. There are millions who want to design something using plastic, but only 7,000 or so buy plastic and mold it. We knew who those people were, and every one of them bought at least something from us. The question was, who bought more from us because of the Website?"

What Podesta did know was that GE Polymerland was doing better than the rest of the industry and competitors like Dupont, Dow, and Ticona. He was pleased but set even higher targets for 2001 and beyond. "We'd like to get 50 percent of our customers to use the Website by the end of the year," he said. He predicted that 30 percent of the company's business would come from the Website in that timeframe, representing $3 billion in revenues.

Going It Alone

When Podesta took over the e-business initiative at GE Polymerland, the Internet landscape was dominated by dot.com start-ups attacking every sector of the business world. Drawn by the lure of entrepreneurial fever and instant riches, the people with talent all seemed to be walking around with millions of dollars worth of stock options in their pockets and disdain for big corporations. With Amazon.com rewriting the rules of business-to-consumer selling, companies like GE worried that dot.coms had the potential to do similar competitive damage in the B2B marketplace. Industry analysts from places like Forrester Research and Gartner Group were making bold predictions about the lucrative future of online marketplaces and the dire circumstances for bricks-and-mortar companies that didn't act quickly. A dot.com competitor named PlasticsNet had begun business in 1996 and in the heat of the dot.com frenzy seemed to be a real threat.

To fight back, many established giants in various industries began to gravitate toward online consortiums, marketplaces, or exchanges in order to facilitate their Internet business models. The exchanges promised to offer customers vast choices, easy access, and huge savings, especially in the B2B part of the world. In the auto industry, General Motors, Ford, and DaimlerChrysler formed Covisint in February 2000 and waited until September before getting approval of the U.S. government that the model didn't violate antitrust laws. In the plastics industry, five competitors—Dow, Dupont, Bayer, BASF, and Ticona/Celanese—formulated plans for Omnexus.com, an online consortium that debuted in the fall of 2000 to compete with GE Polymerland.com.

It was in this marketplace mentality that Podesta began to reshape GE Polymerland's Internet strategy. And like all great radicals, Podesta saw the competition turning right, so he turned left. "A lot of these plans are rooted in the Internet jargon that consultants write," Podesta says. "They say, 'You have to be neutral and offer two or three competing brands for the customer,' things like that. But we decided early on that we would not join any of these online exchanges or marketplaces. We would do it ourselves and not lend a penny to any online start-up."

The logic is simple and tinged with the swagger associated with market leaders. "We believe we have the best overall brand in the plastics industry," Podesta says. "And our individual brands, like Lexan, Noryl, Cycoloy, and Valox, are very big brands in the industry. Why should we give that advantage away?"

Riding the GE Polymerland brand, GE Plastics stood out for its unwillingness to go along with the crowd. To Podesta and GE Plastics CEO Gary L. Rogers, it made simple business sense. With GE Polymerland, the company was selling both GE and non-GE resins, but they were complementary rather than competing products. Beyond that, it could control its own online destiny, offering online distribution, superior service, and a full complement of products. The players in Omnexus would need to figure out how to position competing products and figure out whether to direct customers to the Omnexus Website or to their own individual sites. Podesta saw no logic in the consortium model.

"We have a full basket of products but nothing overlapping or competing," Podesta says. "It is very difficult to sell competing products online. How do you act neutral on that? How do you offer price and fulfillment? And every one of those five companies still has its own Website and sells through physical outside distributors. So now they have three major channels to market. I don't know how they do it. So we decided to go it alone."

Podesta pointed out that this was not a decision that required Jack Welch's sign-off. It is, in fact, part of the GE business model. If you are a leader in an industry, why allow someone else into the game? Whether it's in pricing, new products, distribution, or innovation, if you are the market leader, why give that up by joining a consortium or ceding your advantage to a dot.com start-up that wants to be in the middle? Podesta was particularly wary of the dot.com business model that was built upon the idea that the big traditional bricks-and-mortar players would be forced to go through an established dot.com player in order to do business online successfully.

Podesta also knows that the Internet playing field is a shifting one and that trends have changed quickly in the past five years. Though many dot.coms struggled in the e-commerce space, he is not worried if the momentum shifts back to the pure plays. "The basic concept of commerce hasn't changed since the Stone Age," he says. "Someone sells something, someone buys something. The Internet made everything more visible, more open, more accessible, and easier, but the basic concept hasn't changed. So if something different happens in a year, we can adapt. Even if I made the wrong bet online, they'd still want my brands."

But Podesta is not waiting for the e-business winds to shift against him. Listening to customers revealed an even more pressing need. As each customer's business moved to the Internet, it was clear that one of the bottlenecks to e-commerce was the diverse number of incompatible systems that made the seamless connection between supplier and customer impossible. Customers, particularly big corporate customers, wanted to be able to place an order on their system and have it automatically synchronized with their supplier's system. Elimination of this double-entry dilemma became Podesta's target at GE Polymerland.

As Podesta points out, every company has its own purchase-order system, whether it's a simple Excel spreadsheet or a multimillion-dollar SAP system. That means that every order sets off the tedious process of both companies' having to input an order into their own systems. Podesta believes that this technological issue keeps big suppliers like GE Plastics from penetrating more than 50 percent of its customers for e-business.

"At 50 percent, you start dealing with big companies who say, 'Why would I ever do double entry? I can put the order into my system and hit a button that auto-faxes the order to you and you put it in your system,'" he explains. "You're not going to get that guy to change simply because you offer some great service on your site."

Though this sounds like an IT problem, it reflects the culture at GE Plastics. A raft of independent software makers offers themselves as middlemen to make the server-to-server connection. But Podesta says that he would rather solve this problem in-house, and he is working with a sister division, GE Information Systems (GSX), to create a solution. It is part of a fiercely independent view of the Internet that Podesta espouses. By creating a GE-based solution, GE Plastics can solidify its relationship with its customers and foster a stronger reason for them not to look elsewhere for products.

"Double entry has been our biggest objection," says Scott Blaine at ADC, Inc. "But they've been good at coming out and getting us around the obstacles. They asked for our feedback and were eager to listen. And they worked very hard at trying to tailor the system to meet our needs."

More than that, Foss says, GE Polymerland has moved forward even though all the technical glitches were not ironed out. "You can't wait for perfection," Foss states. "You have to go faster. People tend to wait for everything to be going perfectly before rolling it out."

Foss says that the Internet has fundamentally changed the relationship with the customer. "We used to sit and talk about the frontroom and backroom operations," he says. "Today, there is only one room, and the customer is sitting in that room looking right at you." Customers' access to corporate databases and purchasing systems has created incredible transparency in the business, Foss notes.

"Inefficiencies come to the surface quickly," he says. And as GE Poly-merland.com unearthed the need for better business processes, the company had the perfect tool in place to fuel the changes.

Six Sigma

When Jack Welch talks about GE's tardiness in coming to the Internet, he blames it on fear. "Big companies like us were often frightened by our own unfamiliarity with Internet technology," Welch said. "We thought the creation and operation of Websites was mysterious, Nobel Prize stuff, the province of the wild-eyed and purple-haired. But as we have gotten more deeply into e-business, we have come to learn that digitizing all our buying, making, and selling processes is the easiest part of the equation."

With its hundreds of factories, warehouses, and world-renowned products and technology, the hardest part is done, Welch says. "We have a century-old brand identity and a reputation known and ad-mired around the globe, all attributes that new e-business entrants are desperate to get. And we have one other enormous advantage—Six Sigma quality—the greatest fulfillment engine ever devised."

Six Sigma is a statistics-based measuring process initiated by com-panies like Motorola in the late 1980s to reduce defects in manu-facturing and production dramatically. GE adopted Six Sigma in the mid-1990s as a corporate-wide initiative aimed at improving quality processes throughout the company. Thus far, more than 100,000 GE employees have been trained in Six Sigma, earning titles such as black belts or master black belts for their prowess in incorporating the pro-cess into their operations. "Six Sigma fits like a glove with e-business," Welch declared, "because it allows us to produce and deliver just what customers need when they want it."

The Six Sigma initiative has had a significant impact on all of GE's e-business initiatives. According to the *New York Times,* "Industry ex-perts say that GE is way ahead of other old economy companies in em-bracing the Web." The Six Sigma effect has played a key role in that surge. "Six Sigma processes let us demystify the whole concept of e-business," Piet C. van Abeelen, GE's vice president for Six Sigma quality, told the *Times.*

For GE Plastics, the Six Sigma initiative did indeed fit its e-business effort like a glove. In 1998 CEO Rogers started a Six Sigma initiative called SPAN, which was aimed at reducing delivery times for orders. It was a simple idea: Get the products to customers when they want them. In the past, the date the customer requested delivery was essentially irrelevant. When customers ordered a product and said they wanted it the following week, GE Plastics' response would be to say, "We'll get it to you in two weeks," and then measure itself on the two-week date rather than on when the customer requested it. With SPAN, if customers say they want the product in one week and it is delivered in two weeks, GE Plastics sees itself as seven days late. It begins as a mindset change and progresses to actual improvement in delivery times.

Podesta and his colleagues were especially struck by the Christmas 1999 Internet shopping fiasco that left millions of consumers disappointed when products they ordered from many retail Websites did not arrive in time for the holidays. "You have this higher expectation when you are on the Internet," Podesta says. "So when the product doesn't arrive, it is the most disappointing thing in the world."

When Podesta took over the e-business process, one of his key mandates from Rogers was to move the SPAN initiative to the Internet. Rogers pushed hard for the SPAN program, which became a GE-wide best practice and is now used company-wide to measure customer fulfillment. Essentially, Podesta and his team realized that without the fulfillment part of the business in line, GE Plastics had no Internet capability. Indeed, the feeling was strong that if GE couldn't meet its customers' delivery needs, it would be better to keep them off the Internet in order to prevent them from having a negative experience.

"Service is the reason you go to the Internet," he says. "And if they go and get bad service, they may not come back again for a long time." Thus the Six Sigma service capability had to precede the ramping up of GE Polymerland's online efforts. Several e-commerce initiatives were delayed because people didn't have their service strategies in place.

Layering Six Sigma onto service is a simple but powerful exercise. Service, in many ways, is statistics. Each shipment has many types of statistics associated with it: When did you take the order? How long to fill the order? How long to ship it? Was it late? How many days late? In order to fix the delivery bottleneck, GE Polymerland had to bring Six Sigma tools all the way back to the factory to analyze production schedules. By plotting thousands of these statistics in a clear, methodical way, the company was able to spot trouble points and trends and target the problems. "Six Sigma grounds you and enables you to make the changes that affect the customer, rather than working off anecdotal information," Podesta says.

Finding defects and reducing them is just the first phase of Six Sigma. The second phase is called Design for Six Sigma (DFSS), which works on the premise that one doesn't just fix defects but designs things right in the first place. Every piece of GE Polymerland's e-business strategy since it started has had a DFSS process. In essence, GE Polymerland changed its entire global fulfillment business based on a Six Sigma measurement that takes the outside edges of the bell curve and creates a much tougher measurement for delivery.

With the Six Sigma plan in place, GE Polymerland squeezed the delivery times to unprecedented levels. Customers can now go online and order products, most of which get delivered the next day. "We can get products to 85 percent of our customers the next day," Podesta says. "We are doing a 70-30 inventory model. That meant that 85 percent of the customers for 70 percent of our products could get delivery the next day, which is really quite amazing in the plastics industry."

So rather than slowing down the e-business initiative, Six Sigma ultimately allowed GE Polymerland to move faster because they were not redoing flawed systems but were building them right the first time.

The Impact of Culture

For many large bricks-and-mortar companies, the biggest obstacle to e-business success is the entrenched corporate culture. Even as the new millennium began, it was shocking to see how many big companies continued to struggle with e-business initiatives because of resistance to change in key sectors of the organization.

But inside GE, there are no blockers once the executive committee issues a mandate. Starting in the 1980s, Welch was able to set off huge changes within GE by making it clear that his view was "my way or the highway." Now that he's basking in his current CEO glory, many people forget that Welch's first corporate nickname was "Neutron

Jack," which reflected his propensity for leaving the buildings stand-
ing while the people were eliminated in massive layoffs and restruc-
turings.

So when Podesta came back with his e-business plan, he knew
there would be no resistance from the leadership of the organization.
"This is an initiatives factory," he says. Big initiatives like globalization
and Six Sigma generally succeed because the corporate leadership ac-
tively leads the way. But like other radicals, GE didn't leave anything
to chance. Knowing that the fear factor can create foot-dragging when
it comes to computing, especially among older executives who've
never felt comfortable at a keyboard, Welch instituted an inverse-
mentoring program throughout the corporation. More than 600 of the
top managers in the company were asked to look inside their organizations for a young Internet junkie who could teach them how to maneuver around the Web. Welch himself, at 63, had his own mentor, a
37-year-old GE manager named Pam Wickham, who runs the company's GE.com Website.

According to the *Wall Street Journal*, the program has been a huge
success. GE managers meet regularly with their young mentors for
Web lessons and critique their own and competitors' Websites, discuss
articles and books they've been given for homework, and barrage their
subordinates with questions—many of them, they admit, stupid.

The idea is to get GE's key decision makers savvy enough to understand the competitive online marketplace and understand how to
do business in this new environment. It also helps reshape the organization. "E-business knowledge is generally inversely proportional to
both the age and the height in the organization," Welch told the *Journal*. "I find this to be a wonderful tool, among many others, to change
that equilibrium."

For Podesta, the success of GE Polymerland's e-business initiative
rested on putting together a core group of 50 key people to spearhead
the effort, a number that quickly rose to more than 100. In the summer of 1999, it was difficult to find Internet talent willing and ready to
join a corporate giant like GE. The dot.com frenzy had yet to peak, and
the best and the brightest were focused on start-ups and stock options.

Instead, Podesta recruited from inside. All of the first 50 came
from within GE Plastics, and none had e-business experience. Some
were from the IT organization, but most were from the business

organization. Since then, he has hired only five or six people from the outside. Podesta outsourced 100 percent of the Website development work. "We don't have a single person on the team who can write HTML," he boasts. "We looked for innovators, hard drivers, people who accept new ideas and go fast. In the end, e-business is project management. There was nothing unique about it."

And unlike other corporate e-business efforts that resulted in the creation of a separate e-business company within the company, à la Staples.com, GE decided not to divide its efforts. "We tried to create a dot.com atmosphere, a dot.com identity, but everything is mainstream," Podesta says. "We're all in the same boat, and if you create a different culture that you compensate differently and treat as special, it is counterproductive to getting the boat to sail in the same direction."

It is crucial that the e-business effort be complementary to the bricks-and-mortar business, because in GE Plastics' case that business was "doing pretty well and we didn't want to mess that up," according to Podesta. He acknowledges the importance of having a dedicated e-business team, however, and says that it is key that when his group arrives in the morning, it has one thing on its collective mind: to succeed on the Internet.

All told, Podesta estimates that the e-business initiative will cost around $20 million globally, which seems like a small price to pay for a $7 billion company. Podesta says he is amazed at how many big companies are overspending on e-business initiatives. He says there are a couple of key factors in keeping the price tag low. First, GE Polymerland doesn't use outside consultants. "We haven't paid a single consultant while I've been here, and we won't," he declares. "They don't have any better ideas than we do. We paid people to build what we wanted, but we never paid anyone to decide what we needed."

In addition, GE Polymerland retained its existing legacy mainframe computers and built front-end systems on them rather than invest millions in enterprise resource planning (ERP) systems. Podesta and his IT team decided that rather than spending $100 million on new computers, it would build effective interfaces on its existing systems while slowly moving away from the mainframes.

"Even these big systems from Baan and SAP aren't Internet-capable, so you had to buy a third-party package like Broadvision or CommerceOne on top of that," Podesta says. "On that you'd need to add a database, and even that isn't customized to what you want. For all that, you can pay a user fee, a software fee, an upgrade fee. It's crazy."

Customer SWAT Teams

Podesta acknowledges that with all its successes thus far, GE Polymerland is still in the early stages of e-business and that the landscape is filled with competition aiming at a $50 billion marketplace. He knows that Omnexus.com will be a formidable foe and that the customer base is unlikely to buy from only one source online, just as it is in the bricks-and-mortar world. But he is adamant that the consortium model is not for GE. "What they are doing is hedging their bets," he says of the Omnexus players. "They can't decide what they want to be so they say, 'I'll do a dot.com business, a distribution business, and my own direct business.' And we can't reconcile that. We have one channel to markets and it's called GE Polymerland. It is both our bricks-and-mortar and dot.com brand. Ultimately, all our customers will be electronically connected, and the one who wins the service game will win the order game."

As the game heats up, however, GE Polymerland has made customer education a top priority. Knowing that the customer base is made up of small, technically unsophisticated shops as well as big, savvy players, Podesta's team leaves nothing to chance. GE Polymerland's sales force is pushed to get customers to use the Internet, and they get the same commission whether the customer orders by phone or by the Internet. In fact, they get a slightly higher commission if customers use the Internet.

To facilitate that, GE Polymerland has a customer SWAT team made up of eight customer service representatives whose full time jobs are to visit and train customers on the use of the Website. They are former salespeople who are now called e-business growth leaders. The team tries to visit two to three customers each day. They started with a goal of getting 50 percent of the customers by the end of 2000. According to Podesta, they've heard all the excuses for resistance: "I don't trust my purchasing person to have Internet access"; "I don't have a computer"; "I don't want double entry"; and "I tried it and don't like it."

The team simply doesn't back off until it addresses every excuse or reason and knocks each one down. This aggressive approach is part of the company's proactive culture when it comes to its customers. Rather than simply selling little square pellets, GE Polymerland sells application development. The company invests heavily in building manufacturing plants around the world, but its mission is to drive the specification of its product. "We'll show the car company how to make a plastic bumper or a computer company how to make a plastic CPU for a computer system," Podesta says. Using advances in its technology, GE Polymerland works closely with leading cellular phone makers, CD manufacturers, and all major players in the telecommunications and electronics industries.

For Podesta and GE Polymerland, that is where the growth will come from. While the transaction part of the business has a finite customer base of 8,000 plastics molders, there are millions of specifiers and designers for the endless array of plastic products in the world. All these design engineers need specifications, engineering data, and design help, and Podesta wants to have all that on the Internet. Already GE Polymerland offers wizards for online assistance.

There are simple wizards: A customer comes to the Website and uses a material wizard to help select the correct resin. And there are also more sophisticated design wizards: A customer enters the basic information for a proposed part onto the Website and says, "I want to make this thing. It is this big and this wide." In a matter of minutes, the Website calculates the right resin, the ejection speed, the pressure, and the deflection on the particular part, along with many other parameters—a process that used to take days or weeks.

Customers with CAD drawings are able to interact live with GE Polymerland engineers with both the customer and the engineer looking at the same drawing online to resolve technical problems. Podesta foresees the opportunity actually to do the customer's designs for them online in the near future. "There is a great service and revenue opportunity here," he says.

Ironically, as he becomes more and more successful, Podesta may be working himself out of a job. According to CIO Reiner, the e-business effort will become so integrated into GE's culture that "we will evolve to where we won't have e-commerce leaders. We'll have functional leaders and IT working together to build solutions." Reiner explains that when the e-business initiative was mandated by Welch, most of the company's functional managers didn't have the experience or confidence to lead the effort. But as GE has ramped up across all of its business units, there are already several businesses that have incorporated the e-business leadership with IT.

But GE Polymerland knows that however the organizational chart is structured, there is much work to be done. While reflecting on GE Polymerland's strong start on the Internet, Foss keeps things in perspective. He recalls that a Merrill Lynch analyst recently told him that if GE Polymerland was an independent start-up, it could reap an $80 billion valuation in an initial public offering. But there is a long way to go. "We're in the first inning, and we're not declaring victory," Foss says.

Both Foss and Podesta are certain of one thing: The business model is transferable to other companies. Podesta acknowledges that GE's culture is unique in its ability to do big things fast. But other companies are capable of this kind of initiative if the right leadership is behind it. "It's all about the leadership," Podesta says, "and understanding your power and position in the market."

3

Enron
Redefining Yourself through New Markets

In every company, you've got the radicals, the nuts. We searched them out because they needed to be in these new businesses.

CEO Jeffrey Skilling, Enron Corporation

t would be difficult to find a company making a more remarkable transition from traditional business to e-business than Enron Corporation, the $101 billion Houston-based natural gas and electricity giant. In an environment where speed is the catalyst to e-business success, Enron conceived and launched its e-business initiative in seven months. Since launching EnronOnline in November 1999, Enron has done more than $400 billion worth of transactions over the Internet and is doing more than 3,500 transactions—worth more than $2.5 billion— every day! This represents more than 65 percent of its trading volume.

In so doing, Enron, like other great radicals, has transformed not only itself but also an entire industry. By remaking its business model in cyberspace, Enron has forced its competitors to follow suit and has served notice that the status quo would no longer hold. Jeffrey Skilling, Enron's chief executive officer, says, "We are no longer an energy company. We are a company that makes markets. We create the market, and once it is created, we make the market."

Having quickly discovered how powerful the Internet is in moving and trading its core products, Enron has moved into a raft of new commodity markets, including pulp and paper, coal, metals, plastics, chemicals, and even bandwidth. Much more is on the way because Skilling and Enron chairman Kenneth Lay believe that Enron's business model, layered onto the Internet, will remake countless commodity marketplaces and turn them into fertile businesses. Enron has created a new organization called Enron Net Works to incubate and spawn these new business opportunities. If it works, Skilling says, Enron Net Works, of which EnronOnline is now a part, will become "the Coca Cola syrup of our company."

"Enron has been willing to experiment, and when it makes a decision to innovate and go forward, it puts the people and resources into the business to make it a success," says Jim Walker, a senior analyst with Forrester Research in Cambridge, Massachusetts. "It's a surprise how many companies are tentative and don't want to be first. Enron is willing to be first."

Enron measures its success by the numbers. It has become the dominant player in the global energy markets, and Skilling believes it is possible for Enron to land up to 30 percent of the $1.5 trillion annual revenues in those markets. He figures that Enron has a good shot at grabbing a 30 percent market share in all these new markets as well, which represents at least another $3 trillion in annual global revenues.

"By having a clear vision and striking out on its own, Enron was able to develop these marketplaces very rapidly," Walker says. "A lot of other companies are forming consortia online and spending a lot of time in meetings, ironing out the differences among the companies, about governance and how to put things together."

The competition, though late to the game, has responded. Six of Enron's biggest rivals, including Duke Energy Corp. and El Paso Energy Corp., banded together to form the Intercontinental Exchange, an online marketplace, to challenge EnronOnline. Big utilities like PG&E in California have also leaped into cyberspace to trade energy. But Skilling is undaunted. He claims that competitors have given Enron a year's head start and thus cost themselves the online battle.

"If we're successful in continuing to grow our market share in the energy business and then translate this into other commodity markets, there is a very reasonable chance that we will become the largest corporation in the world," Skilling states. He noted that the company had a market cap of $80 billion in 2000 and that "we've just scratched the surface. Can we be as valuable a corporation as Microsoft, Cisco, or GE? I think so. Because this is just so fundamental. Making markets is fundamental to every business in the country. The old integrated structures are breaking down and being replaced by markets. So the potential is huge."

Like other radicals, Enron believes there are several key catalysts to e-business success. First is moving quickly and aggressively to gain first-mover advantage. Second is building upon a sound bricks-and-mortar business model that is transferable to the Internet. Third and most important is creating a culture in which radical and creative thinking is encouraged and rewarded. Enron has reaped big rewards for encouraging its employees to become entrepreneurs and rewarding them for it.

Indeed, Enron's extraordinary entrance to e-business was not the result of long-term corporate planning and strategizing but rather of the aggressive ingenuity of a single employee with a vision. Enron learned firsthand how valuable it can be, in the quest for e-business success, to foster an open, creative, and empowered culture for employees. Without it, Enron would not likely have grabbed such a significant e-business lead in its industry. In an environment that moves with the speed of e-business, companies bogged down by bureaucracies and stultifying strategic planning are likely to struggle on the Internet. Skilling, a former McKinsey consultant, is adamantly opposed to strategic planning. "The first thing I did when I came to Enron in 1990 was to shut down the strategic planning process," he states. "I have absolutely no tolerance for strategic planners. I don't believe they work."

What does work is to create an open market for employees such as Louise Kitchen, a then-30-year-old gas trader in the United Kingdom who quietly initiated Enron's entrance to e-business. Enron, which perennially makes *Fortune* magazine's list of most admired companies for its innovative and open work environment, is a haven for creative, entrepreneurial people. Its internal compensation and performance evaluation systems are designed to encourage risk taking and radical thinking. In 1999, for example, Kitchen unveiled a plan to her boss in London to put Enron's trading activities on the Internet. Enron had already developed a localized Internet program for Germany and Scandinavia, and Kitchen believed she could take all of the company's trading online and provide a much more efficient way for Enron customers to get information and transact trades.

"I didn't need a pat on the back from Ken Lay or Jeff Skilling," Kitchen told *Bloomberg News*. "It was obvious we should have been doing this ages ago." According to Bloomberg, Kitchen had no experience building Websites, but as a trader she knew a lot about how buyers like to purchase commodities.

Using money from her unit's existing budget, in just two months Kitchen pulled together a team of 380 Enron employees from all over the world to help launch her plan. Working after hours and on weekends, the team quickly built a prototype for what would become EnronOnline.

Ironically, Skilling had been outspoken about his disdain for e-commerce "as it had been traditionally approached," he says. "I didn't want to spend money doing a traditional business-to-business (B2B) site because basically, it's just a bulletin board," Skilling explains. "I'd been pretty explicit about that." So the London-based team purposely kept headquarters in Houston in the dark until just before they were ready to launch. In the fall of 1999, Kitchen's boss, John Sheriff, flew to Houston for a meeting with Skilling.

He told Skilling he wanted to talk about e-commerce. "I said, 'John, you know where I stand on that,'" Skilling recalls. But Sheriff insisted that this system was different. It was a principal-based system, meaning that Enron is a buyer *and* seller in every trade. The site provides liquidity rather than just a bulletin board. "As soon as he said that, I got it," Skilling says. "I said, 'Oh, that's good,' and he breathed a big sigh of relief. I said, 'What's the matter?' and he replied, 'Well, we're rolling it out next month.'"

Past is Prologue

Skilling and Lay admit to being stunned at the swift and vast payback of EnronOnline. The $20 million investment to build the system has been dwarfed by the returns. Skilling says that he wouldn't have been surprised to reap such numbers over the next five years, but that in just under a year "the numbers are unbelievable." He points out that with the combined natural gas and electric businesses in North America, Europe, and Japan, "a marketplace of a half-trillion dollars a year is being fundamentally restructured by this."

As with other radicals, Enron owes a significant portion of its success to the underlying business model that had evolved over the past decade. Simply layering an inferior business model onto the Internet will not create success. In order to understand Enron's Internet success, one must understand the genesis of its business model, which was shaped in large part by Skilling.

Enron was created in 1985 as a traditional gas utility and pipeline company with the leveraged buyout of Houston Natural Gas by an Omaha-based company called Internorth in a deal orchestrated by junk-bond king Michael Milken. But in 1986 the new company was wrestling with a debt ratio of 80 percent, and then, unexpectedly, oil prices collapsed. Deregulation of the natural gas business was killing margins in the gas pipeline business, and to add insult to injury, the Peruvian government took control of Enron's offshore oil fields in Peru. Enron teetered on the brink of collapse. For two years, the company struggled to find a profitable course of action, and none emerged.

Skilling, then a McKinsey consultant called in to help put out the fires, sat in on a 1988 gathering he calls the "Come to Jesus" meeting. In that meeting, Richard Kinder, Skilling's predecessor as president of the company, suggested just a bit facetiously that Enron could either make drastic changes to take advantage of new market trends or declare bankruptcy. Opting to stay in business, the management committee decided to create two new businesses: the North American merchant business, buying and selling energy and other commodities, and the international power plant and pipeline business.

These two businesses were started from scratch, and Skilling was asked in 1990 to take over the merchant business. In 1990, 80 percent of the company's earnings came from the traditional pipeline group. None came from the new businesses. Today, 80 percent of the earnings come from these two businesses. What was notable about the formation of these two businesses under pressure-packed business conditions was that both ended up with similar cultures, according to Skilling. The cultures are very aggressive, risk taking, market-oriented, and accepting of change. In fact, one of Skilling's first acts as president of the merchant business was to initiate an analyst program and recruit talented young people and nontraditional thinkers to be trained for the new business environment.

"In every company, you've got the radicals, the nuts. We searched them out," Skilling says, "because they needed to be in these new businesses." In most cases, they didn't need searching out; they came on their own, drawn by the chance to try something new.

What they were brought in to do was nothing less than change the industry. Enron, which had been a marginal player in the traditional and staid gas-pipeline business, went through a metamorphosis. Skilling's plan was no longer simply to move energy resources through the company's pipelines but to trade natural gas and later electricity like commodities. Though this is now common practice, in 1990 it had never been done before and was considered heresy in the conservative industry. But Skilling, always a radical, saw things in a different way.

Why simply sell energy at fixed prices like everyone else, he wondered, if you could create a whole new market by matching supply with demand? If a utility in Boston needs extra natural gas to handle a December cold snap, Enron could buy surplus gas in Michigan from another supplier and get it to Boston immediately. The magic lay in the ability to move fast, be able to deliver, and stay ahead of the pricing curve. While competitors dawdled at the onset of deregulation, Enron started moving quickly, convincing customers that they could package and price energy any way a customer wanted it. It was revolutionary in an industry that had become torpid with outdated regulation.

Similarly, when electric power deregulation started in the early 1990s, Enron moved swiftly to offer similar options to its customers. With its status as the largest gas trader, Enron was able to leverage that power and create complex deals for electricity as well. What Lay and Skilling learned from the experience was that the fastest, most aggressive entrant into a market has a huge advantage over later players. As *Fortune* magazine put it, "The more customers and more suppliers Enron has, the more options it has in cobbling together a deal. When Enron agrees to provide electric power to a big utility, it may be repackaging power it bought from ten different suppliers under ten different conditions. The more suppliers it has, the more artfully it can pick out a kilowatt here and another one there before putting them on a plate for the customer. The same advantage derives from having more customers than the competition; it means Enron has more places to unload those kilowatts at good prices."

Skilling's model worked so well that it did indeed change the energy industry. With the trading model in place and flourishing, Enron began to build a futures market and risk management products as well as financial services offerings for its customers. Seeing the viability of its new businesses, Enron moved quickly across Europe and then into India and the Far East, building power plants and pipelines. It is now the biggest gas and power trader in Europe, and it invested $3 billion to build a power plant and liquefied gas terminal near Bombay. Though its spectacular growth since the November 1999 debut of EnronOnline gets the attention, Enron was on a fast track already, a B2B player before the term was invented. From profits of $226 million on sales of $4.6 billion in 1990, Enron grew to $1.3 billion in profits and $101 billion in sales in 2000.

The innovative business model was revolutionary enough before the Internet came along. Now the changes have shaken Enron to its core. In 2000 the company conducted nearly 550 million online transactions worth a total of $336 billion. "We've had to significantly change the way we operate to accommodate all this," Skilling says. He explains that the job of Enron's traders has shifted dramatically from a proactive to reactive one. Trading is the key component of the business, and when it is functioning properly, Enron knows it is getting the lowest-cost product to package for its customers. Prior to EnronOnline, a trader putting together a gas or electric supply package for a customer had to be on the telephone calling around to find out a price, then calling another source for another price, and when they were satisfied that they had a good value, they would execute the transaction.

By putting its prices on its Website, the push has become a pull and has changed the role of the Enron traders. Customers have instant access to prices on their computer screens, and they can initiate multimillion dollar transactions with the click of a mouse. Once a customer sees the deal he wants, he clicks on it and it is done. And it is more powerful in that it works for all levels of customers; the biggest buyer or seller in the world or the smallest gets the same deal. The transition is dramatic. "In the old days, you could stop and go to lunch or to the bathroom," Skilling says. "In the new world, you can hardly move because you no longer determine when people do business with you. They do business with you when they want to do business with you."

Competitors claim that the flaw in EnronOnline's strategy is that customers are forced to deal with just one company, Enron. According to Lay, "It's hard to imagine what is more neutral than a totally transparent price that's on the screen all the time." Lay pointed out in *World Link* magazine that the system not only is easy but also is free, while other systems require a fee to participate. "We make money on the spread [between the price we offer to buyers and the price we offer to suppliers]," he says. "But obviously with the kind of volume we have, the kind of liquidity we have, we have a very small spread." He noted that the spread has dropped 85 percent since Enron went online, from about 3 cents to about half a cent. "But we also make money on all the other things that are behind the transactions," he said. And how!

Skilling says that Enron is prepared to put its prices on anybody's Website, whether it is a new exchange or even a competitor's site. The key is that no matter where the prices are listed, the customer is still dealing with Enron.

Forrester's Walker says, "Enron's entrepreneurial culture is the backdrop of its success. But Enron has exploded by applying the lessons of the financial markets to the commodities markets: managing risk better than others through superior financial engineering and credit evaluation tools. We believe that the ability to manage price risk is a skill for the Internet economy."

Good-Bye Vertical Integration

For Skilling, the makeover of Enron is based on his view that rigid, vertically integrated industries like energy, pulp and paper, and even telecommunications were long overdue for change. If you view these businesses as horizontal, Enron operates in the seams between various players in the business, pulling deals together in ways that old economy companies cannot do. The Enron model was New Economy before the New Economy got started. "Putting the Internet on top of it is just turning on the afterburners," Skilling says. All of this convinces Skilling that this business model is simply "a better way to do business than what you see in most traditional commodity businesses."

In the old days of business, Skilling explains, the theory of vertical integration was based on the idea that the costs of information and control were very high. The only way to limit those expenses was by integrating everything. A company had to own and control everything. However, with the growth of communications and computing technology, those costs have collapsed. "So the whole logic of how we set up our industrial base doesn't work anymore," Skilling says. He uses Exxon as an example. Exxon does not rank as the greatest oil exploration and production company in the world, nor as the best refinery. Its gas stations are not in the top quartile of the industry. But with a vertically integrated chain across all the individual parts, it remains cost competitive.

"In the new world," Skilling says, "you can't do that. There will be a market for refineries, a market for production, a market for the direct sale of gasoline. And you will be able to choose the world-class player in each stage of that process. So someone who is vertically integrated and isn't the best at each link of the chain is going to get killed." He acknowledges that the energy business will still have its Exxons and Mobils, but by gobbling each other up in megamergers, they are just getting to be "bigger dinosaurs, not smarter dinosaurs, and they are not going to be able to survive" by just doing business as usual.

In order for this new business model to work, there have to be markets between those various functions. "You have to be able to replace that ownership link with a certainty of sourcing," Skilling says. That's where Enron comes in. If he is right, nearly every company in every traditional industry will fundamentally have to tear itself apart and put itself back together in a different way. There must be horizontally integrated components, each world-class and each capable of moving products back and forth, thus creating new markets. "Every time that happens, you are seeing the commoditization of the products that transfer between those interfaces, and we're going to be there," Skilling says.

For Enron, the Internet has helped open its horizons to seemingly endless new markets. The company heavily rewards its employees, whose average age is 33, for trying new things and thinking creatively, as Louise Kitchen did with EnronOnline. She has moved from London to Houston and is a member of the executive office of Enron Net Works. As a result of such incentives, a stream of new market ideas has come from within employee ranks, including swap contracts that allow newspaper publishers to hedge against fluctuations in paper prices, weather hedges, and the sale of bandwidth. For example, Enron Net Works is investigating potential markets for data storage, an idea that came from an employee. "We believe we can begin providing on-demand data storage and provide a spot market and a forward market for that service," Skilling says.

But the company's decision to sell bandwidth as a commodity raised more than a few eyebrows. Enron has heard the nay-sayers in the past claiming, for example, that electricity would never be bought and sold as a commodity. Tell Lay or Skilling that a market will never emerge and they smile. That's just what they want to hear. It keeps competitors from sniffing around and allows Enron to get yet another first-mover advantage.

Spotting new markets is more art than science, but it requires the market maker to see opportunity where others see walls. Thomas Gros, an Enron vice president, wanted to connect his New York office to Houston headquarters. He decided to set up a videoconferencing link to Enron's New York office. He gasped at the price: $20,000 a month for a high-speed line that would only be needed for a few hours each day. In addition, Enron would get locked into a ten-year deal for the service. Why, Gros wondered, can't you get broadband service when you need it rather than be stuck with such draconian deals?

With corporate support, Gros started a bandwidth trading business. Skilling was amazed at what he found when he looked hard at the telecommunications industry. "The communications business is a high-technology business. They apply high-tech equipment to their networks, but the business model is archaic," Skilling says. "It is straight out of Standard Oil in 1882. It's a rigid, vertically integrated, point-to-point concept. Sooner or later, they are going to have to change their thought processes."

Meanwhile, Enron sees an opportunity. The company formed Enron Broadband Services and set out to build an infrastructure so that it could deliver the product. Investing more than $600 million, Enron built a 14,000 mile fiber-optic network across North America and then began the same process abroad. It has also installed 1,500 large server complexes spread out across the continent and in Europe and Japan as well, to act as on and off ramps to the network. Along with that, the company sourced giant switches from Lucent Technologies so that it could create a market.

"To make a market, you have to have flexibility and be able to commoditize, simplify, and standardize a product," Skilling says. "To do that in the communications business, which is the same thing as electricity and natural gas, we needed to have switches. Once somebody gets to our server complexes, the on ramp to the network, we take them to the switch, and at that point, if we have the ability to switch between multiple networks, we can create a market." With the network in place, customers are able to buy and sell bandwidth in pieces that can be measured in hours or days rather than in years.

The strategy is actually two-pronged. Radical thinkers don't allow themselves to get boxed in by corporate heritage. "Why can't Enron provide content if it already has the network?" Skilling and Lay thought. Thus, Enron is also establishing itself as a content transmitter along the network. It signed a 20-year deal in 2000 with Blockbuster to deliver movies on demand into homes as digitized video streams over the fiber-optic lines. Eventually, the plan calls for 7,000 movies and other entertainment such as games, concerts, and even television shows, all available on demand when the customer wants them via DSL lines hooked to their computers or via cable systems on their television sets. Lay points out that the home movie entertainment market is already a $10 billion market, but only $1 billion of that comes from satellite or pay-per-view systems. "We think there's an enormous opportunity to grow that market if you provide the convenience where people can just call up a video anytime they want to," Lay told *World Link.* Enron plans to invest $600 million annually to build this network.

Similarly, Enron got into the pulp and paper business, another massive industry mired in archaic pricing methods. Again, as with Kitchen and EnronOnline, a single employee switched on the lightbulb. According to *Fortune,* David Cox, a high school dropout and former commercial fisherman, got a menial job in Enron's printing department. Outspoken and ambitious, he convinced Lay and Skilling to start an independent printing company to handle its publications. Cox built the business by taking jobs from other Houston companies, and when rising paper costs cut into profits, he tried to negotiate a long-term, fixed-price contract with a supplier. He was told that no such contracts existed in the paper industry. He called Skilling directly and said, "Here's a $175 billion commodity industry and there are no price-risk management tools."

By 1997, not surprisingly, Enron entered the pulp and paper business and met the same kind of industry resistance they'd encountered in natural gas and electricity. Enron was told that such tools were unnecessary, that investors liked fluctuating paper prices and that Enron had no experience in the market. Under Cox, Enron began trading pulp and paper and had traded 18 million tons of pulp and paper products worth $8 billion in trades by the end of 2000. In September 2000 Enron launched Clickpaper.com, an Internet-based transaction system dedicated to the forest products industry, essentially taking the EnronOnline platform, replicating it for pulp and paper, and giving it its own dedicated Website. Through Clickpaper, customers get the same competitive pricing and price transparency they get with other commodities on EnronOnline. The success of Clickpaper, like other Enron Internet-based offerings, lies in the business model. It is not enough to put up a Website. The key is to have the infrastructure necessary to deliver the commodity to the customer reliably.

Skilling notes that because of this, Enron must acquire a "physical position" in pulp and paper and that that remains a work in progress. Asked how a company as big as Enron moves so quickly, Skilling, in radical form, replies, "I think it takes us too long."

It's the People

As radicals also understand, the linchpin to a successful e-business transformation is the people. Enron, unlike other traditional bricks-and-mortar companies, has not had much trouble finding and retaining talented young people to build its e-business organization. Enron has been ranked as the Most Innovative Company in America by *Fortune* for five years in a row and in 2000 ranked first in quality of management. Paine Webber noted that "it had one of the deepest and most innovative management teams in the world."

Forrester's Jim Walker describes Enron as akin to a consulting firm like McKinsey, which is not surprising since that is where Skilling was trained. The company hires hundreds of talented young MBAs and sets them loose in a challenging and dynamic environment, where the best and brightest will thrive. "Enron has 20,000 employees—risk managers, financial experts, commodity traders, and technology gurus—all incentivized to expand Enron's business," Walker says. "Louise Kitchen told me that the access to internal experts was her number-one advantage. As start-up executives repeatedly complain, finding money is easy, but securing talented people is nearly impossible."

As Lay told *World Link* magazine, the average age of Enron's employees is 33, while that of employees in the rest of the industry is in the low 50s. "We tie a lot more of our compensation to performance than most companies do," Lay says. "And we don't punish failure, as long as there's a pretty good reason why something failed."

Skilling says that Enron felt no need to try to instill a dot.com atmosphere inside the company to attract and retain good people. In many ways, it already operated like a dot.com, without dress codes, regular work hours, or strict rules. When Skilling took over the merchant business, he ripped out all the walls to create an open workplace to underscore the aggressive new culture. The result was that decision-making and thought-process time sped up. Dress codes were also abolished (with Skilling the last to give up his usual suit and tie), but he suggests that he never considered "chasing the dot.com guys."

"We're here to do business," he states. "This is a 'take-no-prisoners' kind of place. But I don't control the place—the people control the place—so if someone wants a basketball court on their floor, they can go ahead. I haven't seen anyone do it yet."

In an article in the *New York Times* about Enron's internal entrepreneurs, Cox recounted that Skilling was constantly challenging employees to find ways to take advantage of the turmoil that impending deregulation had unleashed in the gas industry. "He made us feel that there was nothing we could not do," Cox said.

Similar tales abound inside Enron. Lynda Clemmons, a young woman with a degree in history and French, joined Enron at age 22, and by 29 she had taken Enron into the weather insurance business, creating an operation that sells hedges against the vagaries of the weather that confound energy producers. The business she set up essentially lets utilities buy insurance against weather-induced problems like an unexpected heat wave that forces a utility to pay high prices in wholesale energy markets. Clemmons, working within Enron's capital and trade division, worked out all the arrangements to create the new business. Clemmons, who has since left Enron, told the *New York Times*, "I didn't have somebody holding my hand saying 'OK, this is how it's done.'" Instead, she put out the word, like Kitchen had, and attracted other radicals inside Enron to join her. "You create your own network," she told the *Times*. In two years, she and her new staff sold more than $1 billion in weather hedges. Gros added, "When people here see an opportunity, they want to participate. We do not ask permission to spread the word. We just do it."

Like other radicals, particularly since the dot.com bubble burst in early 2000, Skilling doesn't worry about competing with stock options and initial public offerings (IPOs). There is no plan to take Enron-Online public as a separate company, for example. Instead, the lure is that at Enron, people get to change the markets they work in and are given the resources to make those changes. The company had one of the first employee stock option plans (ESOP) back in 1988, which made a lot of people wealthy, he says. There is an ESOP in place today, and Skilling says Enron employees and board members own 18 percent of the company.

According to Skilling, a crucial lesson—perhaps the most important lesson for the e-business transition—is to run a loose/tight organization and try to reduce the barriers to movement and mobility of employees across the company. The loose side is for allowing smart people to try new things. The tight side is for managing compensation and performance evaluations centrally with a single performance evaluation system across the entire company. Enron recently reorganized the company to create this new structure. "Now everyone above a certain level is considered a corporate resource," Skilling says.

What this does is allow people to move from one business unit to another without worrying about losing titles or compensation levels or encountering different performance evaluation criteria in a different department. "If they are reviewed by a single committee for the entire corporation, it doesn't matter where they are," Skilling says. "It's not going to change." Titles are portable, so once an Enron vice president, always a vice president, no matter the function or the geography.

The idea is simple, the execution difficult, but the results profound. "You want your really good people to move to opportunities," Skilling states. "And the really good people are the ones people don't want to lose. So it's a constant battle."

In the transition to e-business, such an atmosphere and culture is crucial. When Kitchen set out on her quest to create EnronOnline, all 380 people she recruited to the project were from inside the company. There is no end of unhappy managers who would prefer to keep certain people in their organizations, but the person who decides to move is the individual him- or herself. A spurned former boss can make a plea, even to Skilling, but there cannot be secret deals or dot.com-like incentives such as a new BMW or country club membership to keep an employee. In a loose/tight organization, Skilling doesn't care what people wear or what their strategies are, but he won't tolerate inconsistencies in contracts or commitments, and most especially in the compensation and performance evaluation standards. BMWs are not part of the compensation philosophy, period.

The result of this structure, if you truly have fungibility of people, is that the opportunities equilibrate. If someone wants to leave an organization, there can only be one of two reasons: The first is that there is a better opportunity somewhere else in the company "and the people know that better than I do," Skilling says. "That's why I don't need strategic planning anymore because I'm the last person to know if a budding opportunity is going to work. It's way down in the organization, but the people in the organization know that." The other reason is that a unit is being poorly managed or there is no longer opportunity in that business.

"When we started our bandwidth business, we had a huge flow of people into that unit," Skilling says. "That's how I knew we had a tiger by the tail, because these are really smart people, and boy were they clamoring to get into that organization." But after the flood, the movement stopped. The situation resembled Yogi Berra's line about the popular restaurant: "Nobody goes there anymore—it's too crowded." Suddenly the best opportunities were elsewhere.

Enron is also accepting of failure, and some of those whose projects didn't meet expectations are now in charge of even bigger opportunities. In a successful e-business, occasional failure has to be tolerated, or the inclination to take risks will disappear.

"No shots, no ducks," Skilling says.

4

Victoria's Secret
It's the Brand,
Offline and Online

Nobody takes all the locations.

Leslie Wexner

n February 1999, just a few months after launching its Website, Victoria's Secret webcast its annual Valentine's Day fashion show live over the Internet. It was a bold step for a company that had been noticeably reluctant to plunge into e-commerce, and it was a disaster, at least from the technology standpoint.

With just a single, thirty-second commercial during the Super Bowl advertising the event, Victoria's Secret started a stampede of 1.5 million people that crashed servers and communication lines supporting its Internet site.

Meltdown is the word corporate executives use to describe what happened. "We just fried ourselves that day," says Dan Finkelman, senior vice president of brand and business planning for Intimate Brands, Victoria's Secret's parent company. "We overloaded every possible capacity you could imagine. You could smell the frying rubber from here."

Far from panicking, or second-guessing their planning for the event, the executives were ecstatic. Edward Razek, Victoria's Secret's president of brand and creative services for Intimate Brands as well as chief marketing officer, saw a great story in the disaster. "So many people came, Victoria's Secret shut down the Internet. Fabulous!" he told Finkelman. Newspaper headlines around the world and television newscasts trumpeted the tremendous response the Victoria's Secret brand had provoked. "We may have witnessed the beginning of a whole new way to market products," gushed Charles Gibson on ABC's "Good Morning America."

From a retailer's point of view, the event was a watershed in the brief history of e-business. More than 500 million hits followed during the week, and *Adweek* magazine named the online fashion show the Internet marketing event of 1999. In one radical Internet moment, Victoria's Secret's already admired brand was suddenly being regarded in the same laudatory tones as mega-brands like Coca Cola, Walt Disney, and Microsoft. The company that was a slow mover onto the Internet had shown itself to be an e-business to reckon with. To Finkelman, the spearhead of Victoria's Secret's e-business effort, the event brought to mind an old joke: "What did Adam say when he first saw Eve in the Garden of Eden? Stand back, only God knows how big this thing can get."

One year earlier, Victoria's Secret had committed itself to becoming an e-business player. But the webcast brought a jolt of reality to company executives as to just how big it *could* get. The somewhat cynical eyes watching Internet retailing at company headquarters in Columbus, Ohio, were opened to new possibilities. As Leslie Wexner, legendary chairman and CEO of Intimate Brands, says, "It was, perhaps, the most tangible demonstration yet of what the Internet could be. And the reason it was such a success? The power of the brand."

Cynics might argue that a bevy of supermodels like Tyra Banks and Heidi Klum parading around in skimpy lingerie and bikinis is sure to attract a crowd, in person or online, and that it takes no special e-business savvy to mastermind such an event. But the fashion show was far more than a provocative publicity stunt. With $3 billion of the nearly $5 billion in revenues that Intimate Brands generated in 2000, Victoria's Secret is a carefully nurtured, highly successful brand, not a mass-marketed product. In the Internet, the company has discovered a powerful new channel to complement its stores and catalog businesses. Just as important, the Internet enables Victoria's Secret to project itself as a ubiquitous global brand without sending bricks and mortar overseas. Though it has opened no stores outside the United States, about 7 percent of the company's direct sales (catalog and Internet) are international, coming from 160 countries.

"Our strategy right from the beginning was to build something that will showcase and support the brand experience with the customer," says Finkelman. "We wanted something that will offer our best products—our most visually appealing products—in an environment where the customer is comfortable."

Steve Kernkraut, senior managing director at Bear, Stearns & Co. in New York, praises the Victoria's Secret strategy, pointing out that it is "far better grounded than most others" on the Internet. In 1998, he says, Victoria's Secret could have tried to become the "killer app" on the Internet by leveraging great traffic counts on its Website and creating an online superstore selling CDs, Palm Pilots, and other items. Instead, they moved more slowly and built upon the core brand. "They clearly set their sights on the Victoria's Secret brand," Kernkraut says. "They built upon that brand, made the Website part of the brand appeal, and let everything else ripple out from there."

Though it received tremendous media attention from the first webcast, Victoria's Secret did not want to leave the image of technological failure in the minds of customers. In May 2000, with beefed-up Internet technology and partners like Yahoo, IBM, and Microsoft, the company webcast its fashion show again, this time live from Cannes. An even greater stampede of people came to the Website to watch live—more than 2 million people in 140 countries. This time there was no meltdown. "It was the most-watched Web event of all time," Razek says.

These forays into Internet showmanship have proven the power of splashy webcasts to draw potential customers online. But Finkelman, Razek, and the Victoria's Secret Direct team, which includes its catalog and online businesses, have learned much more in the last few years about the retailing dynamics of the Internet. The key lessons include the following:

- The brand drives the Website; the Website doesn't drive the brand.

- The Internet turns Victoria's Secret into a 360 degree brand, which means that it provides a foundation for a consistent image and product line across three channels: stores, catalog, and online.

- The best customers are multichannel customers: Those who buy in stores, through the catalog, and online spend more proportionately than those who only shop in one channel. This finding is supported by a recent National Retail Federation study that found that multichannel shoppers purchase more frequently, spend more per transaction, and, as a result, spend more annually than do single-channel shoppers.

- The Web brings the company more information about its customers than it could ever have before if it is mined correctly. The key is how the company uses that data to build a stronger and deeper customer relationship. Victoria's Secret, for example, has collected a database of well over 3 million customers' e-mail addresses to which it sends a regular flow of product information and sales incentives.

- The path to profitability can and should be laid out before the Internet plan is put in place. In Victoria's Secret's case, the Website has been profitable right from the beginning.

Keeping Things in Perspective

To date, the online retail experience has been spotty at best. The dot.com retail revolution, lead by Amazon.com, proved impossible to ignore for many traditional retailers who raced onto the Internet with half-baked strategies and poorly executed plans. In the disastrous online holiday shopping season of 1999, demand outstripped capability, and many orders did not get filled on time or at all.

Industry watchers spent much of 2000 reading obituaries of once high-flying dot.com retailers, and a pattern emerged. The business-to-consumer (B2C) Websites that not only survived but also thrived belonged to traditional retailers with solid distribution infrastructures and well-executed plans. The Internet became a key part of a broader plan rather than the entire focus. Jupiter Research predicts that online spending will total $199 billion by 2005. More importantly, the Internet will *influence* $632 billion in offline purchases. Radical merchants understand that the key is getting customers to buy, regardless of the channel.

Wexner opened his first Limited store in 1963 in Columbus and turned it into a multibillion dollar conglomerate of brand-name retail outlets like Limited Stores, Victoria's Secret, Henri Bendel, Lerner New York, Lane Bryant, Bath and Body Works, and Express. He has long viewed the Internet with a seasoned merchant's eye—that is, healthy skepticism. His retail empire, which is divided into two big, publicly traded companies, The Limited, Inc., and Intimate Brands, includes more than $10 billion in annual revenues, 5,000 stores, and nearly 200,000 employees. Along the way, he achieved stunning successes, endured disappointing downturns, and, in the 1990s, reinvented his own management style to revitalize his entire company.

For Wexner, e-business is not a panacea but an important next step on a continuum of advances that have changed the face of retailing over the past century. He suggests that inventions such as the steam engine, the railroad, jet aircraft, electronic credit, and even air conditioning had more impact on retailing than the Internet. "Imagine trying to sell fall sweaters or coats in a department store in August in Ohio without air conditioning," he states.

Many of his executives believed that the various retail chains should have launched Websites years ago. But where they saw the leading edge of technology, Wexner saw the bleeding edge. Looking at Amazon and its continuing stream of red ink, he wonders, "What price glory?" When asked his metric for success on the Internet, he replies, "Show me the money."

Though he understood this was new, uncharted territory, Wexner tried to envision the economic model for success. "Do you ever get paid?" he asked when thinking about Amazon's inability to turn a profit. "How much investment needs to be sunk before you don't believe? Do you have to drill the hole through the whole world? Is there a better way?"

Spending nearly four decades in retail has made Wexner suspicious of overhyped, underdelivered promises in technology. He says it is the nature of fashion retailers to react to every trend. "If some competitors opened a store on Pluto, my phone would start ringing: 'What about Pluto? How do we get there?'" Under Wexner, the company has not shied away from technology leadership, as demonstrated by the Limited's early deployment of point-of-sale systems in its stores. But too often, he believes, technological hype can send a company off into the technological equivalent of a wild-goose chase.

"I don't think there's a major retailer that didn't lose at least thirty to fifty million dollars exploring cable television and the Home Shopping Network concept as a way of selling products," he says. "They'd have their own stations, buy their own time, and produce their own shows because it was going to be so dominant. One of my observations about the history of the world is that *nobody takes all the locations.* You just can't own everything."

So his desire to push online was tempered by the lack of an economic model that made sense to him. In the long run, he was persuaded by his own talented staff and the response to the fashion show. "You have to know what your strengths are and what your own limitations are," he says. "And you need to have some idea where the end of the earth is. In almost everything, I'm really happy to be a fast second or even a fast third until I understand it."

For this reason, Wexner was content to sacrifice first-mover advantage to others. He listened to his chief information officer (CIO), Jon Ricker, a veteran of Federal Express and Bell South, who said, "There's no substitute for good planning, design, and engineering."

Ricker, who oversaw the technical implementation of the Internet initiative, made it clear that with the power of the Victoria's Secret brand, "Once we opened the floodgates, we needed something industrial-strength before we went live."

Industrial strength clearly wasn't strong enough on that February day in 1999 to handle the unforeseen hordes of online visitors to the fashion show. Still, the Website had been carefully designed and built to handle conventional Web traffic.

A team of Victoria's Secret executives, including Finkelman, Razek, Grace Nichols, Kenneth Weil, and Anne Marie Blaire, met with Ricker and his technology team to plot out the structure of the Website. Ricker makes it clear that despite his boss's low-key approach, Wexner spearheaded the move to e-business. Wexner chairs quarterly technology meetings and is the cornerstone to the Internet effort across the company. "If the CEO doesn't spearhead this, it will die under its own weight," Ricker says. He regularly talks to fellow CIOs and notes, "My colleagues never see the chairman. Les is not a technologist, but he is personally involved and excited about this. He gets it."

Kernkraut of Bear, Stears & Co. credits Finkelman with overseeing the Internet effort "with the discipline of a consultant" and bringing an analytical approach to the table. But he says that Wexner's core beliefs and his experience as a creator and builder of brands are the foundation for the initiative. "Wexner is a long-term thinker and believes in these core brands," Kernkraut says. "He's not going to go for the quick buck and screw up the long-term value of the brand."

The Perfect Brand for Cyberspace

When Finkelman joined Intimate Brands in 1996, the hype about the Internet was reaching a fever pitch. When prime competitor the Gap launched an early retail Website, there was clamoring for action in Columbus.

"Unfortunately, there was no business model that proved you could do anything spectacular," Finkelman says. "There was certainly a lot of hype."

One of Wexner's requirements was that the move into cyberspace be sequential rather than a full-scale assault across the company's many brands. One brand would lead them, forge a path, create a template for success, and then others would follow.

Victoria's Secret emerged as the obvious choice to break new ground. The company, founded in 1977 in San Francisco by Roy Raymond, was built upon the premise that lingerie would sell far better in a fantasy Victorian boudoir environment than off cold steel racks in department stores. When Raymond sold the firm to Wexner in 1982 for $4 million, the brand image was carefully nurtured and grown. Women came in to shop for underwear and discovered something new: Victoria's Secret didn't sell underwear, it sold an aspiration—the aspiration to feel sexy, feminine, pretty, and desirable. Its lingerie was classy, not tacky à la Frederick's of Hollywood, and women flocked to the brand.

The first catalog was distributed by Raymond in 1978, and Wexner built upon that concept as well. The catalog, which originally featured erotically posed couples, was revamped several times, settling finally on a formula of demurely posed, lingerie-clad supermodels, which would likely appeal to men. The catalog catered to those males who were embarrassed at entering the shops to buy lingerie for their wives and girlfriends. Men realized the powerful message associated with Victoria's Secret's signature pink-on-pink boxes with the heart logo: They weren't just giving lingerie, but love.

Today, Victoria's Secret owns more than 15 percent of the $12 billion U.S. lingerie market and dominates the sexy bra category, the most lucrative segment of the business. There are nearly 1,000 Victoria's Secret stores, and the company sends out 365 million catalogs each year. Victoria's Secret Beauty, with lines of fragrances and beauty products, is now a $600 million business with plans to grow to $1 billion.

There was no question that Victoria's Secret had a raft of attributes that made it well-suited to the Web: a very visual brand, a successful catalog business with a sound distribution and fulfillment infrastructure already in place, and the merchant's mentality to move deftly with the speed of the Web. With brand awareness already high, the Website could leverage the $145 million the company spends annually on marketing and advertising. A more subtle but no less powerful distinction: Shoppers online had no trouble finding the site. Unlike many dot.com pure plays that scramble to attract customers, the number-one way consumers reached Victoria's Secret site was to type *victoriassecret.com*. Numerous hotlinks through cross-marketing deals with other Websites also increased traffic.

But coupled with Wexner's deep misgivings about overhype and underdelivery, Finkelman was mainly concerned that the Internet would present "a distraction to the business." He'd heard stories about how Web efforts could drain resources and attention away from the traditional business. "It's this really neat thing and everybody wants to be involved, but, in fact, we've got this $700 million catalog business to consider," he recalled.

By 1998 there was no longer any danger of Victoria's Secret's being an Internet pioneer. If anything, it was considered late to the ball. "We simply couldn't see what it bought us to be first," Finkelman says. "We had consultants banging on our doors saying, 'You've got to be first.' And later, 'You're behind. If you don't catch up, you'll be dead.' I just fundamentally didn't believe that."

The truth, Finkelman says, is that the basic rules of retailing haven't really changed with the advent of the Internet. "You have to be thoughtful, aggressive, and effective," he says. "You have to provide what your existing customers and potential customers want, like, or find interesting. You have to be some combination of snazzier, easier, faster, nicer, funnier, prettier, cheaper, higher quality, and more valuable to win. It's the same world you live in today. The Internet has not changed the fundamental competitive equation. It is still much better to be right and accurate and on target than it is to be first."

Taking the Brand Online

From the outset, the focus was clear: Use the Website to drive brand awareness and support the brand. Finkelman met with Ricker's group, Limited Technical Services (LTS), which offers information technology (IT) services for both corporations, to set plans in motion. He brought in a local consulting firm to design the Website and told the technologists, "I don't want to see anyone's picture on the cover of *Geek Today* touting our Website. Our objective isn't to win any technology awards. Our objective is to make customers happy."

Ricker, a savvy businessman in his own right, understood the parameters. Despite the climate at the time—a wave of dot.com start-ups that were turning young entrepreneurs into instant millionaires and billionaires—Ricker believed Victoria's Secret had a huge advantage over the pure plays. With the catalog business's direct fulfillment channel in place, he had a solid foundation upon which to build the Website.

With a year and a half of planning and production, the site was carefully constructed. Everything had to be considered. Victoria's Secret brand, for example, is heavily dependent on lush photography of beautiful women, and its catalog has gained legendary status—especially among teenage boys. The company spends millions on photography and production. The Internet team was handed existing visual material, but Ricker and Finkelman knew that pictures had to load quickly because visitors to the site would not tolerate minutes waiting for a photograph to download on the screen.

The team understood the unspoken eight-second rule for Websites. If Web pages don't download in eight seconds or less, a visitor is likely to log off. In fact, in a recent study by Keynote Systems, an

Internet performance tracking service, Victoria's Secret had the fastest download time of any retail site in the survey: 1.16 seconds. That compared quite favorably to Amazon's 4.45 seconds, Walmart. com's 8 seconds, and Macys.com's 13 seconds.

Tim Plzak, director of advanced technologies at Intimate Brands, says the site was designed for the home PC user with a 28.8K modem and a 200 megahertz computer, certainly not the most advanced capabilities available. "We always look at new technologies, but at the end of the day, we focus on what is the customer experience. We're not targeting the high end."

In an era of lavish spending and breakneck speed on the Web, Victoria's Secret's caution was radical. The effort that had begun slowly in the fall of 1997 moved into 1998 at a similar pace. Finkelman didn't feel he could create a realistic budget for the project because there was no precedent for how much such an effort would cost. The press was regularly reporting corporate investments of $25 million or $50 million in their Web ventures. The amounts were unimaginable to Finkelman. "If I spent $25 million on this, I'd be unemployed," he figured.

To date, the Web initiative has cost closer to $5 million, the biggest expense being the technical support needed to wire the back-end fulfillment part of the Web onto the catalog systems.

On a practical level, the core group grappled with the requirements needed for the site. How would it look? What options were essential? How would it work in concert with the stores and catalogs?

Finkelman asked for benchmarks. He had his designers scan the top 25 retail sites and assess their functionality and performance. In the race for technology supremacy, few had taken the time to do this type of benchmarking. Finkelman found it especially helpful. "You hear that you *have* to do this or that, be able to store names, addresses, phone numbers, and send love letters on your birthday. Well, guess what. Only one Website does that, and it's not very good. Hmmm, well, maybe we don't need that."

By December 1998, with little more than hope that the technology planning had been on target, the initial site was launched. It was too late to expect any payback from that holiday season, so the company did nothing but send out a press release. People found the site anyway. The first day, $6,000 worth of goods was sold, a trivial amount, but eye-opening for the team. It meant people were online searching for Victoria's Secret. It was confirmation that the brand was real and, better yet, international. Orders would eventually come in online from 160 countries.

Each day brought more surprises. A $100,000 day before Christmas set off celebrations. Finkelman figured that 18-year-old males surfing the Net would find the site, but clearly women were logging on as well because people were buying. Mostly, it confirmed that the system worked.

The decision to webcast the February fashion show was made in a marketing meeting. Finkelman knew the site would never be ready to handle the traffic, but he believed in "strategy by rapid prototype," and such a radical move was perfect for kick-starting the online brand. Big-bang marketing events might not work for every e-business, but for a brand with the star power of Victoria's Secret, the fireworks were justified.

For Ricker, the webcast meltdown provided a litany of technical lessons and a clear quantative measure of what was needed to move further. From this experience, the company learned exactly how to plan for the proper technical and communications capacity the following year. LTS, with 700 employees and development resource centers around the United States, had the expertise to build the back-office connections to bring the Website together with the catalog fulfillment systems. It also had numerous partnerships with outside vendors like IBM to bring to bear on the project. So there wasn't the urgency to recruit hot young Internet talent or worry about losing key people inside. Victoria's Secret didn't feel the drain that the dot.com revolution was putting on a lot of companies moving to the Internet. Indeed, a common trait of radical e-businesses is that none panicked during the short-lived dot.com frenzy.

A Channel to Customer Intimacy

Radicals understand that the essence of the brand equity is the customer relationship with the brand. Every encounter with a salesperson in a Victoria's Secret store or on the toll-free phone line was a measure of that relationship, and so it would be online. The Website had to provide the same kind of high-quality service that customers expected in the stores. That meant real-time pricing and product information, clear navigational tools through the site, and the ability to translate the fulfillment capability to the Website.

The Website is the conduit to a community as well. Early on, Finkelman saw the potential of e-mail as a path to customer intimacy—far more, in fact, than was possible in the stores or catalogs. Victoria's Secret began collecting e-mail addresses of its customers with the promise to send out regular announcements about products and promotions. Customer registration pages are a documented turnoff in cyberspace, often leading Website visitors to click to another site. To the surprise of Victoria's Secret's staff, customers flew in the face of conventional Internet wisdom. In the first month, the company received 350,000 names. After a year, there were more than a million and a half people logged in the database, and that number has since grown to more than three million.

What Finkelman learned, aside from the fact that so many people would be willing to give their names and addresses so quickly, was that the tenor and tone of the e-mails had to be in concert with the brand. "This brand is all about making women feel good about themselves," Finkelman says. "That is a very important relationship, so we have to be very careful how we talk to her. And we are."

At the same time, the management team saw an unexpected benefit to the e-business emerge. Men had long been uncomfortable entering Victoria's Secret stores and trying to explain to the saleswomen their wives' bra sizes. The catalog helped to some degree, but one had to *have* a catalog to order from it. Despite the many millions sent out each year, the catalog had limited reach. On the Internet, however, men can shop in the sanctity of their own homes, aided by the ability to sneak in and check their wives' sizes in the dresser. During holiday buying seasons, Victoria's Secret has measured a massive spike in men's online buying—upwards of 60 percent of sales during those periods is to men, which is triple the usual number.

Over time, Victoria's Secret continues to add new touches to the site to enhance the shopping experience and cement the brand relationship for both men and women. Incorporating the popular e-mail connection, for example, the site now offers a Wish List feature. With the click of a mouse, a woman is able to create a personal shopping list, replete with desired items, colors, and sizes, that is e-mailed to her husband or lover. The e-mail is password protected so that it cannot accidentally be put into wide circulation.

While this feature has obvious benefits for the shopper, it tracks right to the bottom line for Victoria's Secret. "Return rates are 10 percent lower on the Web," says Ken Weil, Victoria's Secret's vice president for new media. "It is the lowest-cost channel." An online order, for example, saves the company anywhere from $2.50 to $3.00 compared to one placed by phone.

And all of the Website's features are filtered back through the mandate for ease of use. Complex and confusing downloads of information are avoided. "This is not about technology," says Anne Marie Blaire, director of Internet Brand Development for Intimate Brands. "A customer should never have to guess how to do something on the site. It has to be easy."

Staying on Brand

Radicals also believe that some of the most important decisions are ones you don't make. Finkelman has been blanketed with technology suggestions since the site went live. At first, he heard about the virtual model that several other apparel Websites, such as Lands' End, have adopted. The virtual model allows customers to plug their sizes into the Website and create models of how they would look in particular items. "I kind of liked that idea," Finkelman says. "Unfortunately, I believe that if you put it on our Website, every 13- or 14-year-old boy in the world is going to get on the site and try to build Barbie. That's not on brand for us."

Another popular suggestion is electronic sizing. Finkelman recounts a phone conversation with a 29-year-old executive of a dot.com company seeking to partner with Victoria's Secret on such a project. "I want you to imagine the following scenario," Finkelman told her. "I want you to be my customer. I want you to come into a Victoria's Secret store, go into a room in the back, and I want you to strip naked to the waist. Then I'm going to take a digital photograph of you, and I promise it will be confidential and no one else will ever see it, and then I'll put it up on the Web so you can access it. You like the idea?"

After a silent pause, Finkelman continued, "This is not my brand.

My brand is a very personal relationship with this customer. I don't want to embarrass her or scare her. I don't want her to feel like she's being manipulated or used. I want her to feel sexy and glamorous and confident. And I figure that asking her to strip naked so I can take her picture so she can look at herself online wearing a bra is a bad idea."

What it boils down to is simple, Finkelman says: It's not about the *reality* of what you are; it's about the *aspiration* of what you'd like to be. "Before Victoria's Secret was around, every department store in the world sold underwear," he said. "The magic of Victoria's Secret is that women don't want to wear underwear. Women want to wear *lingerie*. They want to feel sexy and beautiful, and this is the underpinning of the brand. We apply that to everything we do on the Web."

Consultants and financial analysts regularly come to Columbus and ask the same question about the Web business: "Are you going to spin it off as a separate unit?" Despite the fact that a separate dot.com business might immediately generate a couple of billion dollars in market cap, Wexner has no interest in such a move. Finkelman and Grace Nichols, Victoria's Secret's CEO, had spent years redefining the brand, realigning the catalog, upgrading the beauty business, and generally remaking the company. The idea of spinning off the Website into a separate business whose life depended on driving volume independently from the stores and catalog seems absurd. Retailers like Barnes & Noble had done so and paid a dear price for mishandling the venture. Wexner never gave it a serious thought. Added Ricker, "Our technology is so woven into the fabric of the business that we couldn't separate it out if we wanted to."

The next most popular question: "When are you going to put every other brand on the Web? Why aren't they all there now?" Against conventional Internet wisdom, such as General Motors' "launch and learn" view of the Web, Wexner refuses to send brands into the fray if they are not ready. Pragmatism is the retailer's walking stick, and one must constantly come back to the basics. If the productivity in a store isn't right, if it isn't executing the basics of fashion properly, if the brand isn't right, then a Website isn't going to help at all. "There's this sense that if a brand isn't doing very well and has real, immediate problems, if only they had a Website, happiness would return to their kingdom," Wexner says. "In fact, it actually complicates and distracts."

Understanding the subtleties between apparel and intimate apparel is crucial, Finkelman adds. "Victoria's Secret is a unique animal. I don't think that if we opened a Website for our other women's apparel businesses that they'd see near the volume that we get at Victoria's Secret."

In fact, Intimate Brands turned the electronic channel into a status symbol within the company. According to Ricker, the various brands now view an Internet presence as an affirmation that all the piece parts of their operations have been done right so they can get an e-channel. "They consider a Website a badge of accomplishment," Ricker says.

A key lesson, Wexner says, is to be wary of ideas that promise to be panaceas. "I have a theology about utopian ideas," he says. "Everybody would like to believe there's a utopia out there, but it's a terrible premise for planning."

A Strategy of Cohesion

Amid the cacophony of hype and expectation, what the Internet has actually brought to the retail table is detailed information about the customer—and it has brought it better, faster, and cheaper. The old adage, "Be careful what you ask for because you just might get it," is pertinent. Armed with a bewildering array of customer data, the task of making sense of the information and using it to pad the bottom line is difficult, expensive, and time-consuming. But e-business radicals share a common penchant for measuring everything and putting great stock in the numbers. For Victoria's Secret, the data are the foundation for enhancing customer service, deepening the customer relationship, and even expanding the brand overseas.

Catalog retailers, for example, once worried that the Web would cannibalize catalog sales. Like Staples, Inc., most have found out that just the opposite is true. Multichannel shoppers spend up to 30 percent more than single-channel shoppers. Victoria's Secret decided not to be intimidated by the fear of the unknown. Rather than pit the two channels against each other, Victoria's Secret merged them into one business unit, now under Victoria's Secret Direct CEO Sharen Turney. There is no evidence yet that the catalog model is obsolete, though futurists would argue that digital will eventually obviate the need for paper. "If I could convert every one of my catalog customers to the Web tomorrow, I'd make a lot more money," Finkelman says. "Paper and printing are far more expensive than a view of the Website. But there's huge value to that catalog as well." Indeed, the idea is to offer a 360 degree brand, available in some form or other 24 hours a day, seven days a week.

Contrary to hurting offline sales, the online brand is changing the *entire* brand. Ricker points out that the immediate communication channel with the customer available online is actually reenergizing both the stores and the catalog. "We couldn't reach the customer this way before," he says. "The stores and catalog pick up the newness and freshness brought by the electronic channel. It motivates customers to rediscover Victoria's Secret."

In fact, the Internet has helped Victoria's Secret reexamine its policies in the store and in the catalog. In the mid-1990s, Ricker says, a customer who didn't buy $100 worth of merchandise from the catalog was dropped from the mailing list. Victoria's Secret has since learned that many customers who never buy through the catalog are the company's best in-store buyers. These customers use the catalog to decide what to buy in the store. Had they continued to be dropped, they likely would have wandered off to competitors' stores. Now, the Internet is allowing the company to measure quantitative correlations among the channels. In this way, Victoria's Secret can better target its promotional activities.

Perhaps more important to Victoria's Secret is the role the Internet is playing in the globalization of the brand. Rather than expand with bricks and mortar across borders, the company is using the Web to cultivate a global brand. Finkelman points out that there are few examples of American retail fashion brands that have been successfully exported to Europe and Asia. "One can argue there are virtually none," he says. Companies that have tried have found the going painful and slow. Thus, building stores overseas has been eliminated from the strategy, and not a brick has been laid in foreign soil.

Ever the pragmatist, Wexner suggests that fast, relatively inexpensive delivery methods as well as internationally accepted credit cards are crucial to the success of global e-business. But he is excited about the Internet's potential to expand beyond current borders. He says that it wasn't hard to foresee the Internet as a means for customers to access products all over the globe. But the winners will be the powerful brands with world markets that have the ability to fulfill the orders. In this regard, Wexner says, "The Internet is going to change the nature of retail." Strong brands simply won't need bricks and mortar in every country to achieve a profitable economic model.

Finkelman believes there are huge opportunities remaining in the domestic market, and thus the company remains more focused on the North American marketplace. Why, he asks, should he invest a lot of money in a 5 percent market when the company can make 20 percent in its home market?

But he is already seeing the power of the Internet in foreign markets. Nearly 10 percent of sales volume comes from overseas, and that without any serious overseas marketing efforts.

No Substitute for Stores

It is always difficult to measure success so early in the advent of a new technology, but Finkelman insists that the online channel has already exceeded expectations. It has not only been profitable since the beginning but has provided payback in numerous unanticipated ways. The Web has been as profitable or more than the catalog business already, and volume has grown exponentially, tripling in 2000.

But the Internet future is even brighter, Wexner believes, because the digital world offers a very new and different way to provide an entertainment experience at the point of purchase. A radical merchant like Wexner has always understood that shopping isn't about going to a place to buy something; it's about entertainment. "The shopping experience, whether it's going to the market in Rome or Jerusalem or the high streets of Europe or to shopping malls or downtowns, has always been entertaining to people," Wexner says. "If I had to prophesize the future, I think that's where technology will have its most remarkable impact, in the stores themselves. I don't know what technologies will yet be developed, but people want to get together, whether it's in Wal-Mart or McDonald's or Victoria's Secret. What makes these places successful is far more than just the goods that are there; it's the social entertainment value for people."

5

Nortel
Agility, Not Speed,
Fuels Success

> If you're going to dabble, you might as well not do it. It has got to
> be top priority.
>
> *CEO John Roth, Nortel Networks, about e-business*

I n less than three years, John Roth transformed Northern Telecom, a stodgy, century-old Canadian supplier of telecommunications equipment, into Nortel Networks, a high-flying Internet powerhouse and a paragon of the New Economy. By the middle of 2000, Nortel had a market cap of $250 billion, making it the eighth most valuable company in the world. Industry watchers were favorably comparing Nortel to Wall Street favorites like Cisco Systems.

Like other great radicals, Roth, who became Nortel's chief executive officer in 1997, propelled the company's transformation into an e-business by leading the charge himself and making it his number-one priority. Nortel, which sells the very equipment companies need to become e-businesses, had to learn to walk in its own moccasins and remake *itself* while preaching the Internet gospel to its customers.

Under Roth, whom *Time* magazine called "the most successful businessman in modern Canadian history," Nortel has become the dominant supplier of high-capacity fiber-optic systems that transmit digital data through the Internet. In so doing, it has surpassed both Cisco and Lucent Technologies in optical networking, which analysts believe is a key sector in the future of the Internet. At the same time, the company has embraced Roth's e-business vision and has made it a reality inside as well as outside the company. Of the $21 billion in Nortel revenues in 1999, nearly $10 billion worth of its equipment and services were either sold or influenced by Nortel's Website. That number grew to $15 billion in 2000 as Nortel's revenues increased to $30 billion and profits rose 42 percent to $2.3 billion.

Using its online muscle, Nortel has integrated customers, design centers, internal manufacturing, suppliers, and contract manufacturers on the Internet in order to maximize supply chain management, improve productivity, and deliver products to customers more quickly. Operating in 150 countries, Nortel receives and resolves nearly 70,000 customer service inquiries per month over the Internet, and customers download 900,000 pieces of training and documentation literature as well as 12,000 software upgrades each month. This results in more than $65 million in customer service cost savings each year.

The company has included its authorized resellers and distributors in its e-business strategy as well. This may not sound radical, but Nortel was the first in the industry to do so and thus prove that e-business success cannot be achieved in a vacuum. Using the Internet to help its customers help their customers, Nortel developed nearly 80 customer *extranets,* personalized sites for some of their key accounts. In six months, a base of 600 users grew to 4,000 users. The use of these e-business applications results in more than $250 million in revenues and $7 million in operational savings each month. Rather than measuring hits or visits to its Website, Nortel is measuring return on relationship and tracking how many customers return because of the value they are receiving. More than 87 percent of Nortel's revenues can now be traced back one way or another to the Website.

With all this, Roth will be the first one to tell you that Nortel's transformation continues to be a work in progress. With 80,000 employees, many of whom were there when the Brampton, Ontario–based Nortel was a subsidiary of Bell Canada, dramatic change has never been a hallmark of the corporate culture. Monopolies die hard. Indeed, Bell Canada Enterprises continued to own 42 percent of Nortel until January 2000. Like other high-tech companies, Nortel got hit hard by the slowing economy at the end of 2000, and its share price plummeted.

But in 1997, as he was about to become CEO after a 29-year career with Northern Telecom, Roth understood that dramatic change was the only option for long-term survival. An industry visionary, Roth believed that virtually all telecommunications would take place on the Internet within 10 years. He also believed that Internet-based telephone conversations would become mainstream and that data traffic over the Internet would explode. The companies that provided the infrastructure for the new Internet would be the winners. In this new world, Nortel had to remake itself and its brand or sink into irrelevancy.

Cisco Systems, its fiercest rival, had become an Internet behemoth, not only selling critical Internet equipment, such as high speed routers and switches, but doing the bulk of its business online. E-business success personified, it presented a massive challenge to Nortel. In a now-legendary memo to all employees, Roth declared that the company would make a right-angle turn and become an Internet company. He believed that Web "tone" would soon be as pervasive, reliable, and taken for granted as a telephone's dial tone. Nortel, he stated, would become one of the catalyst companies making that happen.

In order to do that, Roth took radical steps to inject new life into a moribund culture. All the sacred cows were taken out to the pasture to be shot. The corporate bureaucracy, so endemic to quasi-governmental organizations, had to be dismantled brick by brick, and Roth had no qualms about doing so. Veteran heads began to roll. Five-year-old R&D projects with no results were scuttled. Complex bureaucratic project reviews were eliminated. Much of manufacturing was outsourced. Acquisitions to bring in needed technologies were set in motion. Stock options were given to all employees. And U.S. operations were broadened to attract the talent that refused to go to Canada, with its draconian tax laws. Nortel became a James Bond martini—shaken, not stirred.

By making his role visible and consistent, Roth has been able to overcome the inherent cultural obstacles. "To be successful, you've got to have the alignment of all your organization," says Steve Santana, head of operations for the company's Website. "But nothing turbocharges that as fast as when your CEO puts a stake in the ground and says, 'You're going to do this by this date.'"

Santana describes a presentation he made to the President's Council, Nortel's executive committee, about the Website immediately after its launch. "It was a bit stodgy, and a few people started asking a few questions about the Website," Santana says. "Then John Roth stops everybody and starts describing in detail areas of the site that he has gone through. He found products and information, used the search engine, and was obviously very hands-on. It got a lot of the others in that room to jump on the Web and start looking at it for themselves. And when you have that kind of leadership, a connection of the dots from the CEO on down into the company, that is very, very powerful."

"People credit John Chambers with driving Cisco where it needs to go, but in a lot of ways, the job John Roth is doing at Nortel is more significant," says Chris Nicoll, a telecommunications industry analyst at Current Analysis in Sterling, Virginia. "The transformation of a stuffy old company into an aggressive, nimble player is a difficult one."

Embracing Agility

Like Jack Welch at General Electric, Roth made e-business the company's mantra. He made sure his mandate was sharp and clear. He didn't want people studying the issue to death, or shifting it to the back burner. "If you're going to dabble, you might as well not do it," Roth says. "It has got to be top priority." Inside Nortel, they call it *Roth's Law*. Like Roth himself, the message is not subtle: "If change is inevitable, get over it. Adapt and get over it."

With Roth at the wheel, Nortel has opted for agility over speed. He loves fast cars and uses car analogies to drive home his point. "Being a car nut, speed tends to mean going fast in a straight line," Roth explains. "You can go fast right over a cliff or through a turn. We focus on agility, which is a combination of speed and the ability to change direction. Being agile is the correct thought because just being fast means you can go fast in the wrong direction or in a direction that suddenly becomes irrelevant."

What should a radical do? In a July 2000 interview with the *Wall Street Journal,* Roth provided his list of rules to support his right-angle turn:

- Our strategies must be tied to leading-edge customers on the attack. If we focus on the defensive customers, we will also become defensive.

- In a world that moves at Web speed, time cannot be sacrificed for better quality, lower cost, or even better decisions.

- It doesn't matter whether you develop or acquire leading technology. Our job is to provide the technology and products our customers need.

- When change in the marketplace is inevitable, lead it, don't follow it. Success is achieved by leading change, not waiting for it.

- Never be complacent. We are paranoid about our leadership—willing to cannibalize our own products to maintain our edge.

In Roth's view of the world, a company doing business in an era of high rates of change must be able to adapt and find the right direction. As that direction inevitably shifts and changes, the company needs to be fast enough to anticipate where the markets are going next and get there sooner than anybody else. This was Nortel's formula for grabbing nearly 40 percent of the optical networking market. Rather than be stymied by disruptive technologies, as Clayton Christensen describes in *The Innovator's Dilemma,* an agile technology company of Nortel's size and financial clout can buy its way into a competitive advantage.

With Bill Conner, Nortel's aggressive president in charge of e-business and enterprise solutions, leading the charge, Nortel went on an uncharacteristic buying spree beginning in 1998, to acquire needed technology rather than build it in-house. As a distant relative of Bell Labs, Nortel had inherited a corporate not-invented-here (NIH) syndrome. In an engineering culture like Nortel, engineers would regularly scout innovative technologies coming from entrepreneurial start-up companies and return to Nortel with the pronouncement that they could build the same thing in-house. The fact that it might take years to do it never seemed to faze anyone. That mindset had to be scuttled. To be a successful e-business, Conner and Roth agreed, acquisition was a critical part of the strategy.

"The whole concept of doing acquisitions was absolutely foreign to

Nortel," Roth says. "That kind of thinking had to go." There was simply no time to indulge in endless internal design cycles to produce the necessary pieces of the technology puzzle. "We realized that Nortel doesn't have to develop this stuff; we only have to have it for our customers," he adds. The company has since spent more than $20 billion on 16 acquisitions, including nearly $7 billion in 1998 for Bay Networks, an Internet equipment maker. The acquisition binge has put added pressure on Nortel's internal development teams to move faster and produce results on a pace with the outside market. Roth says Nortel engineers are now thinking like this: "If I ever hope to get any funding in this company, I'm going to have to be a lot faster in order to get this project underway before the company goes out and buys what I'm thinking of."

Like other big companies trying to transform themselves, Nortel continues to struggle with corporate values that are no longer plausible in the world of e-business. Nortel, for example, has a deeply ingrained tradition of "trying to get the best out of everybody as opposed to trying to get the best people," Roth told the *Wall Street Journal*. "Our reluctance to deal with the bottom quartile is our biggest challenge." If somebody has been with the company for 10 years and remains in the bottom quartile of the company, can they realistically hope to rise to the top half? Roth believes you can hire someone who would be in the top half of the company within six weeks. An agile company cannot hold on to underachievers and hope to become an effective e-business.

In addition, Nortel has struggled with geography. Being based in Canada, with its outdated tax policies and business strategies, has set off a brain drain and forced Nortel to relocate many of its businesses in the United States and abroad. Only 25,000 Nortel employees remain in Canada, and Roth has been outspoken in his criticism of the Canadian government, calling for e-commerce tax breaks and federal support for a bigger venture capital market.

Conner says that the perception two years ago was that Nortel was still a Canadian company. "We're not that anymore," he states. "In fact, most everyone knows that most of the people in our headquarters in Canada are staff. We're very much decentralized, and all the people who run the businesses are in the United States or overseas."

If anything, Conner feels that he must still convert the perception of the Nortel brand and get people to understand that Nortel is not only an e-business provider but also an e-business practitioner. That is a process that moves from the inside out.

Bringing In Bay

The Bay Networks acquisition, more than any other, spurred Nortel's remake of its corporate culture. Bay Networks, itself the product of a turbulent merger, had been a direct competitor to Cisco in the router and switching business. Though financial analysts disparaged the acquisition as too unwieldy, Roth and Conner saw infinite potential. Not only would Bay's product line bring Nortel into a crucial market, but its Silicon Valley culture would have a profound effect on the cranky, hierarchical structure within Nortel. Rather than subsume Bay and wipe out its culture, Nortel borrowed liberally to shake up its own workforce.

Soon after the acquisition, Conner asked Phyllis Brock, a Bay Networks executive, to head up a unified Web team for Nortel and set up Web headquarters in Santa Clara, California. Like other radicals, Nortel understood the importance of creating a dot.com atmosphere in order to attract and retain high-quality people. Though the dot.com bubble burst in 2000, the Silicon Valley remains a hotbed of entrepreneurial excitement, and Nortel needed to tap into that excitement to be a player. The best and the brightest in cyberspace were not much interested in moving to Canada, so keeping the Web team in Santa Clara gave Nortel a much-needed Silicon Valley presence.

Brock says that Nortel provides the excitement of a start-up with the resources and stability of a big company, a combination that becomes increasingly popular as the dot.com bubble bursts. She says the number-one attribute of her group is its passion. Hiring passionate people who can bring together the vision as a team is a Silicon Valley trait that had been sorely missing from Nortel. The 40-person team integrated the two disparate Websites into one unified Nortel site in record time and spread the Web gospel according to Bay across the Nortel landscape.

"You need to have a consistent dashboard," Brock says about the

Website. "Every page needs to look the same. You want to reflect the branding of the image and the messages of the company." In the same way, Brock knew that customers wanted a seamless connection to Nortel. They wanted the multiple touch points such as sales reps, call centers, and the Web, all integrated and without cumbersome boundaries to cross. On many levels, Bay Network's 6,000 employees brought a whole new point of view into Nortel.

Obstacles to speedy decision making, such as endless product review cycles, were taken out of the infrastructure, and Nortel, using Bay Networks as a model, started offering stock options to employees deep within its organization. Today, every employee is eligible for stock options, and Roth has been amazed at how powerful a force that is for focusing employees on the success of the company.

Roth credits David House, an Intel veteran who became CEO of Bay Networks, for bringing needed reality checks into Nortel after the acquisition. House didn't stay with Nortel very long, but while he was there, he actually taught courses to Nortel managers about decision-making strategies he learned at Intel.

In order to make good decisions, the people have to keep an open mind to changes. This was not intuitive at Nortel. People also have to make timely decisions, and everybody must be aware that a decision is coming up. "What helped us a lot was that we realized we were not an agile company," Roth says. "One of the big steps in making change is that everybody has to realize that they must change. For example, the development of central office switches took five years. That is not agile. So no one disputed that Nortel was not agile. But we said, let's work at it, and the enthusiasm has gone into making us an agile company."

From this, Roth instituted what he called the CEO Forum. Chosen by their peers, 75 people, all from the rank and file within Nortel, met in three groups of 25. When they met, there were no name tags, no badges, and no titles. Many key vice presidents were not invited, and this sent a strong message to the entire company that change was in the offing. Roth told the *Wall Street Journal* that the event was a turning point for Nortel and led to a spate of great ideas. Among them were the outsourcing initiative and a different approach to managing R&D projects.

By outsourcing much of its manufacturing, Nortel closed 18 of 24 plants around the world. Much of its industry-leading capability in optical networking comes from outside the company. About working with the outsourcers, Roth told the *Wall Street Journal,* "What looks like 100 percent to me looks like 20 percent to them. They can handle 20 percent. My team would really struggle to do 100 percent. And then we were able to focus on those things that only we can do."

In addition, the push toward agility was the perfect opportunity to rid Nortel of outmoded, bureaucratic processes. The requirement for the board of directors to sign off on all R&D projects was eliminated. So-called *gate reviews* that took place during various stages of R&D projects were also eliminated. Instead, Nortel created portfolio management teams that meet every Monday and create weekly priorities for each R&D team. In the past, reviews were only held every eight months. In so doing, Nortel has all but wiped out five-year-long development projects and replaced them with projects that achieve results in a year or two. An agile company gets the fundamental piece done and then adds features later, Roth says. In the push toward e-business, there is no time to wait for perfect solutions.

Roth praises the onset of the agility era at Nortel. Today, development is characterized by small, quickly moving teams that are well focused and don't let anything get in their way. They are focused on market success, not development milestones, Roth says. "E-business could well be hijacked by the technologist," he states. "The big danger is that the IS organization, which is just another technology team, could hijack the e-business agenda and turn it into an elegant major development project for the corporation. You end up focusing on the merits of technology, and who cares about the customer?"

Still, pockets of resistance have remained around Nortel. Chris Nicoll of Current Analysis says that Nortel has not yet achieved a full e-business profile in which orders flow in and out electronically with nearly 100 percent automation, as has Cisco.

"The biggest challenge Nortel faces is changing the mindset," Nicoll says. "People's jobs give them their identities. If I'm an accountant or an order taker, it's hard to realize that there's another value I can add to the company. 'We're doing things this way because we've done it this way for 20 years.'"

Roth understands this conundrum. He says Nortel had an internal system called *bands* in which people were designated at a certain stature and paid according to the band they were in. "Once you were in that band, you would probably never be demoted. In many ways, it resembled tenure," Roth told the *Wall Street Journal*. By eliminating the bands and paying people according to the contribution they were making, Roth ruffled a lot of feathers. A third of Nortel's executives left, either on their own or with a push from the company.

"One of the big traps to avoid in e-business is, if it's not adding value to the customer, if the customer does not see an incremental increase in value every three months from your company, then you are probably working on the wrong project," Roth says.

And just in case there was any doubt about which projects were right and which were wrong, Roth quickly set up a list of all the projects that he felt had been around too long. If they were not agile and were steeped in the old business model, they went on the list.

Ever the radical, Roth makes effective use of the corporate rumor mill to advance his causes. "I let it be known what the list was, and I started making appointments to go see the project team," he recalls. "Everybody knew I was coming, and they knew the criteria for the list. I didn't publish a memo. I just wrote my own little notes and handed them to a few people. 'What do you think of this? Am I working on the right project?' And like wildfire, that thing went through the organization. Photocopies and e-mails were everywhere. 'Roth is coming and he's got the guns up.'"

The first project he visited was "an absolute disaster." Roth ordered the project canceled, and all the people involved were handed pink slips. The project was not only late but also reeked of incompetent management. "There was blood all over the floor," Roth says. "It was a public hanging. Needless to say, I never had to visit the second project."

Build, Defend, Lose: Coveting the Assets

Radicals tend to have the uncanny ability to be realists as well as dreamers. Roth was clear where he wanted to take Nortel, but he also understood the enormity of the task. It's easier, he says, to build a new company than to turn around an old, stuffy one. The most agile company in the world, he points out, is one that hasn't been formed yet, because it can go in any direction. However, this fledgling enterprise has no assets, so it has no competitive advantages either. "So somewhere between having all the assets of a Nortel and having a clean sheet of paper is probably the company you want to be," Roth says. "If you have to be agile, what is the right balance between assets and no assets? I've always observed that the assets that make you competitive today become liabilities on Monday morning."

"I've seen it played out time and time again," he continues. "You go from building your assets to defending your assets. And at some point, over one weekend, whether you realize it or not, you've mentally gone from building to defending your assets. And the minute you're playing defense, you're losing."

Rather than defending your assets, you should be trashing them, turning them into cash to go buy new assets, he adds. Roth uses the move to e-business as an example. As Nortel moves toward its e-business future, people need to be trained in e-business technology and methods. Why not have a course on e-business for employees? The company's training organization is brought in and immediately goes off and starts reading textbooks on e-business. "How long does it take for them to get skilled in e-business?" Roth asks. "They're reading textbooks. Why don't they go hire the teachers who wrote the textbooks?" Roth's conclusion: Why have a training organization at all? Why not get the best pundit in the industry to come and teach employees about e-business?

Similarly, Roth could not understand why the IS organization needed to develop e-business code. Looking for programmers is not moving at Web speed. Why not just find a company that has done e-business development for someone else and hire them to install an e-business system inside Nortel? "Why do I want to start with an IS organization designing code?" he asks. "If I was going to build an airline, I wouldn't start off designing jet engines."

In this manner, Phyllis Brock has outsourced much of the Web development work to outside contractors. Each time she signs a contract with somebody, she is able to check off that agenda item and move to another task. "She can actually get a tremendous amount done by leveraging outside professionals rather than trying to build an internal organization to do it," Roth says. "And at the end of the day, when the project is done, I'm not sitting here with a whole workforce wondering what I'm going to do with these people."

Roth is a student of business history and points out that big companies always put the most resources into their mainstream business, so what is not mainstream does not get the first call on talent or money. "Groups that are supportive services to the organization will always be deprived of talent and money that they really deserve as long as they are inside the company."

Therefore, contracting out these businesses makes infinite sense. People who work in that particular business are doing these things every day of their career. They are battle-tested because they've addressed these issues time and time again. They compete against the best in the business for contracts as opposed to being a captive group with a monopoly inside the company.

Roth uses the subject of health care as an analogy. Why go to a community hospital for a certain coronary surgical procedure where the death rate is 30 percent when the same procedure done in some of the teaching hospitals is under 2 percent? "Having a 30 percent chance of dying or a 2 percent chance of dying really makes you incented to look for those hospitals that do this as a business," Roth says. "I maintain that the death rate on community IS projects is as high as 30 percent, and if you go to someone who's in the business, the failure rate is as low as 2 percent."

In order to be radical in e-business, a company must consider all the warning signs that indicate that it is headed in the wrong direction. Roth has created a checklist of the telltales, as he calls them:

- If you are listening to a project description and the word *customer* doesn't come up, it is the wrong project.

- If the numbers are big, you're talking about the wrong project.

- If the time frames are long, you're designing the wrong project.

- If you are not getting quick hits, you are not learning what the customers really want. Only by putting something in front of the customers can you determine whether they like it and whether you are giving them value or just causing a distraction.

Radicals understand that this shift away from vertical integration is a huge cultural change for big companies. Moving away from total self-sufficiency can be traumatic, especially for corporate veterans who grew up in an era of land barons and turf wars.

The danger of implementing an initiative as pervasive as e-business is that it can encourage people to view it as a career path rather than a way to serve customers. An eager manager says, "I'm going to build that function and run that business. I'm going to have a unit within the company, and that will be my career. My organization will be big because this is going to be huge."

Quite often, Roth says, e-business becomes an excuse to build an internal fiefdom instead of saying "What did I deliver to my customer?" In this regard, radical managers know that they must watch out for the rat holes that can sabotage the effort, because e-business is nothing if not a great funding opportunity.

"When I go talk about e-business, people start talking about budgets, and they are monstrous budgets," Roth says. "I say, 'Wait a minute. What are we doing here?' Then I hear about these huge internal development programs and all the people they need to hire. When I ask what this will deliver to the customer, they say, 'We haven't figured that out yet.' My response is, 'What will the customer see on Day One? What can we do by Tuesday?'"

Thus, says Roth, the steps to make the right-angle turn must be incremental and understandable in order for people to embrace the turn. People must have steps to follow, and they must understand the logic of the transformation. "You never tell people to follow your orders," Roth says. "You want them to follow your intention." Therefore, employees must understand the logic and capture the vision of the changes. "They have to be able to amplify it and fill in the holes in your logic," Roth says, "because one thing about visions is that they're not detailed, so people must fill in that detail. That's what makes it exciting for the organization and leaves lots of room for innovation and discovering the real value."

In addition, employees must believe that this is not only something they should do but also something they *can* do. In territory as uncharted as e-business, it is crucial to build confidence and courage that something meaningful can be done. "It's just like exploring," Roth says. "Every step you take, you see further into the distance so you have a better sense of whether or not you are heading in the right direction."

Disruptive Customers

And most important, e-business isn't just about what your company is prepared to do but what your *customers* are prepared to do, Roth says. "The only reason you're doing e-business is to create greater value for your customers or to reach customers to whom you could not deliver your products or value before," Roth explains. Rather than simply making the e-business commitment for the sake of being in the game, companies must consider the value proposition above all else. Does e-business allow me to provide greater value to my customers at a lower cost? Does it get me to customers I couldn't reach because of economic considerations? Are there customers waiting to discover me because before e-business they had no way to know that I existed?

Roth says that as Nortel moves along the e-business path, it discovers a range of rates at which customers are prepared to move. Some still don't want to touch the Internet; others are pushing to go further and faster. He calls the latter *disruptive customers*.

"We're an industry that sells to other companies," Roth says. "We don't generally sell to consumers. And what we've found, because we're basically an industrial products company, is that more important than disruptive technologies are customers who are prepared to disrupt their marketplace. They are the people who are going to buy the disruptive technology and put it to work and change the game in their industry. So those are the people I focus on." You have to pay attention to these customers, Roth adds, because they will find the technology someplace—if not from you, then from someone else.

More challenging still is finding and winning those disruptive customers. Nortel's customers have bought a lot of equipment and have a vested interest in its current assets' continuing to have a long shelf life. They don't want big change because it makes their lives more difficult. It's the new customers, the disruptive customers, who come in and demand something entirely different. This, in turn, pushes Nortel toward big, dramatic disruptions that will change the industry.

Having embraced the e-business tools that it is selling to its customers, Nortel has to become a role model and a guide. To that end, the company is now measuring itself in Web years, or six-month years. Roth set a goal in late 2000 that 80 percent of all merchandise be sold online. "Merchandise is dead easy to do, and it's the thing customers are the most comfortable doing online," he says. He acknowledges that Nortel's work in building high-capacity networks for customers is tougher to transform into an e-business offering. But all sales or order replenishment as well as all order tracking and customer follow-up should be up and running for all customers quickly.

"If the customer wants to know the status of an order, why should they have to bother my salesman to find that out?" he asks. "I'm a great believer in the old 80-20 rule. Focus on the 20 percent of the activities that the customer sees 80 percent of the value in, and the rest doesn't matter. A lot of people in e-business want to get a 100 percent solution, and they'll never get it done."

Like General Motors, Nortel is exploiting all aspects of e-business, working independently on some initiatives and partnering with competitors in others. In June 2000, Chahram Bolouri, Nortel's president of Global Operations, took Nortel into an online exchange called e2open, along with IBM, Hitachi, Toshiba, and several others, in order to reduce inventory costs drastically and deliver products to customers more quickly. Nortel expects to buy more than $5 billion in goods and services each year through the exchange starting at the end of 2001. Nortel plans to engage in several such exchanges over time.

Nortel's complex offerings create added pressure on the e-business initiative. The supply chain, for example, is unlike the popular Dell Computer model, which incorporates buying, selling, moving, and servicing products for customers. "Our customers and our supply chain are quite different," Bolouri says. "We're not shipping hotboxes to customers. We're implementing networks."

"So we have to focus on how you define networks—how are you going to install networks, and how will you take care of these networks? For example, a customer wants to put in place an optical network from New York to Los Angeles. That's 4,300 miles of network, which is going to include hundreds of different sites. You need to plan, manufacture, install, commission, and test those. And in some cases, you need to put them in service in between 50 and 70 days." Add to that the complexity of the product itself. Optical networks come in 160 different wavelengths, and Nortel must manage these and combinations of different product lines in order to deploy networks for its customers.

To meet Roth's vision, Nortel has ramped up its online relationship with important customers. Customers who have special relationships with resellers can research and configure products on Nortel's Website and then link directly to their reseller of choice to complete the purchase. Nortel is also offering special online services to its channel partners, such as instant product configurations and price quotes, online ordering, and inventory management. In this way, customers are able to get the products they need in minutes instead of days.

"This is more than a Web portal," says Conner. "It's about seamless customer interaction. I mean, why is a Web agent any different than a call-center agent? So customers should be able to come in via the Website or via a toll-free number and get the information they want. It's your direct sales force and your service force. I call it 'clicks and conversations.' Either through clicks or through a conversation, they get the content and information they want to complete a transaction."

With Conner driving the marketing aspect of Nortel's e-business, he is acutely aware that in selling technology and services that are unproven in the marketplace, the company must don its own shoes and learn to walk. In his view, Nortel has done a good job of e-enabling its data networking business and must do the same with its software and services businesses. He says this is all part of the company's cultural revolution, and if he can bring all the myriad pieces of the business into the e-business fold, it will give Nortel a huge advantage in the market.

Like Roth, he is aware of the challenge of pulling all the pieces of a vast organization into a cohesive e-business strategy. But the alternative—fractious segments of the company warring against each other—is a clear path to failure. "We'd look like six different points of light instead of one bright light," Conner says.

And for Roth, the burden is his to carry the e-business lantern. "The number-one lesson here is that it has to start at the top," Roth says. "There has to be a compelling belief by the CEO that this is so important to the company, because if it is viewed as anything less than a front-burner issue, it just ain't going to make it."

6

David Bowie
An Interactive Community
That Rocks

If I was 19 again, I'd bypass music and go straight to the Internet.

David Bowie

Calling David Bowie radical hardly begins to describe this rock-and-roll icon, actor, and pop philosopher. During his 30-year career, he has shown the remarkable ability to reinvent himself, from Ziggy Stardust to the Thin White Duke, from glam rocker to disco king to mainstream pop star. Now comes Bowie's latest, and perhaps most ambitious, incarnation: Internet Music Man.

Inspiration can come from unexpected places. In Bowie, business executives can see the result of bold thinking and hands-on follow-through in harnessing the Internet's potential in a seemingly unlikely field. As the music industry continues to flail about seeking a comfortable and profitable way to embrace the Internet, Bowie, now in his fifties, has already established himself as an Internet visionary, transforming himself from a traditional rock star into an online entrepreneur and impresario.

It is not unusual for entertainers to hire a Web designer to set up a vanity address on the Internet for posting upcoming events and "inside stories." But Bowie helped build his site himself, and it's far from an exercise in egotism. Rather than creating a static Web presence, he designed an interactive *community* called DavidBowie.com. In so doing he has become an Internet service provider (ISP), an online bank, and a partner in a company that builds Websites for other entertainers.

Most important, Bowie plays a central role in the site and spends significant time in cyberspace with his fellow travelers. Each morning he logs on to his chatrooms using various pseudonyms so that he can mix with his fans anonymously and gain valuable insight into their opinions and desires. They know he's often there, which adds excitement to every interchange. With the Ask David feature, he directly interacts with his Web visitors.

Bowie's willingness to put himself—not just his music persona—online has helped him achieve an early e-business advantage in the music industry. "Post an intelligent question on the DavidBowie.com message boards and you may well get a response from Bowie himself," says Chris Mitchell, an Internet journalist and editor of *Spike* magazine. "How many CEOs can say that about their Website? For that matter, how many CEOs have the faintest idea how their own Websites work? DavidBowie.com works because Bowie gets the Web."

Bowie's daily presence adds significant value to his burgeoning Web business and its shareholders. In effect, Bowie has transformed himself into DavidBowie.com, thus becoming his own Internet brand.

Just as Bowie was already well into music videos long before MTV took the record industry by storm, he has been at the forefront of the Internet surge and is quite clear about the Internet's even more dramatic impact. "We're undergoing a most enormous eruption, a revolution. This is for real. It will change everything we know—absolutely everything," Bowie told *Yahoo Internet Life* magazine.

Recognizing his efforts, in 1999 *Computerworld* newspaper, a leading industry publication, named the British rocker one of 20 Internet visionaries for the new millennium, the only entertainer who made the list.

Finding Opportunity in the Chaos

For Bowie, like his fellow Web visionaries, the Internet is mainly about new channels of access. The Web builds direct links between customers and suppliers that can be adapted continuously to a changing business—or entertainment—environment. Successful e-businesses, like Enron or Victoria's Secret, take the best of what they do as conventional organizations and blend the Internet into the flow between company and customers.

Many have stumbled trying to forge these new links amid the chaotic and amorphous Internet. Perhaps as a rock musician, Bowie has a high tolerance for confusion and can see opportunity where others see disorder.

"The chaos factor is a very important part of the Net," Bowie told *Computerworld*. "The most attractive thing is its decentralized nature. Someone said it's almost like having 1,000 books on your floor and not knowing where to start. That's how I live. That's how I think! The Internet really is a technology model of how I think. It thrives on its own chaos. It's willing to change its mind overnight, combine things that shouldn't be bedfellows. I see it as a brother."

DavidBowie.com has become the prototype for the next level of Internet portal, replete with superior visual content and an expanding number of offers, from credit cards to merchandise to music. Most important, DavidBowie.com offers a high level of interaction between the CEO and the customer—in this case Bowie and his fans.

The Path to the Internet

For David Bowie, the Internet is an inevitable endgame to a unique career that began in the 1960s folk scene in England. As a musician, writer, and performer, Bowie has always pushed against the grain. Instead of staying in one genre for long, he has forsaken any single style or image for a chance to investigate any and all forms of music and ideology. Over the course of his remarkable career, he has displayed an uncanny ability to change costumes and characters as well as musical styles, from glam rock to heavy metal.

With his 1969 hit "Space Oddity," Bowie gained international acclaim and quickly transformed himself into the glittery, sexually charged Ziggy Stardust. His stage shows became legendary for their outrageous theatricality.

In the 1970s, his career skyrocketed with hits like "Fame," which he cowrote with John Lennon. During the 1970s and 1980s, he wrote, produced, and performed a string of commercial hits such as "Young Americans," "Let's Dance," and "Modern Love."

But just as he willfully crossed musical boundaries, Bowie refused to stay pigeonholed as a singer. He turned actor, artist, and producer. Along the way, he became fascinated by technology's ability to transform his artistry. He pioneered many high- and low-tech effects on his concert tours, sometimes with unexpected consequences. On the Diamond Dog tour in the 1970s, for example, he descended toward the stage in a giant metal hand—but was stuck mid-air for 45 minutes when the hydraulic system broke.

Since the mid-1980s the cerebral Bowie has written song lyrics and created artwork by computer through the Photoshop and Painter programs. In one experiment, he used software designed by a Silicon Valley friend to cut up his words randomly à la beat writer William Burroughs. The result: an unusual variety of songs from an unusual song writer.

As far back as the 1983 Serious Moonlight tour, Bowie and his operations people conducted global communications by the nascent medium of e-mail. "It was quite barbaric then," Bowie said in *USA Today*. "It took hours. But it was always available, more efficient than telephones, and we could actually keep in touch with headquarters in New York from anywhere in the world."

His own introduction to the Internet came in the early 1990s through his son, the infamously named Zowie, who now calls himself Duncan. Duncan, an avid technologist and aspiring filmmaker, showed his father how to maneuver around the World Wide Web, and Bowie was hooked.

At the time, the Net was littered with dozens of Websites devoted to Bowie and thousands more dedicated to other musicians. He visited countless sites to see what others were trying to do and came away with the feeling that it wasn't enough. Like a true radical, he saw in the Internet the power to transform the musical experience, not just reflect it.

"If I was 19 again, I'd bypass music and go straight to the Internet," Bowie says. "When I was 19, music was still the dangerous communicative future force, and that was what drew me into it. But it doesn't have that cachet any more. It's been replaced by the Internet, which has the same sound of revolution to it."

Battle Lines Drawn

Bowie has long been a trendsetter, not just with his music but in his business dealings. After his business manager upset his financial fortunes in the early 1970s, Bowie took greater involvement in his own finances. He retained the rights to his first 25 albums, an practice unheard of among rockers. Then, in 1997 that same business manager suggested a radical plan. Bowie raised $57 million by floating an innovative bond backed by future royalties of those albums. A cadre of stars has followed suit. In 1998 Bowie was named Britain's richest rock star, with a net worth of nearly $1 billion, surpassing even Paul McCartney. Those close to Bowie question that figure but acknowledge that he has quite successfully parlayed his career into great wealth.

While other aging superstars of rock, like the Rolling Stones, Beach Boys, and Moody Blues, earn massive income by performing their early hits, Bowie continues to look to the future rather than replay the past. The future for him, he knows, is on the Internet.

Many musicians and record companies have struggled to form profitable relationships online in an environment that has become adversarial, often pitting the artist against his or her audience. Advances in digital and broadband technologies give listeners unfiltered access to music in ways heretofore impossible. Some artists and companies are fighting the unbridled use of these capabilities, seeking compensation for every downloaded song.

Bowie has chosen to embrace the possibilities of the new technologies. In 1997 he set some of the controversy in motion by becoming the first major artist to release a new single on the Internet. The song, called "Telling Lies," was offered for free. It is a testament not only to Bowie's continued star power but also to the growing appeal of the Internet that more than 300,000 fans downloaded the uncompressed file, even though it took nine hours.

Bowie is outspoken in his opposition to shutting down companies like Napster and stopping the digital flow of music. In fact, he believes the Internet will become the primary distribution medium for music.

"Mark my words," Bowie told *USA Today*, "this is where the consumer industry is going. We are not going back to record companies and through shops. Within five years, it will have morphed so spectacularly that no one will recognize the music business." Further, he told *Computerworld*, "The record companies are just like King Harold sitting there on the beach, on his throne, trying to order the sea back. They don't stand a chance."

Like other radicals, Bowie is not fighting the tide, but surfing ahead of it. He understands that the Internet breaks down standard lines of commerce. Through his Website, Bowie offers his customers (members, fans) numerous ways to experience and buy his products—and he can do it on his terms, bypassing retail outlets. This disintermediation of the traditional recording industry is being repeated in a raft of industries, from automobiles to telecommunications.

Bowie is not a complete online anarchist. A savvy businessman, he is invested in selling his own catalog of music, which is licensed and sold through EMI, one of the world's largest record companies. But he is certain these labels must find new ways of selling that incorporate rather than reject the radical online model.

Successful Internet venturers like GE's Jack Welch and Enron's Jeff Skilling take a Bowie-like view of the landscape. Rather than resist the technological wave, they swim with it even if it means upending entrenched operations. E-business requires new thinking, which is admittedly difficult for people who have succeeded under the old thinking and old ways of doing business. Most recording artists, for example, are hesitating to embrace the Internet on Bowie's terms. They are litigating to defend their territory, couching the fight as being about intellectual capital and copyright protection. Bowie is crossing the battle lines and inviting his fans to do the same. On DavidBowie.com, all become part of one peaceful community.

From Vanity to Community

In 1995 Virgin Records provided Bowie with a vanity homepage. It didn't take long for Bowie and associates to begin formulating their own ambitious plans. He drew up a set of metrics by which to assess how his Website could, and should, be used:

- Find the things that can't be done in any other context and exploit them.

- Use the medium to create a real intimacy with customers so that they have a reason to return again and again.

- Let that intimacy morph into a true community so that customers form relationships with other customers in a true example of viral marketing.

Instead of worrying about the sheer number of fans he can draw to his site, Bowie concentrates on making them feel like part of a community once they get there. "The Net will become more and more exploratory, reducing itself into many, many smaller and informal units," he told *Computerworld*. "Portals will emerge and dissolve with regularity. Corporate brand name Internet providers will lose their flavor. People will want to keep the village aspect of the Net. We're banking on that. We're not sitting there counting eyeballs at DavidBowie.com."

For Bowie, the Internet is a way to make his career sustainable over the long haul. Rather than have an occasional dialogue with his customer base during a tour to promote a new album, for example, the Internet assures him constant contact with his core audience. Now in his fifties, the rocker is not content to be a nostalgia show for baby boomers. He's going to where the new customers are, and that is the Internet.

Ultrastar

Robert Goodale, Bowie's former business manager, became fascinated with the Internet's potential in the early 1990s and regularly shared his discoveries with Bowie. On behalf of the singer, Goodale explored new technologies that might represent an opportunity for Bowie as an investor or performer.

Himself an Internet music pioneer, Goodale worked with William Zysblat and Joseph Rascoff, business managers for 25 years for the likes of the Rolling Stones; Paul Simon; Crosby, Stills, Nash, and Young; and the Elvis Presley estate. Goodale also earned a slice of fame for producing the first live concert on the Internet. In 1994 he convinced the Stones to do one song during a Dallas concert date that would be digitally multicast across the Internet. It was a complex and technically primitive offering, with tiny, grainy, black-and-white images moving at one frame every five seconds. But the musical world, including Bowie, took notice of the new frontier opening up. In 1997 Goodale created the first Internet-only CD sale for a group called the Cure.

A year later, Bowie, Goodale, Zysblat, and Rascoff began discussions about the business and artistic opportunities on the Internet. The four took a look at existing entertainment-related websites and decided there was opportunity, and profit, in significantly enhancing the fans' online experience.

In August 1998 the foursome founded Ultrastar, a privately held Internet entertainment company based in New York City. With Bowie as founder and executive producer, Ultrastar quickly unveiled the first artist-produced and designed Internet Service Provider: DavidBowie.com.

Through Ultrastar Bowie can spread his Internet vision to other entertainment entities. The New York Yankees, Baltimore Orioles, and Cleveland Browns sports franchises signed on as well as the popular teen group Hanson. With Ultrastar, clients get a branded, revenue-producing community on the Internet rather than just a static Website.

Ultrastar ultimately decided not to do business with sports franchises because there was simply too much sports-related material available for free on the Internet. But it continues to design and build Websites for entertainers. It recently built a Website for Bill Gaither, the most successful hymn writer of the last century. Gaither sells millions of CDs and videos and Ultrastar built a Website to help create an online community drawn to Gaither's hymns and gospel music.

Ultrastar's driving concept is to entice subscribers with high-quality service and interactive online activities that take full advantage of the Internet's power. For some clients, it will provide incremental income from a branded online community that is happy to participate and buy merchandise from the site. For Bowie, it is the essence of his transformation into an online rock star.

Communing with Customers

From a pure design and execution point of view, DavidBowie.com has exceeded all expectations. It has won numerous awards, including Yahoo's Music Site of the Year award in 2000. The reviews have been uniformly positive. "Every page on DavidBowie.com is luscious in layout and style. The sweat, time, and energy needed to cut and polish this gem is evident," said *High Five* magazine. "The real jewel for us was the connectivity this site allows for David Bowie and his fans."

The Website is both deep and wide in its offerings. There are, for example, vast amounts of archival material, including digital files of every song Bowie ever recorded, available for sampling or downloading for a fee. At least 600 recordings are listed, more than any other individual artist site on the Web, by Goodale's count.

In the fall of 2000, Bowie released a new CD titled *Bowie at the Beeb* and discovered that a live version of "Ziggy Stardust" had inadvertently been omitted from the CD during production. He used his Website to allow buyers of the CD to download the song for free.

Bowie, a renowned pack rat, has placed on his site diaries and memorabilia dating back to the early days of his career. He keeps a daily online journal as well, speaking about music, philosophy, art, and his own family life. Also available are paintings, drawings, photographs, videos, poetry, and unreleased musical tracks, all posted by Bowie himself. Lest it smack of complete self-interest, the site also features work from and chats with numerous other artists and entertainers who have worked with Bowie over the years.

But for all its cornucopia of material, the heart of the Website is Bowie's desire to get close to his fans in ways that rock stars never could before. Bowie is a voracious reader and knowledge seeker. His many metamorphoses are a result of the historical and cultural influences he has ingested over the years. The discourse section is filled with opportunities to converse with Bowie, both in chatrooms and on message boards. Every morning, from his home in Bermuda or New York, he goes online under various pseudonyms to participate with his community.

"David loves it," Goodale says. "This has allowed him an intimacy with people who not only care about him but many of whom are extremely intelligent, cultured, and thoughtful. These are people with a shared interest in art or music, and they can talk about all sorts of things they've discovered."

"You have to get your ego in place," Bowie told *USA Today*, "because it's all there, from absolute adoring fandom to bitter vitriol." In the Ask David section he not only answers questions from members but also asks questions of them as well. The discussions range from hot new bands to trends in art and design.

To inspire interactivity, the site breaks down message boards by subject matter and allows members to post their own philosophical or mundane musings, along with artwork, poetry, and songs. A special feature called Karma encourages members to rate the questions and postings with a positive or negative karma rating.

Customer intimacy may be the single most important lesson of DavidBowie.com. Simply designing a transactional or informational Website does not an e-business make. "Being able to chat live with Bowie in a chatroom or swap posts with him on the discussion boards is the key to DavidBowie.com's success," says Chris Mitchell. "It not only offers fans unprecedented access to their musical hero, but it is an indication of Bowie's genuine interest in the welfare of the site and in the fans. Take away Bowie and DavidBowie.com becomes just another fan site."

As powerful as the Internet experience is, Bowie understands that it cannot replace live performance entirely. But the two can reinforce each other. In June 2000 Bowie played three concerts at the Roseland Ballroom in New York, and one of the nights he devoted to David Bowie.com members only. He made tickets available to them through his site and later webcast the event from DavidBowie.com. He also posted his live performances from a 1997 tour and chose 15 tunes for remixing into a double CD offered to DavidBowie.com members only. Once a month, he made one track available for streaming so members could listen to new songs unavailable anywhere else. Bowie didn't stop there. He invited members to create the CD package and liner notes themselves by sending in stories, photos, and artwork of their Bowie concert experiences.

In essence, Bowie invites his Web fans not just to visit David Bowie.com but also to become part of it. He cultivates the sense of intimacy through an ever-increasing number of interactivities. For example, fans can use innovative software on the site to digitally remix existing Bowie songs and personalize them.

In 1999 Bowie instituted an interactive song-writing contest. The Write a Song with David Bowie competition drew more than 200,000 entries. Bowie posted on his site the music and partial lyrics to an unfinished song. He invited fans to finish the verse with their own words. The response overwhelmed the site and necessitated using a screening software program to whittle the lot down to 125 finalists. Bowie himself chose the winner, a 19-year-old man from Cleveland, Ohio, who was flown into New York to meet the superstar singer and sit in on the recording session for the song.

Taking advantage of new software technology from Lucent Technologies, DavidBowie.com invited members to watch and chat during the recording. The software offered viewers a 360 degree view of the session without the need for any special hardware. Members could move the view themselves to get the perspective they wanted. In the chatroom, Bowie and members of the band kept up a running dialogue. Rolling Stone.com turned the entire event into a webcast. The result was a song Bowie liked enough to put on his new album. The contest winner left New York with enough money to go to college, buy a car, and make a down payment on a home. By appearing live on his own Website in this way, Bowie took Internet intimacy to a new height in the music business.

This litany of offerings from DavidBowie.com may seem off the point to some corporate thinkers, but it adds up to a crucial e-business lesson. The devil is indeed in the details, and through this Bowie has unearthed the central value of the Web: control of the customer experience. Rather than be constrained by middlemen such as record companies or promoters, the Internet allows Bowie and his customers to decide what they want, how they want it, and when they want it. "If I write 50 songs in a year, I know I'll get backlogged and frustrated," Bowie told *USA Today,* because record companies would not flood the market with so many CDs. With the Internet, he can release what he wants on his own timetable. Rather than the distribution medium controlling him, he controls the medium.

DavidBowie.com as ISP

With DavidBowie.com as its centerpoint, Ultrastar created a business model that it could sell to other entertainers. All client communities receive three levels of marketing tools with distinct customer benefits:

1. A free general Website, replete with news and information that will draw fans but also serve as the online gateway and navigational console to premium services

2. Subscription-based premium services containing behind-the-scenes content available for a modest subscription fee of $6.95 per month or less

3. A branded ISP service, a higher-priced monthly service that combines features of the free and premium Websites with full-service access to the Internet

Though Bowie had no interest in becoming an ISP, the logic at the time of the initial business discussions made sense. The business plan called for DavidBowie.com to act as both the magazine and the postman. Those who already had Internet access could sign up for $5.95 a month and have full access to DavidBowie.com. But in 1997 legions still had no entry to the Internet, which was an obvious impediment to luring subscribers.

Goodale expresses the analogy this way: "The Website is like a magazine, and we'll get you the magazine. But if you say to us, 'I don't have a postman,' we'll get you the postman, too." For $14.95 a month, subscribers receive all the goods on DavidBowie.com plus e-mail and a 56K dial-up to the Internet, along with the ultra-cool e-mail address of their name@DavidBowie.com.

"It wasn't that we fancied being in the dial-up business," Goodale says. "We just didn't want it to be an excuse for someone not to join."

Radicals, of course, will do whatever it takes to capture customers, even if it isn't in the original business plan.

The subscription base remains the financial center of DavidBowie. com, with 80 percent of subscribers opting for the lower-priced subscription. With 10,000 members, the site's income pays for its own operation, Goodale says. DavidBowie.com's direct costs were just $500,000, and it employs only two full-time webmasters to update the site continually. They carefully monitor content and spend inordinate amounts of time on the phone or e-mailing with Bowie, who is not hesitant to share his views on even the most minor details of the design and execution of the site.

"To have content that people are willing to pay to access is the Holy Grail of almost every site on the Internet," says Chris Mitchell.

"Figuring out ways to do this and making users feel like they are getting a good deal—indeed, a bargain—is the next big step in the future of business on the Net."

Like companies, entertainers who shift their focus to the Internet must sometimes leave old relationships behind and remake themselves with new partnerships. The Ultrastar team set out from the beginning to make the Website a serious ISP, forging associations with the likes of Lycos, Reuters, GTE, Datek, DLJ Direct, Ticketmaster, and a host of other service providers. The site is also affiliated with Rolling Stone Network, a purveyor of music news and webcasts from the rock publication.

In addition, Ultrastar agreed to sell a minority stake to SFX Entertainment, the biggest producer of live entertainment in the world. According to Zysblat, Ultrastar can tap into the SFX consumer database of 60 million people who attend SFX-related events. In 1998 alone SFX promoted or produced 24,000 shows by a wide variety of artists such as Cher, Tom Petty, and Bob Dylan. Its sports group represents athletes including Michael Jordan, Patrick Ewing, and Kobe Bryant. The strategy is that SFX, when mounting its mammoth tours for an artist, will bring those artists to Ultrastar for the creation of Websites for fans.

"We were introduced to DavidBowie.com and saw an enormous business opportunity to replicate that with other entertainers, athletes, and sports teams," says Pam Spevak, president of SFX Interactive. "The Internet is the perfect medium for bringing like-minded people together and for them to get closer to the artists, athletes, and teams they feel close to."

With the same thinking that led them to become an ISP, the Ultrastar team took another radical leap of faith by creating BowieBanc, a DavidBowie.com option administered by USABancshares.com. "Clearly banking is not at the core of what we do," Goodale admits. "But we got interested early on with how the Internet was transforming the world of finance and how that might become a marketing and promotional tool for us."

When Ultrastar was approached by Ken Tepper, chief executive officer of USABancshares.com and an avid Bowie fan, with the idea for a cobranded online bank, Bowie listened. Members who open an account with a minimum $250 deposit get a year's subscription to

DavidBowie.com for free. They also get Bowie ATM cards and credit cards with Bowie's stern visage and penetrating blue eyes staring out from the card. "If we can simultaneously offer a great service to someone and allow them to join us for free, that's a win-win," Goodale says. Ultrastar is scanning the horizon for further such opportunities, be it in telephony, online trading, or even net appliances.

Goodale doesn't want to get bogged down by businesses that require intensive labor and expertise that Ultrastar simply doesn't have, so any future opportunity has to address three criteria:

1. It must have a strong and reliable partner.
2. It must have some marketing benefit for DavidBowie.com.
3. It can't be complicated and require time-consuming operational involvement.

Mostly, it must provide added value for DavidBowie.com customers.

Making Things New

If DavidBowie.com tracks along with the rest of David Bowie's career, it will undoubtedly take many twists and turns as it evolves over the next few years. To those close to him, Bowie is an adventurer and an explorer more than a musician, which makes the Internet his perfect medium. The status quo bores him. He thrives on violating assumptions about music, art, and business.

"His artistry is about blowing up the game and making everything new," Goodale says. "If you are businessman and a partner with him, it can be very scary because he is willing to take huge risks. Of course, he's a pretty clever guy, and in the process he's figured out how to make money while he's doing it. But he doesn't stop doing something because it stops making money. He stops because it is no longer interesting to him."

Bowie continually reassesses his Website and, like an urban planner, seeks ways to enhance the community and build new levels of interactivity. For example, he is well aware that there are additional ways he could flog his music and related merchandise on his Website. But would overselling ruin the sense of community he has tried so hard to create? At the same time, he wonders about illegally made copies of his music and whether he should open a sanctioned bootleg area on the site. If he does so, does he risk a legal and ethical run-in with EMI?

Bowie is convinced that the delivery of music will change substantially, though not completely. He is pragmatic in his view of the corporate giants, claiming that they will each find their own way of delivering online content into retail stores. "I don't think stores will disappear," Bowie told *Yahoo Internet Life.* "People like contact to a certain extent. I think it will be split fairly equally between online and store buying." Customers, he adds, will create their own packaging and art work to accompany the CD—just as he has already experimented with on his own Website.

The lessons from Bowie for corporate titans aiming at e-business are quite obvious, according to Goodale. Rather than struggling to resist the Internet or halfheartedly embrace it, the biggest players should tap their huge built-in advantage as they approach e-business: big existing customer bases, leverage across their industry, and established brand presence.

The challenge of the Internet is a catalyst rather than a deterrent to Bowie. "My belief is that the main focus of his professional thrust these days is the Internet," Goodale says. "This is his next great adventure." With an already established brand and a cachet that gives him a huge presence in his industry, Bowie can "throw himself into this new maelstrom with the kind of heft that makes it double the fun," Goodale says. With a bit of Ziggy Stardust thinking, the giants can do it too.

7

GM

Finding a Catalyst for Shaking Tradition

We don't just want to be big, we want to be big and fast.
And e-business is the way to be fast.

CEO Rick Wagoner, General Motors

On a quiet Sunday afternoon in January 2000, Harold R. Kutner, General Motors' group vice president for worldwide purchasing, got a surreptitious telephone call at home. The caller, whom Kutner declines to identify, wanted to know if he would consider joining forces with archrival Ford Motor Company to build a common integrated supplier exchange on the Internet.

The idea of teaming up with Ford, of all companies, seemed nothing less than "an unnatural act" to Kutner, a 35-year GM veteran. "Are you kidding?" Kutner exploded. "I wouldn't waste five minutes discussing this." But the caller persisted, making an interesting case. GM and Ford had both already launched online trade exchanges as key parts of the massive e-business initiatives at the two giant automakers. And in so doing, they had thrown the vast supplier network into a panic. If every car maker built its own online exchange, suppliers would be forced to create technical links to each one, thus adding needless complexity and costly technological implementations to their already burdened IT departments. Why not build a single common exchange that would benefit all those involved?

Intrigued but skeptical, Kutner agreed to a secret, late-night meeting at the Townsend Hotel, an English-style luxury hotel in Birmingham, a Detroit suburb. When Kutner arrived at Room 301, he found Brian Kelley, his counterpart at Ford, along with Ray Lane, then CEO of Oracle, Ford's software partner, and Mark Hoffman, CEO of CommerceOne, the software maker working with GM on its TradeXchange Website.

The meeting was cordial, though Lane and Hoffman were fiercer rivals than even Kutner and Kelley. They agreed to set up teams from each company to get together to explore the synergies and technical benefits of a group effort. After meeting for ten days in a Dearborn hotel, the teams concluded that such a venture made a lot of sense. Kutner shook hands with Kelley, and an unprecedented cooperative agreement began. The third giant automaker, Daimler/Chrysler, was quickly brought into the mix. By February, the trio announced the formation of Covisint, the world's largest virtual marketplace.

Though it took most of 2000 to gain Federal Trade Commission (FTC) approval for Covisint, the very fact that GM has committed to this "unnatural act" bespeaks the dedication that the world's biggest automaker has shown in transforming itself into an e-business. Though the slow-moving GM has appeared as anything but radical in its business approach over the past few decades, it is indeed radical in its embrace of the Internet. Business page headlines still trumpet GM's sluggish sales and languid share price. But the real story at GM these days is that the company is hard at work ripping apart an 80-year-old business model in favor of a sleek new Internet-based, enterprise-wide initiative that will make Alfred Sloan spin in his grave.

Transforming a $185 billion company with 400,000 employees and 92 years of tradition is no easy task. GM must continue to perform as an Old Economy company even as it makes the transition to its New Economy model. GM continues to face market pressures brought on by excessive inventories, an economic slowdown at the end of 2000, and heavy reliance on an antiquated business model. At the end of 2000, GM announced that it would close its Oldsmobile division because of anemic sales and lay off 6,000 workers in the United States and the United Kingdom. The 103-year-old brand had become the weakest performer among GM's full-line brands, such as Chevrolet,

Buick, and Pontiac. The charges related to the shutdown of Oldsmobile cost GM a significant drop in fourth-quarter profits in 2000.

With quarterly earnings and shareholders' worries as a constant companion, GM must execute its digital metamorphosis under less than ideal conditions. But when Rick Wagoner, a 23-year GM veteran, became CEO of GM in June 2000, he made it clear that big changes were already underway and that e-business was one of the fundamental priorities at GM. This effort "is built around the view that the Internet is just a massive force that is going to change our business and all businesses," Wagoner says. Like other radical e-businesses, GM's efforts are clearly being championed from the top.

Covisint, now up and running, includes not only the Big Three automakers but also Nissan and Renault. It has already become the central marketplace for the flow of billions of dollars worth of material from suppliers to the manufacturers. The exchange encompasses 100,000 suppliers and will do $60 billion worth of transactions in 2001 alone, according to Kutner. Run as a separate business, Covisint will offer shares to the public and is likely to have a major impact on cost reduction and product development for all participating car companies.

As massive an effort as Covisint is, it is only a piece of GM's e-business initiative. Wagoner, who became GM's CEO at age 47, is betting the company on this unprecedented transformation. "This is going to be huge, and it affects everything we do," Wagoner says. "We're in it because of the opportunity, and frankly, it's too big of a risk not to be in it."

For big companies seeking e-business lessons, GM is a petri dish of Internet fever. The company has launched major e-business initiatives across every part of its diverse organization and is spending hundreds of millions of dollars to fuel the effort. In August 1999 GM launched e-GM, a separate business unit, to unify the company's e-business efforts, help dissolve redundancies, and create a single technological blueprint for the corporation.

Most important, GM has adopted a first-mover attitude and philosophy about e-business that has earned kudos from industry analysts and publications. *Business 2.0,* a leading Internet business magazine, named GM as one of five giant corporations that "Get It"—the *It* being e-business—in a June 2000 cover story. GM was the only car-maker on the list. Wagoner is pressing the pedal to the metal because e-business may be GM's last, best hope to regain the luster it once had as not only the world's biggest carmaker, but the most successful as well. "We don't just want to be big, we want to be big and fast," Wagoner states. "And e-business is the way to be fast. It's the key way to change and rally people. Being out in front energizes people."

With this in mind, GM is spearheading major changes in the way cars are designed, ordered, built, and delivered, all relying heavily on the Internet. Leveraging its Internet prowess, GM has already cut product development from 48 months in 1996 to 18 months today. At the same time, GM has saved more than a billion dollars in engineering costs and has doubled its design capacity. Vehicles can be designed faster and taken to market faster, and iterations are possible during the design process today that allow GM to move not only faster but with more accuracy as well. Using e-business methods, GM will not only create new designs, but get to the *right* design—something it has not done frequently enough in the past two decades.

In addition, GM has pioneered the use of computerized in-car navigation and services systems called OnStar. Using OnStar as the platform, GM is bringing a voice-activated Internet link to every vehicle, turning cars into rolling portals and changing major aspects of the driving experience. GM is spreading the Internet effort beyond its car-making, as well, applying its online strategies to its nonautomotive businesses such as home mortgages, insurance, banking, and Direct TV.

Though competitors are all preaching the e-business gospel now, GM has led the way in a radical makeover that will change the entire industry. That this virtual business revolution is being fueled by GM is as shocking as any of the innovations themselves. Two decades of declining market share—from a high of 60 percent in the 1960s to under 30 percent today—and falling profits tarnished GM's image. Writers made the words *bureaucratic* and *hidebound* inevitable descriptors in any corporate profile. GM has plenty of baggage to discard. Remember, it was GM that ousted an exasperated H. Ross Perot from its board of directors in 1986. On the way out, Perot charged, "At GM, instead of just killing a snake, the first thing you do is organize a committee on snakes. Then you bring in a consultant who knows a lot about snakes. Third thing you do is talk about it for a year."

Dan Garretson, a senior automotive analyst with Forrester Research, applauds GM's efforts but says that GM remains at heart a traditional manufacturing-focused company, one that puts cars out on dealers' lots and hopes consumers will buy them. Indeed, in December 2000 GM announced it would cut vehicle production by 14.5 percent because its bloated inventory had ballooned to a 104-day supply of unsold vehicles. That was the largest supply since 1991, during the last recession. In order to transform itself, GM must use the Internet to become a customer-centric company and build to order, not unlike the Dell Computer model. This is no easy task for a deep-rooted culture like GM's. "Their challenge is to really internalize the Internet into the company," Garretson says.

That is exactly what Wagoner intends to do. Using e-business as the platform, Wagoner relishes the chance to zap GM's stodgy image for good. No more snake committees in Detroit. The first lesson he and his predecessor Jack Smith learned about e-business is that you must "launch and learn" or risk getting left dismally behind. "You've got to get into the game," Wagoner says. "You can't sit on the sidelines. You've got to do it personally so you understand enough to know what you're talking about and engage the organization. You've got to push people farther than they naturally want to go. You've got to recognize that if you wait for the perfect answer in something that's evolving like this, you're waiting too long."

A Clean IT Slate

Embarking on an enterprise-wide e-business initiative in a company the size of GM requires equal parts skill, timing, and luck. The luck, in GM's case, happened in 1996 when the company spun off and ousted EDS, the technology services giant it had acquired in 1984, from its role as sole information technology arm for all of GM.

At that time, GM's vice chairman Harry Pearce recruited an outspoken technology veteran named Ralph Szygenda from Bell Atlantic to become CIO at GM. As Bell Atlantic's CIO, he had reengineered that company's entire IT operation. Pearce figured that Szygenda had the temperament and drive to cut through GM's bloated infrastructure. While he was being interviewed, Szygenda, in turn, interviewed every senior executive at GM to determine whether he would have full management support to engineer a turnaround fueled by technology and e-business. "I got that support, and to this day I still have that support," Szygenda says. "It was very important."

By ceasing its complete dependence on EDS for its IT operations, GM suddenly had a clean sheet of paper with which to work. The departure of EDS didn't erase the thousands of legacy systems that couldn't communicate with each other and the moribund technology environment, but it gave Szygenda an opportunity to bring in new vendors and draw up a brand-new plan.

Szygenda began to redo the entire IT infrastructure, changing all the telecommunications systems, driving common computing, and leveraging new Internet "interchanges" across every area of the business. While most IT makeovers cost their corporations hundreds of millions of dollars to implement, Szygenda was able to wring nearly $1 billion out of IT expenses. Today, there are 3,000 fewer information systems in GM than in 1996. This time, all the work was outsourced to dozens of vendors, including EDS. GM was spared the wrenching task of converting thousands of full-time programmers into Web creators. It could tell its suppliers, "You do it, or we can buy from somebody else." This outsourcing model gave GM a combination of leverage and speed when it needed it most.

Concurrently, Szygenda says he has spent more than $1.6 billion on Internet applications so that every time the company touches a customer, supplier, retailer, or employee, it is related in some way to the Internet. Using this platform, he could tie the company together and start changing the model as a whole. By essentially starting over, GM was able to build an e-business foundation before commencing the e-business activities. This has proven to be a huge advantage for GM, Szygenda says. There are no islands of automation, initiated back in the 1980s, that plague so many large companies.

Szygenda also had to recreate technology leadership inside GM, a task that focused much of his attention over the next three years. GM veterans had grown cynical with overpromised, underdelivered technology initiatives, and Szygenda needed to restore faith in the process. He decided to use "change agents" to lead the enterprise-wide effort.

With management approval, he recruited and hired "200 of the best information technology/business people in the world" during 1996 and 1997. They were all corporate officers at other companies in a variety of industries. Almost all had run some aspect of the business, but they were also talented technologists. "I seeded them in every business unit of this company, and the requirement was that they had to report to the president of the business units, which was really a stretch for General Motors at that time," Szygenda says. "Information technology had always been further down the management chain."

With his evangelists and emissaries in place, Szygenda began to see positive results quickly. His new people's voices were being heard on management committees, and they were making a difference. Inevitably, however, Szygenda knew these individuals would come to represent their own business units and wouldn't necessarily work across business units. So he began to hire *process information officers* who had functional responsibilities like engineering, manufacturing, sales, service, and marketing. Their role was to link across the business units. "It formed a wonderful checks-and-balances system," Szygenda says. "In every area of the business, I had a vertical and horizontal leader, and when there was a problem, there would be two different opinions. I always knew what was really going on because I had two different opinions."

When Wagoner became president and chief operating officer (COO) in 1998, he moved to consolidate GM and create a "one-company" philosophy—no small endeavor in a company built upon many autonomous business units and brands. In the past, a customer could buy five Cadillacs in a row and walk into a Pontiac dealership to buy his son a Pontiac, and no one would have heard of him. Under Wagoner and Szygenda, that scenario will become ancient history. Combining information warehouses on customers across brands will create real customer relationships with GM. GM will no longer be just a giant monolith in Detroit; it will become a portal to targeted one-on-one marketing with its customers. Wagoner has adopted the process management concept as well and put his own vertical and horizontal leaders in place. As a young, rising star at GM, Wagoner also had a different view of the Internet and the power of e-business.

With three youngsters at home, Wagoner, himself a computer neophyte, was fascinated at how his children embraced the Internet. He began reading more and more about the Internet, but it was over the Christmas holiday season in 1998 that he got religion. "I noticed that the kids were doing everything on the computer and the Internet, and I'd been reading about all the online sales—which turns out to have been an overstatement—but I thought, 'Hey, this thing is huge. Are we doing enough?'"

When he returned from the holiday break, Wagoner called Szygenda and asked for an e-business reality check. Szygenda came back with lukewarm results. GM was probably doing as well as anybody else in the industry when it came to e-business.

"Are we destined to lead if we keep doing what we're doing?" Wagoner asked.

"No," Szygenda replied.

"Could we?" Wagoner asked.

"Yes, we could if we really put some muscle into this and not just have a bunch of divisions inside GM doing their own thing," Szygenda replied.

Wagoner seized the opportunity and initiated plans to form e-GM. The corporation would get into this battle quickly with all guns blazing. The formation of e-GM served notice of how serious the company was about the Internet. "It made people realize that we were really going to be doing things differently around here," Wagoner says. Although all the e-business initiatives were important, he realized at the outset that the most important and difficult challenge would be an order-to-delivery system that would do nothing less than transform GM into a Dell or Gateway of the automotive industry.

Along with his role in creating Covisint, Kutner was handed the responsibility for building the order-to-delivery infrastructure and making it a reality. Radicals understand that the Internet gives the buying power to the customer, and for the big automakers, that shift is explosive. Nearly 80 percent of car buyers already log on to the Internet for information and pricing before they go to a car dealer to make a purchase. Most would be happy to eliminate the traditionally unpleasant haggling that dealers engage in. Indeed, more and more buyers are realizing that they can order the car they want, custom-fitted for them, rather than settle for inventory on the dealer's lot. For a manufacturer the size of GM, which sells nearly 9 million vehicles a year, such a shift in buying style is tectonic. Kutner calls it the "fourth industrial revolution," which will put customers much more in control than they are today.

"Order to delivery or build to order is the glue that is going to transform GM from a manufacturing-centric company to a customer-centric company," Kutner says. "It's going to transform us from a manufacturer that builds for inventory to a manufacturer that builds for customer requirements."

Companies struggling to transform to an e-business orientation realize that there are learning curves to be climbed before grand plans can be turned into reality. Before doing anything else, Syzgenda had to get GM's management team up to speed with the technology. Wagoner understood that the leadership of the e-business transformation had to come from the top. It could not be handed off as a program du jour.

The goal, according to Szygenda, was for every business manager at GM to become an *e-business* manager. All would have to identify metrics for success in building their e-business. In order to do that, they had to have an intimate, first-hand knowledge of the Internet and its attendant tools. As at General Electric, the lack of intimate computer knowledge at the top levels of GM spawned fear and paralysis. It must take Nobel Prize winners to figure this out, they thought. At GM, few executives used personal computers, even for e-mail. A fair portion of the senior management team had never used a laptop computer or a Palm Pilot. "I told Rick, 'It's unacceptable that someone in our management team could be on a plane in a first-class cabin where you usually have dueling CEOs with their laptops open and he would be sitting there with nothing,'" Szygenda recalls. That would really send a negative message to the e-business world, not to mention GM employees.

So like General Electric, Szygenda got coaches for all of his senior executives to hone their computing and Internet skills. He contracted with Compaq Computer Corp. to send young trainers with solid Internet and communications skills to Detroit. Each executive was assigned a coach for one-on-one work, any time, day or night. The results were impressive. "We had some people who literally did not know how to open a laptop," Szygenda says. "Today, every one of those managers is really strong in technology."

It wasn't enough to enlighten managers and leave everyone else behind. The Internet, as Forrester's Garretson says, must become internalized throughout the whole company. GM had an internal portal called Socrates that averaged three million hits a day from employees, but Szygenda knew that no matter how large that number was, it was not reaching everyone. He wanted ubiquitous access for GM employees so they could log on to the company's Websites from anywhere. In late 2000 GM announced a joint agreement with AOL, Daimler/Chrysler, and Sun Microsystems to link all of its employees to the Internet, either through a personal computer or television.

Wagoner, a 6'4" former college basketball player at Duke, remains in awe of the Internet. He is amazed at the "little atoms flying around bringing information back and forth—a remarkable phenomenon." And though he is now quite comfortable surfing around the Internet, he calls the entire experience humbling. It remains a venue where the kids know more than the adults. "At home, my kids call me E-Wagoner, and not with complete admiration," he says laughing.

Becoming E-GM

In a company as big and bureaucratic as GM, the best initiatives can be smothered into submission by inertia and institutional bloat. When it became clear in 1998 to Wagoner, Szygenda, and GM's strategy board that e-business was going to radically change the landscape, especially in the business-to-consumer marketplace, they moved quickly to establish a more focused company-wide e-business effort. By creating e-GM as the company's Internet business division, GM could both eliminate the technological redundancies that had sprung up across the corporation's e-business initiatives and jumpstart the effort to sell vehicles online. By giving the unit the same autonomy as any vehicle business unit, e-GM gained immediate cachet inside the company.

Consumers had already embraced the Web as a crucial adjunct to their automobile shopping experience. The Internet was not just for books, CDs, and videos anymore. Web pure plays like AutoBytel and Cars.com were forcing the bricks-and-mortar companies to pay attention to the Internet's potential. Online shopping was already having a profound impact on the sale of vehicles, and GM had to become a player. Consumers demanded it. If they couldn't buy direct, as this spate of dot.com start-ups had promised and failed to deliver, they could certainly change the buying experience dramatically by shopping online prior to a dealer visit. In 1997 GM launched GM BuyPower, a Website to help consumers choose and find vehicles. GM estimates that a traditional visit to a car dealership takes two to three hours before a sale or lease can be finalized. A customer using BuyPower can handle so much of the shopping experience online that the dealer visit can be reduced to minutes. In this way, the dealers remain part of the process and feel less threatened.

"I was worried that in our vehicle business, our sales, service, and marketing folks were not moving fast enough," Szygenda says. "They were traditional guys who were having enough problems trying to sell cars and trucks in the physical world." To spearhead the e-GM effort, Wagoner chose Mark Hogan, a 27-year GM veteran and general manager for the GM North America Car Group. Like other radicals, Hogan had no Internet or IT background. He was, by all accounts, a "car guy" who had built his GM career in operations and business planning. He was not burdened by formal technology training and was known as a free thinker who moved quickly and got things done.

At the e-GM announcement, Hogan said his job was to shake things up. "We realized that if we didn't make these moves in the Internet, we could become extinct," he said. Hogan's dynamic style has made him the subject of countless business magazine profiles. When *Forbes* did a cover story called "The E Gang" in July 2000, Hogan was pictured in a group that included GE's Jack Welch, Cisco's John Chambers, Enron's Jeff Skilling, and Charles Schwab. That is heady company for a guy who worked in virtual obscurity for most of his career. But as radicals realize, the transformation to e-business requires a dynamic and visible champion to lead the way. Hogan has become GM's e-hero.

Under Hogan, e-GM oversees the company's BuyPower Website and the OnStar division. In addition, with e-GM leading the effort, the company has built a common architecture for BuyPower and made it the engine for all of GM's online vehicle information around the world. On the Website, consumers can shop for vehicles and choose models, colors, and options, as well as locate local dealers who have the desired vehicle for sale. Though U.S. franchise laws prohibit direct sales of cars to consumers, BuyPower was set up to work *through* dealers rather than around them. The next step is to use BuyPower to allow customers to custom order these vehicles. It is through BuyPower that GM's ambitious order-to-delivery initiative will be launched over the next few years.

BuyPower is up and running in 15 countries, and the goal is to be in 48 countries by the end of 2001. In Brazil, GM has already seen the power of selling online. Since GM Brazil launched its new Chevrolet Celta in September 2000, 55 percent of the 15,500 cars sold through the end of November were through the local GM Website in Brazil. "We broke all records in the automotive industry" for online sales, Szygenda says. In November alone, 80 percent of sales of the Celta were done over the Internet. Combining the need for seeing and test-driving a vehicle with the ease of the Internet, dealers in Brazil set up Internet kiosks in the dealerships and did 95 percent of the sales through them.

As part of the program, GM actually designed the Celta to be sold online. The low-priced, one-liter-engine car has just 20 options, as op-posed to thousands of possible combinations of colors and features on most vehicles. By doing this, GM is able to streamline the ordering process and keep inventories low. This back-to-the-future marketing effort is reminiscent of the early days of the automobile when Ford's first Model T was available in a choice of colors: black, black, or black.

Hogan says that plans are afoot to adopt the Brazilian model for selling Saturn vehicles in the United States sometime in 2001. Similar plans have already been set in motion in Vauxhall, England, where more than 1,200 vehicles were sold by the end of 2000. Hogan told Reuters that though the United States has regulatory issues and fran-chise laws, the customer is becoming more and more comfortable with the Internet. Thus, shopping online will lead to buying online at some point in the near future. "We want to be ready to be there for that customer," Hogan said.

In addition, Hogan set up a series of formidable alliances that rap-idly increased the traffic to the BuyPower site. Strategic partnerships with America Online, Kelly Blue Book, Edmonds, and Net Zero, the largest free Internet Service Provider led to a 2,000 percent increase in the amount of traffic coming into BuyPower. Mining all possible angles, GM also made deals with specialized affinity groups at colleges as well as with the disabled. By the end of 2000, BuyPower had directly generated the sale of 50,000 vehicles through dealers, an admittedly small number when compared to the millions of vehicles the company sells. But to Hogan the numbers indicate that when BuyPower is offered in all of GM's major markets, the impact will grow exponentially. When the service started, less than 20 percent of GM's dealers really understood it or embraced it. Today, more than 75 percent of dealers have signed up to be part of the program.

A Cultural Shift

E-GM not only energized the dealers, but it had a swift impact inside GM as well. The business unit is housed near GM's old headquarters building in Detroit and has the jazzy feel of a dot.com start-up, with orange floors, an orange conference room, and open areas for staffers to relax and share ideas. In a company as conservative as GM, it may appear to be the lunatic fringe. And it had an immediate impact. Though the staff is just 150 people, Hogan says he receives thousands of requests from employees to join the unit. The staff is a diverse group of Internet veterans from such companies as IBM, AT&T, and EDS, as well as newly minted MBAs and graduate technical people who would never have considered working at GM if not for e-GM. The summer of 2000 brought 40 interns from such business schools as Harvard, Stanford, Wharton, Michigan, Northwestern, and Carnegie-Mellon. Hogan hired several upon their graduation.

"We were able to pick the cream of the crop because of all the interest," Hogan says. "People see the world's largest Internet start-up as something to sink your teeth into." Like most radicals, those he picked were also radicals. While hiring, Hogan purposely looked both inside and outside GM for unconventional thinkers. "We very consciously brought in what we call, from a Meyers-Briggs' standpoint, extroverts who were not traditional automotive industry-type thinkers," he says. "We knew we had to be a catalyst for change in the company. In fact, it all starts with me. I've never been billed as a traditional thinker. I've spent most of my time outside the white lines."

Hogan says he has learned several key lessons at e-GM already. Though he knew little about e-business when he took the job, he understood the potential. He says having a combination of executives who are Web-savvy yet understand the traditional business is a crucial combination.

He also learned not to underestimate the need to communicate up and across rather than just down into the organization. "I spent the majority of my time in the first year communicating down and out, and I took for granted too much at the top levels of the company," Hogan says. "We needed to do a smarter job of communication with the top ten or fifteen people in the company."

Hogan also echoed Wagoner's launch-and-learn mantra. Traditional companies like GM tend to be so mired in a database mentality—that is, focused on gathering and analyzing endless reams of data—that it's uncomfortable to launch a new initiative without some type of corporate clairvoyance about how it will turn out. "You just can't afford to do that," Hogan says. "Time will whack you in this kind of space. You've got to be fast and aggressive, and you might not have the 100 percent perfect answer."

Another key lesson is to recruit a core of missionaries, not mercenaries, to spread the word. E-business efforts need evangelists—people who are zealous, resilient, and great at communicating. The technological base is important, but having a team that is influential as communicators of the message is crucial.

Table stakes to the game consist of a strong IT staff and leader, which Hogan says he has in Szygenda. Hogan notes that there have been shortcomings in communicating the business requirements clearly to the IT staff, but he says that the situation has improved over time and that Szygenda is a talented leader with a great technical team underneath him.

For Hogan and e-GM, the challenge is nothing less than changing the perception of the entire corporation. Obviously, e-GM will be measured by its success in driving car sales but also in cross-marketing the whole realm of GM products and services. "We really want the customer to think about GM not just as a vehicle manufacturer, but as a provider of mortgages, insurance, banking, Direct TV, and OnStar," Hogan says.

Indeed, to Hogan the biggest measure of success will lie in GM's ability to "reach out and touch customers on a daily or regular basis rather than on an episodic basis once every three to five years. We've got 120 million customers on the road today around the globe, and we'd like to be able to interface with them frequently. If we could do that, we'd be happy, and presumably our customers would be happy too." Through other offerings like GMAC, Direct TV, and OnStar, GM has the potential to be as ubiquitous to a consumer as the phone company or cable TV.

OnStar

If anything at GM convinced Wagoner that launch and learn is the correct e-business philosophy, it is the OnStar system that is becoming a standard feature on almost all GM cars and trucks. OnStar became a separate GM division in 1996. The innovative system began as a way to offer consumers better safety and service directly inside their vehicles. Building upon the initial OnStar technology, which provided pioneering global positioning systems and cellular communications devices as part of the car, GM has, over the years, ramped up the OnStar effort to include a spate of new technologies that bolsters the original offerings and ties the vehicle directly to the Internet. Competitors like Ford have launched similar initiatives, but GM believes its early entry has given it a wide lead.

"When we were thinking about OnStar five years ago, we didn't have all these technologies we have now," Wagoner says. "We got into the game, we started playing, we changed as we went along, we learned, we adapted, we substituted players, and here we are, five years later, so far ahead of everybody else. It's not because we knew where it was going, we just got in and played and got our knees dirty."

OnStar began as a three-way partnership between GM, Hughes Electronics, and EDS. Hughes brought cellular technology, EDS provided its call center expertise, and GM built the cars and trucks. The three companies struggled to work together, however, and in 1996 GM bought out the business and set up OnStar as a wholly owned subsidiary in Troy, Michigan, a suburb of Detroit.

When Wagoner created e-GM, he decided that OnStar was such a critical piece of the e-business strategy that he placed it under Hogan's jurisdiction. For Hogan, OnStar represented a breakthrough, a way to deliver the Internet directly into the vehicle.

Since its early days, OnStar has continued to add technology and features that have turned GM vehicles into moving Internet portals and phone booths. Since OnStar uses innovative voice-activated software, drivers with the system now have a raft of cyber-options available without taking their hands off the steering wheel. The entire system is voice-activated and accessed through the vehicle's stereo system. GM has entered into numerous partnerships with large and small communications vendors such as Verizon Wireless to offer nationwide hands-free cellular service. OnStar also offers digital satellite radio with 100 stations, as well as a new system called Virtual Advisor.

With Virtual Advisor, a driver pushes the OnStar button, usually located on the rearview mirror, and then speaks via a tiny speaker housed under the rearview mirror to a voice-activated call center. The driver asks to be connected to the Web and uses a security code number to gain access. Once online, the driver can access unlimited information from the Internet including stock quotes, weather, sports information, and e-mail, all personally tailored to that driver and delivered by an automated voice response system.

Though GM is still negotiating deals with various service providers, the potential applications are numerous. For example, GM could connect with Fidelity Investments or Charles Schwab to provide stock trading capabilities from the vehicle. A small transactions fee would go to the vendor, and in this way GM avoids the need for any onboard advertising. Consumers won't tolerate lengthy advertising, says Mike Peterson, an OnStar executive. They will, however, accept quick mentions of sponsorships, which will be part of the deal.

Peterson says OnStar is investigating a raft of possible applications to be built into the system. "We're limited only by our imaginations," Peterson says. For example, a real-time personalized traffic advisor is in the works, which will allow a driver to input a typical commute route and then receive information about not only traffic tie-ups on that route but also alternative routes if the primary route is congested. A mobile Yellow Pages is also in the works, which will combine telephone numbers with specific directions to the nearest movie theater or Chinese restaurant, and so on.

In addition, OnStar will be personalized to each vehicle so that core services and mechanical diagnostics in the car are automatically relayed to a GM call center. Most problems can be triaged instantly, and the driver will be given a voice message such as "pull over immediately," followed by service advice and instructions about what to do next. OnStar is already capable of responding if a driver has an accident. If an airbag is deployed, OnStar automatically sets off a signal to

GM's call center, and the vehicle is located and the police are notified. A GM representative actually calls the driver on the spot to ask if there are injuries. If so, an ambulance will be contacted and dispatched immediately to the accident scene. Insurance companies can be alerted as well if the driver wishes. For new, young drivers, the system offers a list of dos and don'ts at an accident scene.

With OnStar, GM is transforming the relationship with the customer, using technology as a Trojan horse. "We aren't interested in simply selling people new cars and trucks," Wagoner says. "We want to sell them the most effective automotive experience. Retail financing is part of the automotive experience, having good parts is part of the automotive experience, and so is OnStar."

OnStar allows the driver, who spends more and more time behind the wheel, to use that time more efficiently and safely. "Everyday we are figuring out more things we can do through this entry into the vehicle," Wagoner says. "We don't know how far that can go."

GM is investigating a raft of innovative applications. One scenario is a software package related to engine performance that would allow an owner to download the software upgrade overnight via the OnStar system. Thus, a Corvette owner might upgrade a 150-horsepower engine to a 280-horsepower engine and perhaps be able to throttle that back when his teenage son is driving the car. Though it has some negative Orwellian connotations and GM does not sanction such applications, the OnStar system could be used to monitor a vehicle's whereabouts, which is comforting to parents of teenage drivers. The ability to locate specific vehicles has already paid off in several car theft cases reported to the police.

"There's a lot of different ways to think about the functionality of a vehicle and what people want," Wagoner says. But he is also a pragmatist. "Never forget that they'll never buy our cars just because we have OnStar and somebody else doesn't. They've got to say, 'Hey, this is a nice vehicle, and I like all these great services too.'"

Covisint

One of the historical quagmires for American automobile makers is the paralyzing relationship with suppliers. Trying to broker deals with hundreds of thousands of suppliers created long bottlenecks in product design, development, and manufacture. When the Japanese showed the world a better way to structure supplier relationships back in the 1970s with their *keiretsu* model and promptly grabbed a dominant position in the world's automotive markets, Detroit was stunned.

Though improvements have been made, big players like GM and Ford never quite found a comfort level with their suppliers. But the Internet has changed all that. From a business-to-business standpoint, the Internet is setting off a revolution in the relationship between manufacturers and suppliers that is reshaping whole industries. GM recognized the potential early on. Kutner studied e-commerce models, from Amazon to Dell to Compaq, to help create a new procurement model. GM's procurement process was effective on the cost and quality side, he says, but was inefficient on the time side. The quotation process, with its attendant meetings and valuations, supplier visits, multiple number of quotes, and endless negotiations, created nothing less than a quagmire.

Seeing successful online exchanges like eBay and Mercata, Kutner decided that a purchasing exchange made sense for GM. With that in mind, Kutner inked a deal with CommerceOne, a new Internet software company, to help create the Internet option called Trade-Xchange. It didn't take long for Kutner to realize that when it came to the Internet, customers had heightened expectations about their orders and fulfillment. "We realized what we were dabbling with was more than just a purchasing exchange," Kutner says. "It was a supply chain–connected exchange so that we could not only do purchasing but vehicle development processes as well."

What GM foresaw was a virtual connection to its suppliers of goods and services so that GM engineers could do design and engineering changes online. By interacting electronically with their suppliers this way, they would take days, weeks, or even months out of the purchasing process. Starting with its own TradeXchange, GM moved easily into the Covisint deal without missing a beat. Already, hundreds of millions of dollars worth of supplies have moved through Covisint. Due to FTC regulations, each automaker retains its own site, and there are clear rules about security as well as firewalls to protect the confidentiality on pricing, costs, and other information. But because volume has such a direct effect on cost, the suppliers are reducing their cost structures by 5 to 25 percent. "Obviously, I'm going to expect some of that cost saving to be transferred to GM," Kutner says.

In addition, the system allows suppliers to go to market in a much different way than they have historically. By using the Internet, suppliers can dramatically reduce expenses associated with armies of salespeople roving around the world and trying to sell on a direct person-to-person basis. The impact is especially powerful for smaller suppliers like Ideal Steel or the Bing Group. When the giant car makers go to market for five million carburetors or testers for truck batteries versus 100,000 of the same part, the cost basis thins dramatically due to the volume. Without the online exchange, the smaller players buy out of catalogs and get few if any discounts. When the volume increases by 10 percent, 20 percent, or even 100 percent, costs will come down by 15 to 20 percent. "We've really created a Webified industry and an industry standard for the world," Kutner says.

The Covisint players contributed a total of $200 million to jump-start the site. If and when Covisint becomes a publicly traded company, each of the players should recoup their investments and then some. Kutner sees two sources of revenue: the transaction fees from the hundreds of thousands of transactions that pour through Covisint, and supply chain management. "Part of our business plan is to have and provide what we call 'best of breed' systems for our tier-one suppliers and their tier-two, tier-three, and tier-four suppliers," Kutner explains.

Like other radicals, GM believes that the move to e-business will fundamentally change the company, and the Covisint connection plays into that theme. Kutner says that the connectivity with suppliers will not only take vital time out of the purchasing process but will also speed up vehicle design at the same time. Working with a seat supplier like Lear, for example, a GM design engineer might come up with an idea that would reduce the cost of truck seats by $20. Prior to the Internet, implementing this change would require drawings sent back and forth between GM and Lear designers and engineers. Once approved, Lear would have to send the drawings to its suppliers, and they would return the specifications to Lear with their changes. This back-and-forth movement along the supply chain could take weeks or months. No wonder a company like GM moves like a giant turtle.

Now, working through Covisint, GM engineers sitting in Warren, Michigan, can connect online and e-mail documents back and forth to Lear and also to key suppliers in the supply chain. The entire supply chain can be talking and working through these changes in real-time. Within an hour, a change decision can be made and implemented. "Instead of waiting weeks and months for this cost improvement or quality improvement, it's going to happen in a couple of hours," Kutner says. "Just think when we put through thousands and thousands of transactions like that on a real-time basis—the benefit to us, our supply chain, and our customers."

Order To Delivery

While Covisint is a key component in GM's e-business transformation, the Holy Grail in the automotive industry today is the ability to deliver quickly the exact vehicle that the customer wants. This capability not only eliminates long waits for the buyer and large inventories for the dealers but also inflates customer satisfaction enormously. GM surveys show that a significant percentage of people who buy their cars off a dealer lot are disappointed with their purchase within six months. They really wanted red but settled for white. They really wanted a CD system to hold six CDs instead of one. "Our expectation is that more and more customers are going to want to have a car built to their specifications versus going on a lot and buying something close to what they want," Kutner says. "And when they are spending $20,000 to $60,000 for a vehicle, they should get what they want."

The GM brain trust knows that all its Internet efforts must lead to this capability in order to transform GM into a twenty-first-century competitor. The disparate GM efforts in cyberspace are all aimed at this target. Bloated, 104-day inventory levels just won't fly in the new millennium. According to Hogan, GM is already using its e-business initiative to reduce finished goods—meaning vehicles on the dealer lots—inventory radically, as well as inventory in the pipeline. Toward the end of 2000, Hogan noted that the company had taken 10 to 15 days worth of pipeline inventory out of the system.

Today, 80 percent of GM customers buy off a dealer's lot. Hogan predicts that in three to four years, as customers get more and more comfortable with online ordering, that number will reverse, and only

20 percent will buy off the lot. The rest will be purchased online and delivered through a dealer, he says.

The idea, Szygenda says, is to link together planning, manufacturing, distribution, and the retail experience electronically in a seamless environment—nothing less than changing a process that has been entrenched in the automotive industry for 80 years. "Whoever does that first is going to revolutionize the industry," Szygenda says. "We're in pretty good shape to do it." Indeed, today GM carries $40 billion worth of inventory. Hogan and Szygenda believe that GM will cut that number in half over the next three to five years using the Internet and order to delivery.

Cynics may scoff at such a notion. GM hardly has the reputation as a revolutionary. Because it is so huge, changing directions is slow and cumbersome. Yet that is exactly what radicals focus on: initiating change in the face of daunting obstacles.

No one knows better than GM, for example, the perils of endless design and production cycles. Trying to predict what customers will desire four or five years in advance has been more art than science. GM has often stumbled on this slippery slope and paid the price in marketshare decline. In the summer of 2000, for example, the company unveiled a radical new design in its Pontiac Aztek sport utility vehicle. Though it was aggressive and bold in design, the Aztek got hammered in the marketplace, with reviewers saying it was ugly and overpriced. Sales were disappointing, and in December 2000 *BusinessWeek* reported, "The Aztek is the vehicle people love to hate."

The same article pointed out how the design process for the Aztek began way back in 1994 and morphed through several iterations and design committees over six years to its current status: an unwanted and unloved vehicle. In order to stay competitive, GM can't afford such lengthy design cycles nor such tepid results.

Kutner acknowledges that "every business process in this company is going to have to change in order to respond to this more discriminating customer." Planners and designers don't have six years to fiddle with designs. Engineers have to plan and design a new vehicle in two years and factor in faster assembly along with plug-and-play options and content in order to respond more quickly to customers' needs. Without the Internet as the platform for change, it cannot happen.

In addition, the logistics chain, which today requires 10 to 14 days to move a vehicle through the dealer network to a customer, must move to what Kutner calls *dynamic routing.* Using the Internet to track a vehicle at any time and in any location will cut the time in half to get that vehicle to a customer.

To that end, GM teamed up with the Palo Alto, California–based trucking and air freight company CNF Inc. to form a joint venture to manage the flow of materials to GM assembly plants and the distribution of GM vehicles to dealerships. According to the *Wall Street Journal,* GM receives more than 180 million pounds of material daily from 12,000 places. By creating one system, which they will call Vector SCM (for supply chain management), to oversee the flow of materials electronically, GM hopes to cut the 14-day vehicle delivery time to between five and ten days. At the same time, Kutner hopes to reduce the cycle time for a *custom*-ordered vehicle from 60 days to between 15 and 20 days.

GM is spending more than $400 million on its order-to-delivery initiative. The goal is to create a seamless system that will tie the supply base into the customer ordering system. In this way, the network becomes almost a living organism that can sense GM's requirements before the physical order takes place. Suppliers online will know when customers are making inquiries about a certain vehicle so they can anticipate needs rather than wait for an order to be delivered.

All of this will be done in real-time, and Kutner is confident that the dealers will become a vital part of the process rather than be excluded over time. "There isn't a business in the whole world that won't be touched by the Internet," Kutner says. "The dealers are all going to recognize this. Many already have their own Websites where they are selling cars in their city over the Internet."

It's the Products, Stupid

Of course, GM understands that beneath all the technology lies a fundamental relationship that cannot be ignored: the customer and the car. At the end of the day, the product is the thing that translates into profits and halts the slide in market share. In order to compete with the Japanese and Germans, GM has to build innovative vehicles that inspire customers to buy.

Hogan points out that well over half of GM's products in the pipeline have no predecessor in the current lineup. "We're really heading out on a track of innovation that will change the way the public views our vehicles," Hogan says. He acknowledges that the Aztek is a controversial addition to the GM family—a love it or hate it proposition—but says, "It is a statement of our intent to do things differently."

He mentions upcoming models like the Buick Rendezvous, Cadillac Evoq, Chevrolet Avalanche, and Corvette Z06 as examples of vehicles that are not your father's GM cars. GM is going to unveil the Chevrolet SSR (Super Sport Roadster), an unusual-looking crossover vehicle that combines a roadster with a pickup-truck bed.

But in a company that sells nearly nine million vehicles each year, the hot cars sometimes go unnoticed among the more familiar vehicles that are required to accommodate such a vast customer base. The Internet itself is helping to push the design envelope, to get people thinking far outside the box. Hogan says there is an online-design experiment in the works for a vehicle called the X-Games, aimed at Gen-Xers and Gen-Yers who are into extreme sports like snowboarding and mountain biking. The vehicle has flexible seating, unusual storage, and a unique interior that can be hosed out, and it doesn't look like anything GM has ever built.

"We're doing some iterations online with prospective customers who are helping us tweak the design," Hogan says.

In the end, for a company the size of General Motors, the e-business transformation is a matter of culture—both internal and external. "Culture is the biggest issue here," Forrester's Garretson says. Syzgenda acknowledges that the "magic of culture change" is extremely difficult to achieve. "The Internet is a tremendous benefit," he says. "Because our people really like this stuff, they want to be part of it. They go home and their five-year old is doing schoolwork online and their 78-year old grandma is sending e-mail, so it is hard not to be part of it when you're at work."

Wagoner echoes the sentiment. He has instituted a "go fast" culture inside GM and challenged the company to change its mindset and leave the past behind. He realizes that the process isn't necessarily natural inside a company like GM, but the biggest problem is not people seeking to avoid the new Internet world. The biggest hurdle, he says, is "how can we learn, how can we stay ahead, how can we engage our partners—the dealers and the suppliers? Are we thinking broadly enough about all this? Can we keep our computer uptime so I can go home and not have to spend twice as much time sending e-mail from home as I do at the office? You simply can't forget the small stuff."

And as radicals realize, having the CEO personally committed to driving the entire e-business surge is crucial. "Having the CEO involved is incredibly important as to whether they succeed at this," Garretson says. "They wouldn't be able to do this without Wagoner leading the transformation."

It is difficult to picture GM executives holding online meetings, communicating regularly by e-mail, and building a future around the Internet, but that is what is happening in Detroit. Wagoner acknowledges that none of this has yet impressed Wall Street or moved the stock price. But he is unwilling to back off even an inch. "If I take anything away from it at this point, it's how much we don't know," Wagoner says. "We've learned so much that we know there's so much left to do. But that makes it kind of fun."

Southwest Airlines
Simplicity Wins,
Complexity Confuses

I'm not a surfer, but I know I wanted things to remain simple. I call that
the "Aunt Maude" approach. I want our product to be so user-friendly
and so simple that even Aunt Maude could figure out how to use it.

Herb Kelleher, Southwest Airlines

ove Field, Texas, is a rather quiet place, for an airport. About 330 commercial flights take off and land here each day, compared to 2,200 at
Dallas–Fort Worth (DFW), 20 miles down the road. But Love Field is a
fitting headquarters for Southwest Airlines (NYSE symbol: LUV),
which dominates the airport with about 85 percent of arrivals and de-
partures. A bit off the radar screen of the larger carriers, Southwest
has concocted a unique blend of business by offering travelers inexpensive tickets, frequent short-haul flights, and decidedly no-frills service. In April of 1996, the company added one more attribute to its
strategic mix: selling tickets online, and being the first major United
States carrier to do so.

By the end of 2000, Southwest was generating an astonishing 30
percent of ticket revenue from its Internet site in an industry where
competitors are spending millions to inch sales out of the single dig-
its. In dollar amounts, the airline was the first to pass the $1 billion In-
ternet sales mark for a single year, and it did so in just the first nine
months of 2000. For the year, it took in about $1.5 billion online.

That Southwest got to the Internet first is not so surprising. The lone rider of the industry was essentially kicked out of three computer reservation systems in the mid-1990s and was thus forced to explore other ticket-delivery options. What *does* confound business logic is how a company running on slender resources could exploit a capital-intensive activity, such as by establishing itself on the Web. With start-up costs estimated at just $5 million, Southwest obviously did not change its lean-is-better philosophy to enter e-business. In fact, the air-line has bent the Internet to its own principles.

Who orchestrated Southwest's success online? CEO Herb Kelle-her, 70, claims it wasn't him. It's easy to believe him since he still suf-fers from the perception that he has trouble figuring out how to turn on his personal computer. Nevertheless, Kelleher's imprint is all over the site. No executive surpasses the Southwest CEO when it comes to keeping things simple, and this operating philosophy is embodied in the Website.

"We have been extremely successful in taking the simplicity of booking travel on Southwest and putting it online in an easy-to-use for-mat for our customers," he says. "It's just one more way to reach us, and the feedback tells us that we're doing it right."

Web monitoring firms confirm Kelleher's self-assessment. In Oc-tober 2000 Southwest ranked first among air carriers, according to Top9.com, with 2,871,000 unique visitors, compared with 1,908,000 at AA.com and 1,794,000 at Delta.com. Southwest may also lead its com-petitors in terms of revenue produced at its online site, but that com-parison is difficult to make since most airlines do not break out rev-enue and costs from their Internet operations. What can be said is that Southwest's consistent reputation as one of America's most ad-mired companies, as measured by *Fortune* magazine's annual rank-ings, has now added a new dimension: most successful airline Web-site.

The Texas Triangle

Southwest began life in 1967 on a cocktail napkin, a crudely drawn tri-angle linking Houston, Dallas, and San Antonio. Businessman Rollin King and his friend Kelleher, a lawyer, sketched out their idea in a San

Antonio bar. Air Southwest, as it was called at the time, faced lawsuits before it even took wing. Not until 1971 did the renamed Southwest Airlines schedule its first flight from Love Field.

Love became Southwest's theme. In the 1970s stewardesses wore hot pants while serving up love potions and love bites, known as drinks and peanuts on other airlines. When these other carriers flocked to DFW at its opening in 1974, Kelleher argued that Southwest should stay put, and its dominance of Love Field began.

At its conception, Southwest embodied a radical competitive focus. Instead of going toe-to-toe with more muscular rivals in the air travel industry, the company created its own market: point-to-point, short-haul flights. Kelleher, Rollin, and colleagues understood that in this side of the business they would be competing primarily against car travel, not other air carriers.

Surface transportation has several attractive attributes that traditional airlines find difficult to challenge: cheapness of travel, for instance, and the flexibility of when to leave and return. Instead, they counter with amenities such as meals, films, and video games. Southwest bets every day that these luxuries are actually secondary in the minds of a large number of travelers.

To compete against the cheapness of auto travel, Southwest set ticket prices at half that of regular carriers. For flexibility, the airline geared itself to frequent flights all day long. In the majority of the 59 cities Southwest serves, travelers can come and go pretty much whenever they want.

To avoid the congestion of larger airports, Southwest chooses smaller venues: Midway in Chicago rather than O'Hare; Islip on Long Island rather than LaGuardia; Providence, Rhode Island, or Manchester, New Hampshire, rather than Boston's Logan. In these secondary markets, there is less stacking of incoming flights, fewer holds at gates, and reduced taxi time, which enables Southwest to keep to a tight, and economic, schedule.

To standardize maintenance parts inventories and staff training, Southwest decided to fly only Boeing 737s and now operates a fleet of nearly 350, with 52 more to be delivered by the end of 2002. Single-class service and open seating make boarding not just more egalitarian, but faster as well, which helps keep turnaround time on the runway at the Southwest goal of 20 minutes, twice as fast as other airlines. All of these efforts are geared toward one result: keeping customers moving as quickly and inexpensively as possible between cities where they have the option to drive.

In effect, Southwest insinuated itself into a competitive space that no one had recognized before—between traditional air flights and personal car travel. Once there, the quirky airline from Texas held on with a single-mindedness that has beaten back encroachments on its territory from the major carriers on one flank, and upstart regional discounters on the other. Southwest's reward: 28 years of continuous profitability.

Finding Opportunity in Crisis

Why did an airline operating off the beaten track, known more for freethinking than for free spending, become the first to invest in an online operation?

Swift action in the midst of danger is probably the best answer. In 1994 Southwest faced a crisis when three of the four Computer Reservation Systems (CRSs) that travel agents used for booking demanded that Southwest pay their rates to stay included, a total of $100 million, according to Kevin Krone, the senior director of marketing automation. By contrast, Southwest's net income in 1992 was $97.4 million.

In the mid-90s, about 60 percent of Southwest's business came from travel agents, half of that from the Sabre system. Being shut out of all CRSs except Sabre meant that Southwest had to find some way of booking the remaining 30 percent, or lose the revenue. Travel agents could still handwrite tickets on Southwest, but the extra time and hassle of doing so were major disincentives to their directing business to the airline.

Travelers who normally bought through agents began calling Southwest directly, putting an enormous strain on the existing distribution infrastructure. The company's options were either to build more call centers and hire many more people—an expensive alternative that would take months to implement—or to find other electronic ways to connect to travel agents and customers.

Southwest accepted banishment from the CRSs and countered with a crash development of ticketless travel, a perfect way to circumvent the loss of agents. In four months, a team of forty people linked back-end computers with front-end reservation systems to accommodate what was at the time a novel idea: passengers traveling without tickets in their hands. Today more than 80 percent of Southwest's travelers fly ticketless.

Fortunately for Southwest, the development team did not have to start from scratch. The concepts of ticketless travel and an Internet site were already taking shape in the minds of a small group of marketing and information systems people. They were working on these projects, Kelleher proudly notes, out of sight and "without permission."

Many conversions from traditional distribution methods to e-business stem from forward-looking executives' pushing the organization onto the new path. In Southwest's case, as with other radicals like Enron, the impetus came from the bottom up. "The beauty of the evolution of our presence on the Internet is that I didn't give anybody a mandate," Kelleher says. "People were already working on it when we had a crisis."

By March 1995 the information-only Website was inaugurated, the first by an American airline. According to Anne Murray, director of integrated marketing, Southwest was not expecting to see any immediate value from this effort, but one soon appeared. Instead of having to mail costly information packets to every inquiry from investors, journalists, and students, Southwest started directing them to the Internet, where the data dispersal was essentially free.

Krone, now head of the Internet operation, was part of the team that created the Website. "The only thing dynamic you could do was look up schedules and fares," he says, "you couldn't purchase anything." While many in the company were satisfied with that limited functionality and were not contemplating extensions to it, Krone says the idea in marketing was always to turn the site into a distribution vehicle. "The reactions varied from either indifference to 'Yeah, let's do this.' Nobody said, 'This is dumb, I vote we don't do it.'"

In April 1996 Iflyswa.com added the booking feature to its

Website, and the nature of doing business in the airline industry began to change dramatically.

Web Economics

In her book *Customer.com*, Patricia Seybold spells out the strategic reasons to develop a significant Web presence. Two of her points seem written for the airline industry:

- Reduce your costs per transaction substantially.
- Reach your customers in the most cost-effective way with targeted offers.

Krone figures that a reservation booked by an outside agent costs Southwest $10, compared to just $1 if that customer logs on and purchases at Southwest.com. A phone reservation directly to Southwest costs something in between; the company hasn't pinpointed the exact amount. Salomon Smith Barney calculates the costs for nondiscount carriers at $12 per ticket bought online to $45 per ticket bought through an agent.

Obviously, luring people to the Web makes terrific economic sense. For airlines, the three biggest costs—aircraft purchase, labor, and fuel—are often untouchable because of contracts set years in advance. The largest cost centers that can be addressed are ticketing, sales, and promotion, which together comprise roughly 20 percent of total expenses. One ticket sold online by Southwest results in an immediate savings of 90 percent over one bought through a third-party agency, and perhaps 40 percent savings over one taken by a phone representative. In an industry in which most airlines still rely on agencies to connect to customers, Southwest takes in 70 percent of its sales directly either online or by phone.

Overall, Kelleher figures his company saved $80 million in 2000 by selling online tickets that otherwise would have been purchased by phone or through third parties. The annual expense to maintain the Internet operation is just $21 million. *Fortune* magazine cites Southwest's low costs (22 percent below the industry average) and high operating margins (16.5 percent above the average) as evidence that it is "the best-run airline" in America.

Southwest draws customers to its Website in three main ways. First, it guarantees that the price of any ticket bought there will be the lowest that the airline offers, typically 60 percent off full fare. More important, this lowest price is available *only* online.

Second, Southwest made its Rapid Rewards program more rapid for frequent fliers. Instead of requiring eight round-trips for a free ticket, the program requires only four now—if they are bought online. This benefit has proved so popular that Southwest extended it at least until its 30th birthday in June 2001.

Third, Southwest created Click 'n Save specials, which are sent weekly by e-mail to almost three million people who have signed up for the notices.

In practice, no one-way ticket booked from the Website costs more than $109, even for travel from Chicago to San Antonio, or Los Angeles to Nashville. Can such bargain prices really power Southwest's earnings?

"We think this [fare schedule] is still profitable for us," Krone says. "It's a 21-day-plus advance sale, so it helps us in our inventory control and revenue management. We're taking bookings that are many days or months out and layering them into the system. That helps smooth out demand."

In addition, the mushrooming number of Click 'n Save subscribers provides Southwest with the second strategic advantage Seybold mentions: a vehicle for reaching customers. "It's a great trial device for us to put offers in front of people," Krone says. "We look at it as a marketing vehicle, and a relatively inexpensive one because the e-mail is basically free. We shave a few dollars off the fare—that's the price on getting the word out." When Southwest launches service to a new city, it can spread the news fast to Click 'n Save subscribers and offer them introductory specials.

In March 2000 Southwest launched its first televised commercial spots dedicated to promoting its Website. The company targeted professional sports audiences with its wry sense of humor in the "Symbol of Freedom" ads. The ubiquitous tag line: "You are now free to move around the country." In one such ad, a man gets his glasses all fogged while unloading the dishwasher, which inspires him to log onto Southwest.com and book a trip. In the next scene, he and his wife are enjoying an outdoor hot tub at a ski resort. His glasses are still fogged.

In 1999 Southwest moved 57,500,213 people around the country, making it the fourth largest American airline in terms of domestic passengers carried. In the fourth quarter of 2000, profits rose 65 percent to $155 million. For fiscal year 2000, profits grew by 32 percent to $625 million. This balance sheet is the envy of the airline industry.

The Internet Favorite

Travel is the single biggest sales category on the Internet, outpacing software, books, records, and toys by wide margins. Jupiter Research, a Jupiter Media Metrix company in New York, sizes up the online travel market for the year 2000 at $11 billion. About three quarters of that total—$7.85 billion—come from airline bookings. About 10 percent of all air tickets are being bought online today, a figure Jupiter Research predicts will grow more than 17 percent, to $15 billion, by 2005.

As a big-ticket item, travel lends itself to consumer research for the best deal, and there is a mind-boggling number of options for window-shopping today. Travelers can log on to Priceline, Travelocity, Cheaptickets, Expedia, and dozens of other so-called agency sites promising *the* lowest fares. These general service providers take a traveler's desired schedule information and scour their databases of participating airlines, hotels, and rental car companies for the best price.

By and large, broad travel sources rank much higher on customer satisfaction than direct supplier sites run by Delta, Marriott, or Hertz, for example. The reason: People clearly want choice.

"Consumers prefer the agency sites because they like to shop and compare prices," says Robert LaFleur, an analyst at Bear, Stearns & Co. in New York. "They're much happier when they feel they've done their research and gotten a good deal."

Southwest is the anomaly. It does not make its tickets available through the agency sites, except Travelocity, which is powered by the Sabre database. Essentially, it's a leap of faith for a traveler booking on Southwest to believe that the price offered is the best one available anywhere.

Other airlines are scrambling to partner with each other in an array of alliances that seems unusual, if not downright unlikely, for fierce competitors. In Hotwire, for example, American Airlines, Continental Airlines, United Air Lines, Northwest Airlines, US Airways Group, and America West Airlines have become limited investors in a Website operation geared to selling seats on underbooked flights at big discounts. By mid-2001, a controversial and much-delayed joint venture dubbed Orbitz is expected to be up and running. The five founding members—United, American, Delta Airlines, Continental, and Northwest—are majority owners of a consortium that travel agents see as a threat to their livelihood. Southwest is the only major airline that has not yet signed up to participate.

Will Southwest join Hotwire, Orbitz, or any other alliance of airlines to sell tickets? Herb Kelleher's answer is straight to the point: "No." Considering the dot.com massacre that occurred throughout 2000, radicals who avoided succumbing to dot.com fever when it was at its boiling point now look visionary.

Kelleher, the indefatigable CEO, a man who pilots his airline on the margins of the industry, can afford to go it alone. Like many radical executives, he has helped his company carve out a business niche that is seemingly impervious to what major competitors do. For example, Delta announced in September 2000 the creation of an internal division dedicated to e-business, with separate business-to-business, business-to-consumer, and business-to-employee branches. From new revenue, distribution cost savings, and equity investments, the Atlanta-based airline estimates reaping a $150 million benefit per year by 2002.

Not content with doing e-business internally, United is investing $100 million to build a separate company to handle its Internet initiatives. The headquarters for United NewVentures will be in Chicago, rather than Elk Grove, Illinois, in order to attract e-business professionals and create a unique business atmosphere.

Instead of constructing whole corporate structures to manage burgeoning Internet affiliations, Southwest focuses on a simpler business prospect: its online relationship with customers. The value proposition of a sale on Southwest.com cuts both ways. The buyer buys a ticket at a rock-bottom price, and the seller sells at one-tenth the cost. Why complicate the process?

Staying Ahead

Making a strategic move first can confer a sizable advantage, whether in traditional business or in e-business. Maintaining that initial advantage over time, though, shows that the company knows how to implement a good idea, not just conceive of it.

LaFleur from Bear, Stearns & Co. sees two basic ways of using the Internet, depending on the attractiveness of the company's product. "If you have a so-so product in the marketplace, then you can try to draw business to your site in order to leverage your brand. If you have a great product, then you can use the site as a convenient booking mechanism. With Southwest," LaFleur says, "the product is driving the site—not the site driving the product. They already have differentiated themselves. They need a Website to process orders, and they have used it effectively to launch new routes."

In essence, Southwest has maintained its brand identity—low-cost, convenient, efficient travel—even while shifting customers to a new technology. The product has remained primary and the distribution method secondary. Larger carriers such as Delta, United, and American lack Southwest's unique brand identity and so must pursue more ambitious Web relationships.

"For a novice, the user friendly format of Southwest.com is clearly a winner over other airline sites," LaFleur says. "The advantage Southwest has is that they don't fly everywhere and their prices don't change eight times a day. People know that if they want to go from point A to B, Southwest is going to be the lowest cost. They underpromise and overdeliver."

While other airlines have a bewildering display of destinations, fares, frequent flyer promotions, and blackout dates, Southwest remains an island of simplicity that translates well to the Internet. A customer leafs through a pull-down menu of cities, desired travel dates, and number of people. By the fifth screen, the purchase can be complete, and a customer does not have to be part of the frequent flyer program to do it, as with other airlines.

Kelleher describes the guiding principle behind the Website. "I'm not a surfer, but I know I wanted things to remain simple. I call that the 'Aunt Maude' approach. I want our product to be so user-friendly and so simple that even Aunt Maude could figure out how to use it."

Shore from Jupiter Research phrases this Internet philosophy succinctly: "Simplicity wins; complexity confuses."

Just the Basics

In its summer 2000 report, the Internet monitoring service Gomez.com said about Southwest, "Well, another quarter has gone by with a minimal number of changes and guess what—it doesn't really matter. Southwest has one of the most successful sites in the airline industry as its loyal customers continue to flock there to book their travel. If you're among the loyal, why bother going anywhere else?"

In August 2000 Southwest.com did change the booking screen, the first major alteration since 1996. During the design exercise some suggested adding an opening screen asking the general question, "What do you want to do today—book a trip, look up your Rapid Rewards account . . . ?"

Krone reports the result of the discussion: "We said, no, we can't do that. We have to keep it simple and straightforward and not require any more clicks than are there already. Even adding one screen upfront gives someone an opportunity to say, 'Oh, forget it.' Once people get involved in the process they tend to stay with it, so we don't want to put any roadblocks up causing them to exit the process prematurely."

That is not to say that Southwest isn't tinkering with its Web presence. The Rapid Rewards double credit was offered in February 1997. In August of the same year Internet-only fare specials were added. In May 2000 corporate travel managers were given the online ability to monitor their employees' business with Southwest in a Web-based program called SWABIZ.

As an Internet pioneer for its industry, Southwest had no airline models to follow. Among all sites, Krone points to Yahoo as one that clearly knows its mission and doesn't need to present a fancy face to the world. He cites Amazon.com for its marketing strategy of telling consumers, "If you like this book, you'll probably like this other one."

Is there a lesson for Southwest? Krone says, "At first blush it doesn't make sense for us to say, 'If you like San Diego, you'll like West Palm Beach; they both have palm trees.' I don't think there's that kind of way we can use it. But there might be if somehow you could find out that someone is a baseball park junkie and you could say, 'If you like Fenway Park, you might like Coors Field.' But you have to get a lot more information about them."

Four years after initiating its booking feature, Southwest began creating the databases that might make use of customers' online buying habits. The company is wary of being intrusive by asking too many questions and making customers feel uneasy that their privacy is being invaded.

Krone believes that Southwest.com grew slowly in the beginning because of frightening stories in the news media about the insecurity of buying on the Web. But now, with people routinely buying books, groceries, records, and almost every other product imaginable on the Internet, security has receded as a consumer concern, he says. "If you're already on the net buying groceries or doing banking, it's easy to buy an airline ticket."

Maintaining Its Philosophy

Establishing a new means of doing business can tempt a company to change with the technology. Southwest studiously ignores many of the possibilities of the Internet, but it isn't for lack of vision. It's a matter of choice.

Corporate philosophy in Dallas has long held that focus groups, user surveys, and many other standard marketing tools are too costly. Listening to the customer, Southwest-style, means that every employee is encouraged to send in customer feedback from the field.

The marketing purse strings have not opened up just because Southwest is meeting its customers online. With millions of people clicking on to its site, the company could amass a mountain of information about customer preferences, then tailor offers down to the individual traveler. It does not.

"Currently we don't do anything like one-to-one marketing or personalization at all," Krone says. "We don't do much as a company as a whole. In a few places we have detailed information about customer buying, but we haven't done anything with it in terms of direct marketing. One-to-one marketing is expensive in the physical world. In the electronic world it is cheap, but it's expensive to compute it, get the programs to go through your database looking for patterns, and develop offers based on them. Down the road we'll do that, but now we're focusing on getting the basics out there without getting too fancy."

Part of Southwest's reluctance relates to the very nature of its business positioning. An aggressive discounter has a much more difficult time thrilling customers with targeted offers. A full fare of $99, for example, might drop to $49 if bought on the Internet. To go beyond that and excite the customer, Southwest would have to almost give the ticket away. Competitors, on the other hand, might start out with a $600 fare that they could offer for $300. The traveler perceives greater value, even though he's still paying hundreds more dollars.

This situation is ironic: Southwest, the airline that revels in providing the personal touch in its flying experience, is hamstrung in projecting that same personal touch on the Internet.

Krone says, "A lot of times people see one-to-one marketing as 'see what he bought and make him an offer based on that.' I don't think that's going to work real well for us. But we can be more personalized by providing other, non-fare-based content that might be relevant, such as schedule alerts or fare alerts."

Instead of worrying about targeting individuals or special groups of people with $5-off offers on a $49 fare, Southwest is concentrating on making booking tickets easy and consistent for everyone, all the time. No matter how easy the process, though, some potential buyers will log out without completing the purchase. Converting these lookers to bookers is a major effort of many sites, which are supplying onscreen help icons, toll-free phone assistance, and direct e-mail. Companies find themselves in a curious position: They've tried to lure customers online because of the reduced costs of doing business there but now are finding that they must add back the costly human touches in order to complete many transactions.

Southwest does none of it. In fact, if a customer requires phone help or changes his itinerary after booking online, the double Rapid Rewards benefit is nullified. Southwest expects and requires customers to complete their side of the process on their own.

But in an age when almost every Website has a "contact us" option, why not Southwest?

"One thing we feel strongly about is responding to you," Krone says. "If you call, write, fax us—if you write in on the back of a napkin—we think you deserve a personal response, not a form letter. Our fear is that because e-mail is so easy to do, we would be flooded with e-mails and we'd have to make a philosophical change and say we aren't going to respond to everybody or not respond personally."

What scares Krone are stories of competitors receiving 250,000 e-mails a month. By contrast, he guesses that Southwest responds to about 30,000 letters a *year.*

Shore at Jupiter Research sees other airlines investing in the technology that can route priority e-mails, such as people having difficulty completing a ticket purchase online, and provide automated responses. But she also understands Southwest's thinking. "Most sites are still measuring their response time to e-mails in terms of the number of days, but consumer expectation is in terms of hours. If you can't respond in a timely matter, one of three things will happen: You lose the person as a customer, they e-mail you again, or they migrate to a higher-cost channel (such as a telephone representative) for help. So while I would prefer Southwest allow e-mail or have live chat, if they can't handle it, it's better not to. Opening up an e-mail channel if you can't afford it is the worst customer service you can offer."

Keeping to the Mission

Many Websites are studded with advertising and links, two common ways to earn money and cultivate business on the Internet. Again, Southwest hews to its own concept of value.

"The flagship mission of the site—the value to Southwest employees and shareholders—is selling tickets at a dollar a piece instead of ten dollars," Krone says. "So it doesn't make sense to put a banner up that we get a penny per impression from an advertiser and then perhaps lose a sale because the customer sees a great ad, clicks on it, and they're gone."

At that point, four things could happen, three of them bad for Southwest. The potential customer might come back to Southwest.com and buy the ticket. On the other hand, he or she might buy the ticket on another airline, buy it on Southwest through a third-party, or decide not to fly at all. Advertising, in other words, provides little financial benefit at a possibly high cost.

Through 2000, the only connections a Southwest.com visitor could make were to conventions and visitors bureaus. The company added the ability to book rental cars in December 2000, and in 2001 Southwest added hotel booking capability, catching up to features offered by competitors.

"It's a matter of resources," Krone says. "It takes programming to make it work that a person who just booked a flight on us to Albuquerque can be linked to relevant offers on cars or hotels. We are constantly in a battle—we have a long list of neat ideas, but then you have to think about your programming hours. We will double staff in the next two years to accommodate developing some of these things."

Where's the Fun?

Southwest.com admirably expresses one famous aspect of the company: bare-bones, efficient service. But the site decidely lacks one of the other hallmarks of the airline: a sense of surprise and fun.

A flight on Southwest may yield surprises—a ticket agent dressed in a costume for Halloween, for instance, or a stewardess rapping out the safety precautions before takeoff. The corporate mindset is playful and casual, as evidenced at the Dallas headquarters, where nearly everyone strolls about in shorts and sneakers.

To convey his no-nonsense style, Herb Kelleher operates one of the country's most profitable airlines from a spartan, windowless office. The flamboyant CEO, who once arm-wrestled another executive for use of the "Just Plane Smart" slogan, will do whatever it takes to publicize the Southwest message.

"If Southwest can be described as a person, it would be efficient, fun, and wacky," says Susan Kirkelie, senior director of marketing programs. "It's a balancing act when to be efficient and when to be wacky. When you're booking a ticket, you just want to book, so we defer to the number-one word people use about us: efficient."

As the gatekeeper of changes to the Website, Krone thinks hard about the balance of business and fun. "The site has to reflect our culture," he says, "but we go to great lengths to keep it simple and consistent. Once a customer learns the system, then the next time he comes he finds we've changed it because we're trying to be funny, hiding a button or putting in a tricky icon—you can't do that. Some people might get a kick out of it; most people would say, 'I'm going elsewhere.'"

So where in the virtual Southwest experience is the surprise, quirkiness, and laughs that are so much a part of the physical Southwest experience? They can be found online, but not anywhere near the booking process. If you want to download a vintage commercial, click on Programs and Services, then Education, then Videos. If you want to see Herb Kelleher handing out peanuts in flight, click on About SWA, then Photo Gallery.

"The great thing about the Internet," Krone says, "is that you can perform all those tasks at one store, so to speak. But you can't confuse what each part of the puzzle's purpose is. In the entertainment section, you don't want to say, 'Buy a ticket, buy a ticket, buy a ticket.' And in the ticket section you don't want to divert people with entertainment."

Southwest.com is crafted with one purpose in mind: to sell tickets. On an average day the site may see 10 million hits, a far cry from the 40,000 in 1995. Curiously, Southwest doesn't measure the more meaningful number of unique visitors.

The Website was built to accommodate anticipated volumes, but as Krone says, "We didn't want to build the church for Easter Sunday—we didn't think that was a wise use of our resources."

Easter Sunday came in July 1996, when Southwest celebrated its 25th anniversary with a $25 fare. "That lit up the sky," Krone remembers. Lines snaked through the corridors of airports. At pay phones people handed the receiver over to the next person so they wouldn't have to redial. Callers overloaded the AT&T network, and when they couldn't get through, many people shifted to the Internet, which overwhelmed that channel as well.

At that time a busy day for the Website was 115 reservations. Today Southwest.com is completing well over 10,000 on a daily basis, Krone says. He calculates that if demand were spread out over the day, the site could handle 60 to 70 percent of total bookings.

Handling more than half of bookings online is a fantasy that only Southwest among airlines has the luxury of dreaming at the moment.

Catering to Business

Roughly 50 percent of Southwest's passenger traffic comes from business travelers, and the Website has proven a valuable tool for cultivating this profitable group.

In May 2000 the company launched SWABIZ, an online means for corporate travel managers to track trips taken by their employees. Any travel booked by the company's identification number will be posted within 24 hours and available for review by managers. The information includes the traveler's name, confirmation number, type of transaction, and fare booked. A travel manager can sort by tickets bought for a month or year, by city pair, and by dollar amount.

Before SWABIZ, corporate travel managers had no easy way to keep track of corporate travel. "It's a piece of the business we want to compete in," Krone says. "Because we don't participate in CRSs, the reporting has been an Achilles' heel for us. Putting reporting and booking features in one product helps us to compete more vigorously."

The 400 companies connected right now tend to be small to medium size, like Simply Fashion Stores Ltd., a Birmingham, Alabama, chain of 225 stores. "When Southwest called us up and told us about it, we joined right away," says Bob Greenlee, the corporate auditor.

Simply Fashion is Southwest's dream company. Budget-conscious employees fly almost exclusively on Southwest. In 1999 they took 250 flights, worth $62,000 in tickets. Before SWABIZ, Southwest sent a paper receipt for every flight taken, which the auditor's office had to match to the bill.

"SWABIZ gives us the ability to look at all of the flights, whether someone in the central office or in the field books it," Greenlee says. "We just go to the Website and pull up the account."

Home Depot, Inc., signed on for SWABIZ in September 2000. Out of a total 75,000 flights taken by employees each year, the company books 8,000 to 10,000 on Southwest, representing 3.5 percent of its airline dollars.

"Before this," says Cathy Spivey, senior manager of travel services, "we had a real tedious process in place where we would call Southwest reservations for every booking and then manually put in a shell of the reservation on our system."

Reinventing Competition

In the halls of Southwest, the lure of cyberspace encourages many to ponder using the Website for one promotion or another, one marketing vehicle or another. Kelleher admits his faith in the Internet as a strategic tool, but such talk makes him remind everyone of Southwest.com's singular purpose: to sell tickets. No feature should be added that would hinder the reservation process.

"A great many competitive forces over the years have tried to oust us from our low-fare niche, but we have always persisted," Kelleher says. "The Internet has proven to be an effective means for us to distribute our product at a very low cost. Keeping our costs low allows us to continue our mission."

When it started online booking in 1996, Southwest saw the new distribution channel potential for reinforcing its profitability. Many companies across all industries are still seeing red ink after five years on the Web. Newer entries, such as the well-financed Travelocity and Expedia travel sites, have racked up multimillion dollar losses.

Southwest doesn't care how any other airline or company uses the Internet. Just as it defined its own niche in the commercial aviation business, it has created its own imprint on the Internet as well.

Southwest competes by devising its own game with its own rules. Other airlines use commuter feeders and interlines with competitors for baggage handling; Southwest does not. Other airlines operate from a hub-and-spoke configuration; Southwest flies point to point. Other airlines—most other companies, in fact—declare customers as their first priority; Southwest states that its more than 30,000 employees come first. Other airlines are trying to figure out how to maximize profit from selling tickets online; Southwest has already done it.

Southwest's claim that it invented competition is certainly exaggerated, but in terms of airlines that sell tickets on the Internet, it is true.

9

Progressive Innovation Driven by Pragmatism

The man with a new idea is a crank—until the idea succeeds.

Mark Twain (as quoted in Progressive's 1999 annual report)

n searching for role models in the transition to e-business, the insurance industry wouldn't likely leap onto the top of one's target list. The staid and heavily regulated industry, not unlike much of the financial services world, has not been quick to embrace the Internet and e-commerce. Culturally, the Internet seemed like nothing more than the lunatic fringe to many key players mired in entrenched business models and archaic bureaucracies. They've all since leaped into the fray, but few have emerged as true pioneers or even Internet luminaries.

But there are always exceptions. Progressive Corporation, the $6 billion auto insurance company based just outside Cleveland, Ohio, has long stepped to the beat of a different drummer, mostly because of its iconoclastic and eccentric chief executive officer Peter Lewis. Progressive, at Lewis's behest, began an earnest transition to e-business in 1995 and has emerged as the leading online insurer in the United States. Though the e-business push is not solely responsible, the company's revenues have soared from $3.4 billion in 1996 to more than $6.2 billion in 2000, and Progressive has moved from the sixth- to fourth-largest auto insurer in that time. Its average growth rate of 21.6 percent during that same time period dwarfs the 3.3 percent growth rate for the auto insurance industry as a whole.

Progressive remains heavily dependent on its relationship with a network of 30,000 independent agents, through whom it sells 80 percent of its policies. But that relationship is undergoing dramatic changes as insurance, like virtually all other industries, is impacted by the advent of the Internet. Progressive was the first to sell policies directly to consumers via its Website, and it has essentially remade itself as an online organization—from selling to claims adjusting to forming intimate customer relationships with a new, younger audience.

Progressive has won a spate of awards for its Internet initiatives, including a number-one ranking among insurance Websites from Neilsen/Net Ratings and "Best Online Insurance Carrier" by Gomez Advisors, a leading e-commerce tracking company. Progressive's Website is attracting 750,000 unique visitors each month, which surpasses all other insurance-related Websites. They are being drawn by Progressive's growing reputation as an online force. Through technology, Progressive has built a brand with a simple theme: "It doesn't have to be this difficult. We'll take the hassle out of auto insurance." The tagline in the company's aggressive advertising campaign is "Not what you'd expect from an insurance company," a message that has gained more credibility as the company's Internet business has grown.

The company, for example, uses its Website to allow its customers to do comparison shopping for prices, openly posting competitors' prices regardless of whether they are more or less than Progressive's. Customers can then buy a policy online with the click of a mouse. Using PersonalProgressive, a password-protected site, customers can make secure, real-time payments, track current claims, modify policy information, and interact with Progressive agents and service reps via the Website and toll-free phone lines.

In combination with wireless technology and a vast fleet of emergency response vehicles, Progressive is using the Internet not only to arrive at an accident scene quickly—often before the police or tow trucks—but also to settle the claim and write the check on the spot. With the Internet as the new foundation, Progressive's customer service and claims handling capabilities are winning impressive new business for the army of independent agents who sell the company's products. Though the Internet allows Progressive to compete with its own agents in selling direct to customers, most agents are finding that Progressive's move into cyberspace is actually helping more than hindering their business.

"Progressive is light years ahead of anybody when it comes to automation and the use of the Internet," says Tom Masters, an agent with the Sirak-Moore Insurance Agency in Canton, Ohio. "They've helped me increase my business tremendously."

Like Enron and other radicals, Progressive has built its online initiative on a foundation and business philosophy that were already in place and thriving. Under Lewis, Progressive nourishes an innovative culture in which employees are empowered to think creatively and take risks. They are rewarded handsomely for success and find wide paths of upward mobility in the organization. Companies with such cultures tend to embrace the potential of the Internet and allow their organizations to mirror the Internet itself: an open environment where communication flows and information become the currency.

For its Internet initiative, Lewis has depended heavily on Glenn Renwick, former chief information officer and now chief executive of insurance operations, and Alan Bauer, the company's Internet business leader. Bauer, for example, pushed hard to turn the company into an e-business after his own early brush with the potential power of the Internet. But all initiatives must filter through the management framework that Lewis has built within Progressive over the past 35 years as the company's CEO. For Lewis, e-business is a crucial piece but not the only piece that completes the puzzle. Technology has always been a pragmatic tool for the company, not a means to an end. Innovation, Lewis learned from his father, the company's cofounder, is always driven by pragmatism.

"Progressive is a hybrid," Lewis says, "a clicks-and-mortar company. Technology has always been important to what we do and how we do it, so offering our products and associated services on the Internet was a natural next step. But the key issue is staying very focused on the consumer, rather than the Website."

To do that, Progressive is a company that measures everything, and it has carefully monitored its Internet initiative with metrics for success. Bauer explains that Progressive carefully tracks raw insurance data as it relates to the Internet. Do Internet customers stay around as long as non-Internet customers? Do they have similar claims? Do they feel the Website performs well? All this information drives the Internet initiative. "I have taken the view that we want to be pretty early with technology but not first," Bauer says. "We want to be biased toward functionality, not glitz." For example, Progressive avoids massive graphics files that download at a snail's pace on most consumers' personal computers, opting instead for a clean, functional site without logjams.

In 1999, Progressive saw the Internet become the market of choice for customers ages 18 to 35. This demographic group is the most likely to actually *shop* for auto insurance (as opposed to opting for the same insurer as their parents or listening to an agent's advice), so Progressive is keenly interested in finding ways to attract their business. That year, Progressive sold more than $70 million of auto insurance on the Internet, which represented just 7 percent of sales but was the fastest growing market segment. It provided more than one million quotes and serviced more than 65,000 customers online. In the first three quarters of 2000, the numbers grew significantly to $170 million and 13 percent of direct sales.

And Progressive understood early on that the Internet business model would continue to grow and be a key factor in the future. According to the National Association of Independent Insurers (NAII), an estimated $14 billion of insurance will be sold online by 2004, a tenfold increase over 2000. Progressive also understands its audience better than most competitors. People tend not to change insurance companies or policies once they pass age 35, so Progressive is focused heavily on the next wave of consumers.

"We've got to be thinking about what a 14-year-old is thinking," Renwick says. "What are they doing in school; how are they working with music? I don't think they expect to get a telephone call, answer a lot of questions, and find out something later. They want answers now, they want a 'what if' on a real-time basis. They want more control over their product. They want to personalize it more to them. They want more choices, and they want to manage it."

Being out front early has provided Progressive with an Internet template that most of its competitors have yet to create. Executives are willing to share lessons learned from its transformation into an e-business. One of the critical lessons is that the CEO must spearhead the effort and make it the centerpiece of the company's move into the future. Lewis is not a technology junkie and doesn't use a keyboard, but he understands the impact of the Internet and has built a vision of the future around that.

Lewis says there are three keys to e-business success:

1. "Make your offering information rich. We do this by giving consumers comparison rates and giving customers unparalleled access to their auto insurance information and account. It's the consumer's insurance policy—not ours! Information transparency guides a lot of our decisions.

2. "Make it easy to use. For us that means it needs to be fast, responsive, intuitive, and flexible. For instance, we offer a 'what if' capability so that a customer can quote five different sports cars, if they are thinking about buying one. Consumers want information first—we make that easy to get—and then they are more likely to buy.

3. "Make it work with the other ways you do business. Just because a consumer wants to shop on the Internet doesn't mean that's how they want to buy. Don't create barriers across channels—make the transition between businesses seamless and easy for the consumer to navigate. Consumers want to buy in different ways—to the extent we can position ourselves squarely in front of them at each turn, we'll win."

Life Imitates Art

Over the past four decades Lewis has earned countless plaudits for his effective management style. He is also considered a radical in a business where much of his thinking has been anathema to the status quo. Lewis became CEO in 1965 at age 31 when his father Joseph, the company's cofounder, died. He gained dubious renown in 1995 when a *Fortune* magazine profile highlighted his self-proclaimed, inexhaustible sex life and penchant for smoking pot. The same profile also praised his brilliant management style, which turned Progressive from a sleepy insurance wholesaler into one of the biggest and most profitable players in the industry. With Progressive's revenues and profits on a steady upward spiral and shareholders reaping huge rewards, Lewis was granted his eccentricities.

Progressive's headquarters in suburban Mayfield Village, Ohio, feel more like an art museum or university than a corporation. The glass and concrete campus, designed by William Bialosky, houses much of the 5,000-piece contemporary art collection that Lewis began to obtain in the 1970s. The hallways and open spaces were designed to become promenades for the permanent exhibition. Though the collection includes priceless works by Andy Warhol and David Hocking, it consists mostly of works from obscure emerging artists who tickle Lewis's fancy.

The artwork is not simply to cover blank walls. For Lewis, it is a reminder to all 19,000 employees to think outside the lines, to enhance creativity and originality, and to remind people of the necessity for risk-taking and innovation at Progressive. The company reorganizes annually to give people different jobs and functions so they keep growing and changing as the company does.

In a *BusinessWeek* interview, Lewis said, "A business organization is like an accordion. When you're flourishing, you tend to delegate and spread out authority and push innovation. When things aren't going so well, you tend to centralize. Our idea is to act mentally like you're flourishing all the time. Our attitude is that we will try almost anything that makes sense and we'll stop it when it stops making sense."

Under Lewis, Progressive has always been a radical in a straight-laced industry, opting for higher risk or nonstandard personal auto insurance. For example, it got into the motorcycle insurance business in 1969 and became the nation's largest insurer of motorcycles, usually considered a high-risk market segment and thus one to be avoided. The company figured out ways to measure risk— a driver's age rather than the size of the motorcycle—and ended up with a customer base of older riders who were much better risks. These formulas were put to use to measure and discount other types of auto insurance and create far better risk ratios than the competition. Lewis also commanded that the company earn an underwriting profit instead of depending on investments to make a profit, as did most competitors.

It was in this environment that the seeds of Progressive's e-business initiative were sown and key players began to push the company online. Like that of other radicals, the online odyssey was initially conceived and championed by one enterprising person within the ranks.

Bauer had been running Progressive's West Coast operations for six western states when he heard the siren call of cyberspace. An early user of Compuserve and e-mail, Bauer grew more intrigued with the Internet's business possibilities after trying the first Web browsers in 1994. For fun, he volunteered to put together a Website for a local musician and was so pleased with the response that he called his boss, Progressive's chief operating officer, and said, "We ought to do something on the Internet." He suggested a billboard site that would be little more than good public relations. His boss gave him the green light.

He launched Progressive's first Website in 1995, and despite the relatively small Internet population in those days, the site immediately started getting a response. In typical fashion, Progressive began to measure and Bauer was impressed with how easy it was to grow traffic by 10 percent each month. The driving force was e-mail. "We had people telling us things on e-mail that they might not have told us otherwise," Bauer says. "There were unhappy claimants, happy claimants, people whose bills got lost, people who thought their bills were lost, all coming through e-mail. It gave senior management a view of the business it didn't have any other unified way to achieve."

As Bauer began to expand his vision, he saw clear synergies with Progressive's already radical business model. In the 1980s, Lewis had decided that Progressive would no longer sell auto insurance. Auto insurance, to most consumers, was nothing more than a necessary evil, and auto insurance companies were big, bloated bureaucracies that cared little for individual policyholders. The new vision, according to Lewis, was to "reduce the human trauma and the economic cost of auto accidents in a cost-effective and profitable way." That may sound like corporate doubletalk, but for Progressive it became the rallying cry to rethink its business model and break away from the industry status quo. "The idea is that your insurance company ought to be there to help you, not to lift the hassle factor to another degree," Renwick says. At the core of the new mission was speed and transparency.

Progressive had always operated as more of an insurance wholesaler, content to stay in the background and let the agents interact with the consumers. But a series of industry-changing events forced Lewis to rethink the corporate mission.

Proposition 103

In November 1988 voters in California passed Proposition 103, a law designed by consumers to roll back escalating auto insurance rates. To Lewis, the initiative was essentially meant to punish auto insurance companies for overcharging, for being uncaring monoliths unwilling to listen to consumers' concerns, and for being noncompetitive. For Progressive, which did 20 percent of its business in California, the cost was greater than the $60 million in refunds it was forced to pay. It was a wake-up call for the entire company. Though Progressive fought it at the time, Lewis now says Prop 103 was the best thing ever to happen to the company.

According to Renwick, who became president of Progressive's California division, Proposition 103 was the turning point that made Progressive a consumer company. "We realized we would have to change the product profoundly to create a value proposition in the marketplace that was fundamentally different from what consumers had been willing to accept," Renwick says. "Californians said, 'We're not going to take it anymore,' and that was the genesis of a major change in the way we handled claims."

Under Renwick, who later served as the company's business technology process leader, Progressive embarked on a path that would lead directly to its e-business initiative. After Prop 103, Renwick decided that Progressive could do the one thing that insurance companies traditionally had never done: openly share information and allow customers to make informed choices. Both Lewis and Renwick had attended focus groups in which customers chided the industry for not being competitive enough. This was astonishing to them because there were more than 300 companies writing auto insurance, and just a one percent shift in price by one player could shift the business dramatically for all the others. How could the industry possibly be more competitive?

Customers weren't buying it. Auto insurance was simply one of life's inconvenient necessities, and the insurers made sure that it was near impossible to shop for the product. Auto insurance was complex and inaccessible from the customer's point of view. Every state had its own arcane insurance regulations and pricing structures. Lewis and Renwick believed that a company that simplified the buying process would have a huge edge. Why not emulate the jolly old Kris Kringle character in the classic film *Miracle on 34th Street* and send Macy's customers to Gimbels if Gimbels had the product and Macy's didn't?

Renwick initiated Express Quote, which began as a phone-based product that allowed customers to do comparison shopping. By 1996, Bauer suggested that Express Quote would be a perfect tool to move to the Internet. "It has zero marginal cost; people would like it; it would bring traffic to the site. It was perfect," Bauer said. At the same time, he began to link the Website to the company's call center so that all data records created online would be accessible to a call center rep. With this tool, prospective customers can go directly to Progressive's Website and do comparison shopping. When they ask for a quote, they will get prices from Progressive, Allstate, State Farm, and the next largest insurer in their state. Sometimes Progressive's prices are better, sometimes not. If a customer is buying strictly on price, Progressive may not get the sale.

"When you are buying auto insurance and you make one telephone call or use an agent, you don't have any points of comparison," Renwick says. "There was no way to make an informed decision, and no one was out there trying to fill that space." By deciding to fill that space, Progressive has become a recognized brand that transferred perfectly onto the Internet. Auto insurance pricing is a complex art, and rates change quickly. Regulations in each state make supplying such comparison-shopping data on a 24-hour basis labor intensive. But with all that, Progressive decided there was money to be made in giving customers an option they'd never had before.

The key was to instill in the culture a willingness to be open and share information directly with customers. This was a sea change for many who had grown up in the insurance business, even at Progressive. Renwick says that the comparison-shopping option was expensive and time-consuming when done by voice. The Internet, on the other hand, is the perfect medium for the product.

"The important thing is never to underestimate consumers," Renwick says. "There's always this thought that 'My god, changing your auto insurance policy must be complicated.' You know what? It is. But it doesn't have to be that way in terms of the presentation to consumers." In fact, the Web has become a haven for comparison-shopping across all kinds of industries, and Progressive simply tapped into a growing trend. It won a major first-mover advantage by combining a unique product offering with a perfect medium.

The obvious next step to Bauer and Renwick was adding a "Buy" button to the Website. What good was comparison shopping if you couldn't buy on the spot? Beginning in Minnesota in 1997, Progressive began to sell auto insurance online. Buyers came one by one, and the trickle grew steadily into a larger stream. This led to online after-sales service and a clear lesson for Bauer. "So much of what we did and continue to do is driven by consumers saying, 'Why aren't you doing this or that online?' You read the e-mails, and their expectations are clear and ambitious. One key lesson we learned early on is that people want to do things that they couldn't do over the phone or face to face, such as 'What If' price quoting."

The Internet allows what Bauer calls "a suspension of politeness." People might ask a phone rep the difference in insurance premiums between a Corvette and a Toyota. But after two or three such comparisons, both the caller and service rep would be reluctant to continue. Online, a prospective buyer can play that game all day. Bauer says there are a raft of consumers who are fascinated with the tool. "What that said to us is play to that strength, allow people to have access to those things. We also found that our conversion rate, which is a fundamental metric to us, rose. The number of sales per quote went up as a result of that tool," Bauer says.

Bauer is quick to point out that Progressive's progressiveness was not without detractors. As utopian as the culture sounds, there were voices of dissent in the process. One senior vice president felt strongly that e-commerce was a big mistake because of security problems on the Web. He told Bauer, "You do that and people will be writing checks out of our check printer by the afternoon." Bauer eventually satisfied the executive with a closer scrutiny of security measures, "but the debate took longer than it should have."

He also notes that his vision of the Internet is not the only vision in the company and that sooner or later, visions can collide. He says that such collisions are actually healthy for the process and that his role is evolving from an evangelist to an incubator for new ideas. Having Lewis solidly behind the Internet initiative, which he was from the beginning, has made a key difference in moving forward.

Speed Is of the Essence

Proposition 103 also convinced Lewis that Progressive's claim service, like others in the industry, was inadequate. He decided that speed would be the ingredient that Progressive could add, but it would take a radical move to do it. He told his claims people that he wanted Progressive to be at the scene of an accident right away. The concept would be called Immediate Response Claims Service, and Progressive would retool its claims department from its usual 8 A.M. to 5 P.M. workday and offer 24/7 coverage for response to an accident scene. To implement the process would not only take a revamping of the entire claims department and its technology operations, but would also require a fleet of vehicles to bring its claims reps out to the accident scenes.

Progressive executives thought Lewis had finally lost it and gone over the edge. The costs of such an operation would be prohibitive, they protested. But Lewis saw it differently. Two things happen when you deliver fast, he told *BusinessWeek:* "You give better service and the better you do things, the less they cost in our business. And the faster we get to the losses, the fewer the lawyers that get on the other side."

Despite a huge turnover in the claims-adjusting force and several years to implement the plan fully, Lewis succeeded. Today, in the 48 states where Progressive does business, the sight of the white Progressive SUVs, called Immediate Response Vehicles, has become commonplace at accident scenes. Armed with laptop computers, intelligent software, and wireless access to the Internet and the company's claims department, Progressive's claims reps are able to be at an accident scene in nine hours or less more than 50 percent of the time. They use an internally developed software package called Claims Workbench to enter police reports and download damage estimates and costs for parts and labor at body shops, and they can write checks on the spot for the repairs. In this manner, claims reps are empowered to settle claims in the field, a powerful competitive advantage.

Lewis says the company has saved a great deal of money and time with Immediate Response, which has become the company's best marketing tool. He explained to *Fast Company* magazine how the process has reaped huge rewards for the bottom line. By inspecting autos right after an accident instead of days later, he said, vehicles get repaired sooner, which means that Progressive pays fewer storage-lot and rental car fees. By moving to settle claims quickly, Progressive keeps customers from getting more upset than they already are at having an accident. Thus, they are less likely to get a lawyer and start costly and time-consuming litigation. "We're out to take the lawyers out of the system," Lewis told *BusinessWeek*. "We're out ambulance-chasing the ambulance chasers."

By seeing the damage quickly and in person, Progressive also avoids being victimized by body shops trying to pad their bills or customers faking an injury. As much as 30 percent of the money auto insurers pay out is for fraud. And if a company spends less money settling claims, it can charge lower prices for its premiums, Lewis says. "Fast is cheap," Lewis told *Fast Company*.

Most of all, the brand flourishes as the company's SUVs become recognized around an area, now with the company's Website address prominently plastered across them.

Agents on the Web

For Progressive, like other radicals, the move to the Internet was a natural next step rather than a jolting interruption. Renwick says it is a mindset, more than anything, that is based on offering a higher value proposition for the consumer going forward. Among the key changes that must take place are treating customers as intelligent consumers, giving them more relevant information, and letting them make more intelligent choices and personalize the product to meet their own needs.

It is with this in mind that Progressive has approached its vast network of agents to offer the Internet as a potent ally rather than as a threat. "This is a significant issue for us," Renwick says. "We don't control consumer choices. There are people we absolutely want as customers who much prefer to visit their independent agent and sit down face to face to do their insurance transactions. I have no problem with that."

As the largest writer of auto insurance for independent agents—with 10 percent of the market—Progressive is intent on retaining that relationship even though it is a declining market. Lewis believes the agent market can be a cash cow for another 20 years but that Progressive must become the number-one choice for auto insurance regardless of the channel. To be number one, a company must offer the best deal, and to do that, there must be innovation, which is ultimately driven by technology.

Renwick says the agents understand Progressive's need to supply its product in any way the consumer wants it. "It would be pretty foolish of us not to be moving to address the needs of consumers buying on the Internet. [The agents] get that," he says. "Arguably, they are benefiting from our expertise in the Internet world."

Bauer says that agents have felt threatened by Progressive since the company started selling auto insurance directly to consumers a decade ago. But there has always been an upside as well. Progressive has always been a leader in getting technology to its agents. It was the first company to provide a software link to the agent's office so that agents could share important data, such as applications and claim reports, electronically with Progressive.

Among the first options on the Progressive Website was a Find an Agent application so prospective customers could type in their zip codes and locate a local insurance agent. This has become a commonplace tool on other insurance sites, but Progressive was the first to offer it. Progressive set up an online agent's channel called For Agents Only. This Website allows agents access to information about their customers' policies and offers tracking information on growth of premiums and number of policies and updates.

Tom Masters, the Canton-based agent mentioned earlier, says that although a large segment of the agent population disdains Progressive's moves to sell direct to its customers, he and many others are thrilled with the company's use of technology to enhance the agent's opportunities. "I haven't seen a lot of impact on direct selling yet," Masters says. "There's a lot of shopping going on, but most of the buying is still done through us. But they provide the absolute best in customer service and claims handling. We have hundreds of insured who call us to make changes, and now they can go right to the Internet. We can download their information and know it's correct the next day rather than wait two to six weeks as we traditionally have had to for paperwork."

Masters was invited, along with a host of other agents, to visit Progressive and see several pilot programs the company is planning. One new program is aimed at reducing the hassle factor in getting a car fixed after an accident. Progressive sends out a representative with extensive body shop experience immediately after an accident, and this individual snaps digital photos of the damaged auto, posts them on the Internet, and makes them available to a host of body shops with which Progressive has contracted. These body shops are prescreened and must meet Progressive's high standards. The body shops bid on the auto repair work, and Progressive decides which one will get the contract. The accident victim simply drives the car to that body shop, where a rental car, prearranged by Progressive, is waiting, and they can drive away. When the car is fixed, a Progressive expert checks it, and the owner picks it up, drops off the rental car, and drives away.

"This cuts down the costs dramatically because it is much more efficient," Masters say. "It gives the company much more control over what is being done." Masters was even more impressed with the *attitude* toward technology that he found within Progressive. "The Internet is alive and well within Progressive," he said. "The overall attitude and enthusiasm is unlike anything I've seen elsewhere. They never bring a product out to the agency force that has bugs. When it comes to us, it is perfect. Other companies rush to get things on the Internet, but they are too hard to deal with. If it's too hard, it tends not to get used."

For Progressive, the agent relationship will continue to be crucial for years to come. But Lewis has never minced words, and he intends to make Progressive the number-one supplier of auto insurance regardless of the sales channel. The Internet has long been touted as a platform for the disintermediation of American business, and as online capabilities grow more flexible and user-friendly, there will undoubtedly be a shift in the source of Progressive's business from agent to direct.

But Renwick believes that choice won't likely become an either-or choice for a long time to come. Consumers are impossible to pigeonhole, and trends are often blown beyond proportion by hype. "History is hard to change," Renwick says. "One of the single most powerful determinants of who your insurance company is going to be is whom your father was insured with. Dad can be pretty powerful."

The issue is how to distribute the product so that the cost of goods sold is supported by the product price. "As long as I can find price points that are supportable by those multiple distributions, I'm happy," Renwick says. "So today we offer our product in ways that the consumer wants, face to face with an agent, calling us, or directly through the Internet."

The market share of the independent agent has held steady for a long time. The current trend tends to be consumers who buy from an agent but become more intrigued with servicing their own accounts from their den. Renwick says Progressive is already getting aggressive in its advertising with a message that Progressive.com is more than just a company with dot.com added to its name. E-business is now a full-fledged piece of the corporate fabric, not unlike the artwork that adorns Progressive's walls.

More Change Ahead

Convincing customers to change the way they do business, especially in the insurance business, is no easy task. They won't change, in fact, without a damn good reason. Under Bauer, Progressive is moving forward with new wrinkles for its e-business side. Progressive is forging digital links with a series of body shops around the country so that a customer can get an answer online to a most frequently asked question: When will my car be ready? "We always felt we were done when the claim was paid," Bauer said. "But the customer didn't have their car yet, so they think we're not done." In this way, the Internet is fundamentally changing the business model.

Customers also want the ability to access their service representatives online either to ask a question or to discuss some aspect of a claim. Progressive now provides a single electronic file and gives customers access to ask what's going on with their claims. Now a customer can go to the Website and get an updated status of a claim: "You are here in the process. We've done some investigation, and here's what we think happened." "People have paid the money; there is no reason to keep these things a secret from them," Bauer said.

In addition, Progressive has created a way for customers to track the activities around a claim. If a supervisor tells a service rep to call a customer and give him or her an update on a claim and that employee does not make the call, it is tracked back to a record of the claim that the customer can see. So if the service rep didn't make the call, it will be noticed either by the supervisor or the customer. "It's a good way to improve the quality of service," Bauer says. "Information transparency is a further way for us to differentiate ourselves."

What Progressive executives understand, as do most radicals, is that the Internet is a work in progress and an evolution. The company has no plans to spin out its e-business as a separate entity, believing that the Internet is simply an extension of what Progressive already is. "It integrates so well with the rest of the company that to spin it off doesn't make much sense," Bauer said. "If we did that, we'd have different ownership, different interests, different compensation systems. We're not likely to do that."

Both Renwick and Bauer point out that it is as important to know what the Internet does *not* do well. Loss reporting, for example, could easily be transferred to the Website, but Bauer believes it is a process more suited to human interaction. "It's clearly in Progressive's interest to get all the nuance and detail of an accident as well as intelligently following up on statements made by the person in the accident," Bauer says. "If the person says, 'I'm kind of hurt' what does that mean? The Web is not going to do well with that. Frankly, some things, at least in today's state of technology, are better done by phone."

But Progressive is highly unlikely to be passive about too many things. It is not their corporate style. Lewis may be nearing retirement, and he understands that it is key to serve as both a visionary and an evangelist for the e-business effort. His reputation as a risk taker helps define the Internet initiative within Progressive and gives employees the impetus to push beyond conventional boundaries. But, he says, "It's much more than the CEO—it's the whole company. There's an attitude at Progressive that I support. It's a bias toward action."

Renwick says the key lessons are not about the technology but about the will of the organization. Successful transformations into e-business depend on having a solid understanding of where you want the company to end up. "If it's just transferring your old business model onto the Internet, that's about where you'll end up," he says.

"We've learned how to create a vision about what we want our consumer experience to be and how the Internet gets us there."

In addition, the system must be solid and reliable. For an e-business to succeed, it has to be real-time and be up all the time. "When you say you can do something and start to create a dependency on that, you'd better be there, or the brand damage can be immense," Renwick says.

And the organization must have the guts to stand behind its e-business effort culturally, or the company won't be able to take it. "Consumers can be brutally explicit about what they want," Renwick says. "You better be damn good about delivering it."

Bauer points out that Progressive is aware that its competitors have all targeted the Internet and are making strong inroads of their own toward an e-business infrastructure. "We have the lead in this," Bauer said. "We have the most traffic, and we sell the most business online. Can we maintain it? That's our challenge."

10

Staples
Multiple Channels Mean
Repeat Customers

*Over the next decade, this is going to be huge for us. And without the
Internet, we never could have pulled this off.*

CEO Tom Stemberg, Staples

When Thomas Stemberg, the founder and chief executive officer of
Staples, Inc., went before his board of directors to discuss the company's Internet future in 1998, he expected resistance to his plan. He
pointed out that the company had several options in this new and
uncharted territory. Staples could ignore the digital environment
completely, though that hardly seemed an option with the frenzied
movement to online in the retail community. Staples could also incrementalize its effort, taking a low-risk, piecemeal approach with the
hope that the wave of dot.com start-ups would ignore this lucrative
and attractive marketplace for office supplies. The incremental approach also presupposed that strong competitors like Office Depot
and Office Max would follow the highly unlikely path of ignoring or
downplaying the Internet as well.

Stemberg, a Harvard MBA and ferocious competitor, had a more
radical idea in mind. Like everyone else in retailing, Stemberg had witnessed the transformative effect the Internet was having on business.
He had seen what Amazon.com had done to the bricks-and-mortar
bookselling universe and was convinced that somewhere down the

line, the Internet would represent at least 25 percent of overall revenues in the office supplies marketplace. That, he realized, was a $50 billion opportunity. Staples, a $10 billion giant and pioneer in the office supplies superstore industry, could use the Web to scale up its product and service offerings and transform itself into a vastly more powerful and effective company. Staples simply had to be a player, Stemberg believed.

A voracious reader and student of business trends, Stemberg had spent a great deal of time in the Silicon Valley studying Internet companies. A great believer in finding role models to emulate, Stemberg connected with Meg Whitman, the chief executive officer of eBay, the highly successful online auction site, and convinced her to join the board of the new Staples Internet venture. The sister of an old Harvard Business School colleague, Whitman had known Stemberg for many years and was willing to share her online wisdom. Stemberg studied the eBay model carefully and came away with a deeper understanding of what kind of effort and commitment would be required to succeed in e-business.

Stemberg decided that Staples should attack full bore. When he approached the board, he said, "Let's go for it. Let's see how high is up!" He acknowledged that a full-scale assault on the Internet would be expensive and would entail significant losses over a period of years. But he was convinced that Staples must build a dominant online presence. "This will be the most significant organizational challenge we've ever encountered," he told the directors. To his surprise and delight, the normally conservative board was unanimous in its decision to support a major Internet initiative, an effort that would cost $250 million or more over the next few years. "We don't want it to be on our watch that the company didn't move aggressively when this opportunity presented itself," the directors said.

With that, Staples launched its radical rush to the Internet: Staples.com. What Stemberg has called "a huge bet" is now in play. The new business unit, with its own P&L, has already reached an initial target of one million customers and is on track to reach $1 billion in sales by 2003. Staples' Internet effort has already garnered positive reaction from industry watchers who are monitoring the company's attempt to become an e-business powerhouse. Within two years of its November 1998 launch, Staples.com has become an award-winning

Website and one of the most highly respected retail Websites on the Internet, leading its industry in customer traffic.

Staples.com went from start-up to revenues of $100 million in just one year, and that number grew to $450 million by the end of 2000. At that rate, it should easily surpass its initial goal. Staples has leveraged its brand and marketed its online presence effectively in its 1,200 stores and in its catalogs, as well on its fleet of ubiquitous, red Staples delivery trucks, which bear the Staples.com Web address. But Stemberg is not ready to declare victory. Staples.com lost $150 million in 2000, and Stemberg calls the e-business effort "a work in progress." He is ready and willing to ride the venture to profitability and has grand plans for Staples.com to lead the company into lucrative new markets, such as business services.

Most of the office supply giants were late getting into the Internet space, but they have not suffered from their tardiness as other industries have. Melissa Shore, a senior analyst with Jupiter Research, says that the office supply industry did a good job of keeping dot.com pure plays from commandeering the Internet. "Though they didn't go in until 1997, when they launched, they launched with sites that had real value propositions," Shore says. These value propositions, such as the one Staples.com offers, must be strong enough to change people's behavior on a long-term basis, Shore says. And that is what Stemberg intends to do.

His vision is three-pronged: to become the dominant leader in the sale of office products and services on the Internet; to build a business that is every bit as profitable as Staples' other direct fulfillment businesses—retail and catalog sales; and to build a vibrant dot.com entity through which Staples can serve customers, both online and in the stores, better than they've been served before.

The power move into e-business has not come without critics. Stemberg has had to fend off negative reactions from Wall Street about the Internet initiative. Some financial analysts targeted "unacceptable dot.com losses," which left Staples' stock floundering during much of 1999 and 2000. Like other radicals, however, Stemberg hasn't wavered in his support of the Internet effort. If anything, he has become more enthusiastic as the new organization has grown. In the company's 1999 annual report, Stemberg tried to reassure shareholders that the move to e-commerce was not a gamble but table stakes to the new game. "Aggressive pursuit of Internet leadership is something we must do to protect and expand the brand in which we and our stakeholders have invested so heavily," he wrote. "Our goal is to seize the lion's share of this large and growing market."

Forging a New Relationship With Customers

In order to fulfill the Internet promise, Staples.com has implemented a carefully conceived business strategy. Unlike other dot.com startups, Staples.com was born with a vast distribution infrastructure already in place, a huge advantage in the e-business transformation. With its fleet of trucks and local distribution centers, Staples offers customers ordering $50 or more from the Website free next-day delivery, just as with Staples retail and catalog operations. Modeled in some ways on Staples successful catalog business as well as on the few other successful dot.com start-ups, Staples.com offers consumers yet another channel into the company. But as other radicals understand, Stemberg knew that Staples.com represented far more than a Website and distribution channel. It represented an entirely new relationship with Staples customers and, at its best, would be a platform from which to elevate and expand the already successful Staples brand.

Stemberg also understood that the power of the Staples brand lay in the relationship that it had built with its millions of small business customers. To those customers, Staples had to remain one company, not separate online and offline entities. Thus, the challenge for Staples was to build a dot.com organization and a dot.com culture within a huge, highly energized company that was barreling forward with 50,000 employees, more than 1,200 stores, and 25 percent annual sales growth.

In a prescient move, Stemberg turned inward rather than outward to find the person to lead the new business. Rather than search for a dot.com veteran or an information technologist from outside the company, Stemberg appointed Jeanne Lewis, then 35-year-old executive vice president of sales and marketing at Staples, Inc., to run the fledgling operation.

Lewis, with a Harvard MBA and a background in banking, had come to Staples in 1993 and followed a general management path ever since. She'd run the company's New England division with 1,000 employees in 50 stores, followed by a stint running a merchandizing division. She stepped into the sales and marketing role in late 1996 and came to Staples.com with virtually no information technology or Internet experience. What she had was more important: a deep and visceral understanding of Staples and of how it did business.

It was, in many ways, a bold move by Stemberg. He could have opted for a technologist, as many companies have done. But what he was seeking was a specific skill set. "I said, if I was a headhunter trying to pick a dot.com executive out of our company, whom would I pick?" Stemberg recalled. "The first choice would have been Jeanne. I'd seen the way she operates, and she not only relates to the dot.com world, but she understood how these people think and what they liked and didn't like." Stemberg spoke at length to eBay's Whitman about the top spot before making his decision.

Whitman told him, "Tom, a lot of people will tell you to go out and hire a dot.com person. But you give me the right person and I can teach them dot.com. They've got to be able to make decisions very quickly, be antibureaucratic, and can't have big egos. They have to work insane hours. I'd much prefer to have those attributes and somebody who understands your business."

Jupiter's Shore says that Lewis "is strong, driven, and understands the small-business customer." For the successful transition to e-business, "having someone strong, smart, and strategic at the helm is key."

Stemberg wasn't concerned about Lewis' age. He says that leadership is about energy and intensity more than age. Running a business requires hiring the right people, motivating those people, and setting definable benchmarks. Lewis' management experience within Staples defined her as a leader of the new enterprise.

For Lewis, that grounding in the Staples, Inc., business operation became the foundation for the culture of Staples.com. While other corporations and an unnerving number of dot.com pure plays got caught up in the technological bells and whistles of the Internet, Lewis kept her focus squarely on the business equation. Technology is the platform, she says, but the *digital* value proposition is no different from the bricks-and-mortar value proposition. Staples.com, from its first operational hours, was designed to enhance customer access to the corporation and its products. If done correctly, it would extend and expand that access in new and profitable ways.

Lewis' first challenge was to build a new company inside an existing one. She knew the type of people she wanted: high energy, high competence in their specialty, a willingness to work hard and to learn. She knew she could find a core group from within Staples—managers who were unafraid of the Internet and wanted to be part of the start-up. And most critical for both internal and external hires: Egos had to be checked at the door. In a highly collaborative, fast-moving team effort, communication and cooperation are even more important in the online world than in the offline world, Lewis believes. There is simply no room for building personal power bases. But in the fall of 1998, the task of finding and attracting talent to Staples.com was indeed a challenge.

The challenge was exacerbated by the Internet IPO frenzy that took the world by storm in 1999 and early 2000. It proved to be a fleeting run as some semblance of reality and business sanity returned to the markets in April 2000.

But the birth of Staples.com was marked by an era when the best and the brightest Internet talent were rushing to the pure plays and promises of stock option riches. Stemberg turned to financial whiz William Sahlman at the Harvard Business School to help crystallize the financial objectives and strategies of the new Staples business. Sahlman told Stemberg that Staples' number-one challenge was to attract and retain the kind of people who could build this dot.com business within the company.

Indeed, because the Staples story was already a legend in the retailing universe—Staples had pioneered the office supply superstore concept in 1984 and grown exponentially ever since—the company's many retail MBAs were already the target of dot.com recruiters who prized the business-to-consumer expertise that characterized the Staples culture. Staples became a recruiter's gold mine, and many Staples executives were receiving five or more phone calls every day from headhunters with stock option–laden offers.

So Staples.com not only had to find and attract new faces, but also had to keep the talent it already had. Offering options in Staples itself would not be enough so in 1999 the company initiated a separate tracking stock for Staples.com and offered new hires options in the new venture that might rival that of pure-play dot.com IPOs. If and when the market conditions were right, those shares would go public. At the same time, Stemberg realized he could undermine morale at the core company, so he offered shares in the Staples.com tracking stock to all full-time employees. Staples.com employees were also eligible for shares in the core company, and this cross-fertilization of personal interest in both organizations set the foundation for the sharing of ideas and joint projects across the entire company. In fact, this cooperative, cross-cultural environment became crucial to Staples.com's success. When the dot.com bubble burst in 2000, the stock option issue slipped quietly into obscurity, as did the possibility that Staples.com would go public anytime soon. But it had served its purpose during a chaotic time.

Though Staples, like other corporate giants late to the Internet, suffered through the dot.com hysteria, the company offered recruits a good reason to avoid the risky start-up route. Staples.com had the stability of a fast-growing multibillion-dollar organization with plentiful cash flow to support it along with equity on the options side. And with 545 percent growth, the dot.com organization had all the hair-raising excitement and fast pace of a true Internet start-up—in other words, the best of both worlds to a young talent. The resulting dot.com downturn only emphasized Staples' message, and some who were lured away wanted to come back.

Part of the business model's power is that all boats rise on the same tide inside Staples. Store general managers, for example, receive bonuses based on *delivery* sales, and those sales include not just store sales but sales from catalogs and the Internet. This lined compensation plan runs across the company and has created a company-wide atmosphere of cooperation and support rather than turf wars and feuds. This is particularly true with the catalog division, where fear of cannibalization from the Internet was the strongest. For Lewis, this means she can tap into relationships and expertise with the corporate chief technology officer, the executive vice president of merchandising, and anyone else whose knowledge will enhance the Staples.com effort.

In fact, Lewis immediately set up an internal advisory board made up of leaders of all the company's business units that meets every six weeks to talk about Staples.com. In those meetings, the Website is broadcast on a big screen, and Lewis walks the group through upgrades and changes and asks for input on how to improve the site. "It's an exercise that shows that everyone is part of this effort, not only from a compensation side but from a cultural side as well," Lewis says.

Lewis was also savvy enough to realize that selling the Staples.com concept to nearly 50,000 employees who had been quite happy with the way things were was not as much a cheerleading job as a hands-on, show-me-the-money effort.

The magic, Lewis points out, is in the numbers. "We measure everything," she says. "We are analytical hounds in the truest sense of the word. What got us over the biggest cultural hurdle around the fear of cannibalization was numbers. What guides our business investment are numbers. What tells us whether we are having a good day or bad day are numbers. I don't and couldn't fly blind."

Using a variety of metrics, Lewis is able to calibrate how much it costs to gain a new customer and retain a customer for life. Those same numbers reveal how much each customer is likely to spend every year and how much comes from the retail store, the catalog, or online. Staples estimates that it costs $100 to acquire a customer and that that customer is likely to spend $1,000 a year over his or her business lifetime with Staples. If Staples discounts are factored in, that number is $600 a year. Lewis believes that the $100 figure will continue to drop while customer spending will increase. She notes that the online business model cuts customer service costs dramatically. A catalog customer, for example, calls in and places an order. A Staples representative has to pick up the phone and process the order. With the Internet, the customer enters the order him- or herself. Customer service costs drop on the back end as well, and coupled with the ability to offer a variety of services online as well as surrounding product offerings with valuable content such as reviews from sources like CNET, Staples.com's value proposition becomes even clearer.

Cutting the cost of doing business is the goal of all Internet business plans, and Staples is already seeing the payoff, according to Stemberg. Staples' highest profit channel is its direct channel. The catalog business, for example, contributes 14 percent of profits and has a 30 percent return on investment. But each phone call to order from the company costs Staples $3.39, with an average order of $180. With customers using the Website, the number of phone calls to place an order from the catalog business goes down to under one call per order. "For every phone call not made, we save almost $3.50," Stemberg says. "So there's already a 2 to 3 percent savings in order entry costs." Catalogs cost a lot to produce and send, and the Website allows the number of catalogs to be cut. So the company is already cutting 3 percent of its costs with a projected 5 percent over the long term.

The strongest testament to that value comes in the form of repeat customers. Lewis calculated that in the fourth quarter of 1999, Staples.com attracted 83,000 repeat customers, and in the first quarter of 2000, that number jumped to 143,000 repeat customers, an increase of 60,000 in just three months. Staples.com measured more than 200,000 unique customer visits in the fourth quarter of 2000. "More than half our revenue comes from repeat customers," Lewis says. "This speaks to the power of the Internet in general and our site in particular. If you like what you find and we actually make your life easier in terms of purchasing, you are going to come back."

The numbers help Staples.com determine not only what people do buy but what they *don't* buy as well. In this way, the company can shift to a more targeted, profitable mix of products. With the Internet as its foundation, Staples.com can broaden out the product mix exponentially.

For example, the retail stores stock 8,000 items, but Staples.com offers access to more than 200,000 items. If a customer wants an obscure copy of Apple software, an item the store would never stock, it can still be ordered via the Website. Indeed, part of the rollout plan for Staples.com is to offer, both via internet kiosks in all the stores and from PCs at home, the ability for customers and Staples salespeople to order online literally hundreds of thousands of goods that aren't stocked but that customers might want or need. "We will have every piece of software, every portfolio accessory, every ribbon, every obscure cartridge for every printer that went out of business ten years ago," Stemberg says. "It doesn't make sense to inventory these things but we'll give you access online. And you can track your order at our site. We think over the next decade, this is going to be huge for us. And without the Internet, we never could have pulled this off."

Share of Wallet

Clear from the outset was the staunch belief that Staples.com would never replace the bricks-and-mortar company. Stemberg refuses to believe that the Web could ever account for 100 percent of Staples' business. Rather, Staples.com adds an important new channel between Staples and its existing customers as well as a vehicle for attracting new customers. For example, Staples.com quickly added two new Websites to the fold: StaplesLink.com, a customized site for Staples' contract customers in large and medium-sized businesses; and Quill.com, to serve customers of Quill, the direct marketing office supply firm that Staples acquired in 1998.

The dreaded cannibalization that big companies have feared the Web would spawn is not happening, despite the fast growth of Internet shopping. Lewis likes to point to a study by Jupiter Research, which forecasts that by 2005 consumers will spend $199 billion online and a whopping $632 billion offline via catalogs and stores. But according to Jupiter, that $632 billion spent offline will be influenced in some way by online shopping or browsing. Despite the widely predicted death of bricks and mortar at the hands of the Internet, Staples.com is not intended as an either-or choice. It is an adjunct to retail space based on the belief that consumers and small-business people will always want to touch and feel and see certain items before they purchase them. Staples sells more than staples and pencils. Staples' lucrative furniture and electronics businesses, for example, require showrooms. Stemberg believes this so strongly that Staples continues to open a new retail store every 37 hours.

"The Internet has fueled a huge growth in the consumption of the goods and services we sell," Stemberg says. "So while the Internet may cannibalize a little from our retail stores, it is creating a huge demand overall—of which our retail stores will enjoy more than their fair share."

The reason Stemberg is so confident about the cannibalization issue is that he'd been through it before when Staples was just 4 years old and he started the company's catalog business. Back then, he heard the same hue and cry about cannibalization, and it never happened. Both businesses thrived, feeding off each other. Ironically, much of the business model Lewis used to build Staples.com came from the

Staples catalog business. The customers are primarily business customers. The mix of product—supplies, furniture, and technology—is very much what the catalog business sells. Shira Goodman, the Harvard Law School and MIT Sloan School graduate who runs the catalog business, understood the dot.com opportunity and fully embraced it. She sold it to her own team as well, and despite losing some business to the Internet, the catalog business has continued to grow 14 percent each year.

Among the numbers it tracks, Staples discovered that 70 percent of the people arriving at the Staples.com Website were new customers or customers who had defected to competitors more than six months ago and were returning online.

Thus, cannibalization wasn't happening. Instead, Staples was "gaining share of wallet," Stemberg says. As with Victoria's Secret and other retailers, it turns out, the more *choices* a customer has, the more likely he or she will spend more in all of the retailer's channels. Staples carefully tracks its customers and their spending habits and discovered that a small business customer who shops retail alone is likely to spend $90 per employee per year with Staples. If that customer uses the Staples catalog as well as retail, that number jumps to $150 per employee. And now, with Staples.com in the mix, that amount doubles to $300 per employee.

Thus, Lewis' main job has been to marry the rich and diverse resources available inside Staples, Inc., with the development and business needs of the new online venture. In order to make Staples.com a strong player out of the starting blocks, the task was to put together a team of technologists and businesspeople who understood the Staples opportunity at its core.

Of the more than 200 employees in the new unit (Lewis expects the number to grow to around 300 at its peak), only a third came from within Staples. But within that third is the leadership team of Staples.com, a group of Staples veterans and senior managers. Michael Ragunas, chief technology officer at Staples.com, for example, is a 14-year Staples veteran who joined the company straight out of Harvard and acquired his technical skills while working for nine years in Staples' information technology department. Ragunas and other Staples veterans inside Staples.com know the product, the customer, and the business and have key relationships on the core side of the business. Many have worked in the retail stores or for the catalog operations, and they are also Internet savvy.

The people hired from the outside bring strong Internet skills as well as direct marketing experience, Lewis says. Mixed together, the net result is a learning environment in which the Staples veterans teach the newcomers about the company and the newcomers impart their Internet wisdom. The complementary skills have allowed Lewis to focus on an aggressive business strategy rather than spending time getting people up to speed. "We never lose our way because at the leadership level, ultimately the business knowledge is our guiding light," she says.

The Dot.com Inside

When Stemberg tabbed Lewis to run Staples.com, he asked her if she wanted to run the new operation from a separate location. If Lewis was going to create a dot.com environment, perhaps it would be better handled away from the gleaming steel and glass headquarters building in Framingham, Massachusetts. Lewis considered the option and then declined. "We can create a space within a space," she said. "I work really hard to make sure that the core business feels a part of this business because (a) they are and (b) it is crucial that this is a combined effort."

Nonetheless, Lewis made some concessions to the dot.com world. A tour around Staples, Inc., reveals the usual rabbit warrens of cubicles and Dilbert-like space common to most large corporations. Across an open vestibule, entering through a nondescript security door, a visitor to Staples.com is immediately struck by the jazzy colors, the art deco furniture, the open work pods, and the stock ticker–like plasma displays that crisscross the ceiling, sending a steady stream of messages, trivia, and Internet information to the Staples.com population. Present is the prerequisite employee snack bar with free coffee, sodas, and cookies, along with the ping pong and pool tables and ever-popular foosball game. Like other dot.com start-ups, Staples.com expects its workers to put in yeoman hours, nights and weekends, so they must provide the goodies.

Lewis initially championed individual offices, but eBay's Whitman convinced her to choose open cubicles for everyone, including executives, to foster an open, communication-heavy approach necessary for dot.com teams to operate efficiently. The workforce is young and casually dressed. But in truth, the workforce at Staples, Inc., is also young and casually dressed. Trying to create this hybrid internal environment is clearly made easier with a young, aggressive, entrepreneurial culture already in place because cultural barriers tend to be toughest to conquer when making the transition to e-business.

And even with its youthful workforce, Staples, Inc., was not immune from the upheaval of creating a new culture within a few feet of the old one. Problems and clashes inevitably arose. Giving shares in each other's business units was important, but Stemberg and Lewis soon realized that it is the subtle touches that cannot be ignored lest they scuttle the whole ship. "This was very difficult," Stemberg admits. Jupiter's Shore says it is key to get everyone to understand the importance of the Internet to the whole organization. She recalled hearing Michael Dell speak about the difficulty in getting everyone on board for Dell.com when the company first embraced the Internet. "They put Dell.com on all the restroom doors," she says. "It takes a while for large companies to mobilize and get their hands around the Internet and into the lives of every employee."

Free coffee inside Staples.com, for example, became a flash point inside the core company. "This isn't fair," Staples, Inc., employees complained. "Part of the Staples values is that we pay for our own coffee. Are we now throwing the Staples culture down the tube for the dot.com?"

In April 2000 Stemberg initiated a series of "town meetings" for all employees to address the questions about Staples.com. In it, executives from both business units talked openly about the financials and explained why things were done. When the question about the coffee came up, Stemberg was prepared. He explained the math. "I told them, on average you guys in the traditional business have about 150 square feet of office space per person. The dot.com people have about 100 square feet of office space per person. We pay, fully loaded, about $20 per square foot for occupancy costs. So each of you costs about $3,000 per year in office costs, and we've saved $1,000 a year on each dot.com person. I don't think they are going to drink that much coffee, do you? And that is why I said yes to this and why I'm not going to change my mind."

But in the interest of fair play and equality, Stemberg also offered all the departments in the company the chance to convert their space to the dot.com design scheme—including free coffee—if they felt it was a better way to set up their offices. There were no takers.

The Website

While the cultural issues evolve, Lewis and Ragunas have focused their efforts on the Website itself. Lewis cringes when someone suggests that the Internet is just another sales channel. Staples.com not only brings in new customers but also offers something even more important in the business model: It allows Staples to control the customer experience from a quality perspective.

For example, individual salespeople in Staples stores may know exactly the right information about any given item to help close a sale with a customer: "This laptop computer offers this amount of power, storage and battery life for this price and compares favorably to similar laptops from other manufacturers," or, "this printer paper works on these inkjet printers and is far cheaper than several other brands." If the customer only knew these few things about the product, things that the salesperson would have pointed out, they would have bought it. But now, instead of relying on individual salespeople in 1,200 stores, Staples.com can capture that information, put it on the Website, and offer it over and over again to millions of customers. Conversely, by bringing Staples.com into the stores for salespeople to use, this same knowledge sharing can be offered globally throughout the corporation.

With more than 200,000 products available, the site offers sophisticated search and comparison features so that customers are not overwhelmed by the selection process. "The beauty of it is the controlled, positive, information-rich experience, if you do it right— which is an experience you can have not only at home in front of your computer, but in the stores as well," Lewis says.

The site itself has been refined eight or nine times since it was launched in November 1998. But Lewis and Ragunas were never satisfied. "The technology becomes the customer-facing aspect of the business, so you have change and adapt," Ragunas says. The mantra inside Staples.com is "no technology just for technology's sake." Graphics on the site have been kept to a minimum in order not to bog down customers using 56K modems with tedious downloads. The registration process has been shortened and simplified. Pages that were hardly used were removed to cut superfluous information and unnecessary clicks. And even then, Lewis and Ragunas wanted more, so in May 2000 Staples.com unveiled a complete makeover of the site to make it more usable, friendly, and effective. Based on hundreds of hours of usability testing and customer feedback, Staples.com Website designers aimed at making the online shopping experience more intuitive and effortless.

For example, prior to the redesign, Staples.com had added a zip-code request page to the site that appeared the first time a customer clicked to any link off the home page. Perceived as an annoying obstacle intent on gathering personal data for marketing purposes, visitors simply clicked away from the site completely. In fact, the zip-code request was there so that the system could track availability of inventory from local distribution centers and thus alert the customer to expected delivery dates for those items. Perhaps if the visitor knew that, it wouldn't be such a turn-off. So Ragunas and his team added a line of text explaining why the prompt was there, and in a matter of days the number of customers who left the site at that prompt dropped by 75 percent.

The site had already created a unique shopping-basket capability for small business managers. With it, a company could create an online master account and subaccounts for each employee. As supplies are needed during a week or month, the employee simply goes online and adds the item to the shopping list. However, the software is designed so that only one designated manager, usually the CEO or office manager, can approve and send in the final order. This allows that manager to peruse the order list and approve all purchases without the tedious, time-consuming need to sign off on each order from each individual. Though it sounds like a simple tool, it is actually a software tool for which big businesses spend a lot of money to incorporate into their internal procurement systems.

Lauren Marrus, founder and chief executive officer of Chelsea-Paper.com, an online custom stationery Website in Manhattan, says that Staples.com has changed her buying habits for office supplies. "I don't know what I would do without the Website," Marrus says. "We are directly across the street from a Staples store, but we use Staples.com." Marrus says the master account ordering system has made it possible to control costs and manage the buying process "without putting a lot of senior management time into the process."

The site also offers customers e-mail reminders of products that will likely need to be reordered on a regular basis as well as notices of specials on those products or related products.

With the redesign, Staples.com sought to make the site easier to search and navigate. The idea has been to reduce the number of clicks a customer must make to buy a product and minimize the number of pages to find a product. For example, Staples designers noticed in tracking its customers that many kept physical lists of items needed and then typed them onto the site. To relieve that, Staples.com put its shopping cart feature on the right side of every page, viewable no matter how many pages into the site a user delved. That way, the shopping list is always in sight and updated as the user buys an item. If the customer is planning to shop over the course of several visits to the site, the system automatically returns the shopping cart list as it was when the customer logged off. Now, instead of having to click through three or four screens to add an item to the cart, it is always there and updated.

However successful Staples.com is in selling the company's core products, its potential to expand Staples' business model is even more profound. "With the Internet, we become a full-service provider," Stemberg states.

Staples has already been in the services business, for example, offering small business customers everything from payroll and accounting services to Sprint long-distance services. Buy a fax machine from Staples, and you can also buy Sprint, for which Staples gets a commission. But Stemberg points out that the services end of the business was not deftly administered and therefore languished as a business opportunity. "We used to sign people up on a keypad, but we had so much information that we ended up losing a third of the orders," Stemberg says. Customers in the store would find a kiosk touting services and offering an 800 number to call for more information. "That's not going to sell services," Stemberg says. Today, customers sign up for services online in a closed-loop interactive process, and no orders are lost.

With the Website, Staples has upped the ante and made services its next frontier. Through Staples.com, customers can buy payroll, accounting, insurance, office services, and sales and marketing tools, as well as dozens of other services that small businesses generally find difficult to access. "On the Internet, you can be overwhelmed by choices," says Melissa Shore. "Because buyers trust that Staples has done its homework to pick the right business partners, it is like a Staples seal of approval."

Using its brand name and its leverage as a major supplier, Staples finds the best vendors, negotiates the best deals, and brings buyers and sellers together online. For example, small businesses often want to do concept testing or focus groups but cannot afford such high-ticket marketing services. Using the Staples.com site, a customer can run an online survey or focus group and get instant feedback, Lewis says. In seeking professional business services, small business owners often have no idea how to choose or even where to look for suppliers. With the Staples "stamp of approval" as a guide, the customer feels comfortable making such a decision.

Staples.com also offers customers the ability to use Register.com to register their own Websites. Staples owns 10 percent of Register.com and thus gets royalties and equity in the business. "For us, it's just the beginning of doing for small business in services what we did for them in product years ago," Lewis says.

Translating the Brand Online

Like other radicals, Staples is successfully translating its vaunted brand online. Lewis points out that recreating brand attributes online is a key focus of her group. She says there are both *emotional* attributes and *practical* attributes. The practical attributes associated with Staples have to do with saving time and money and building a trust in the long-term relationship with the company. It's about offering good prices, good information, and good services—"doing what we said we were going to do," says Lewis. On the emotional side, Staples has spent large sums on massive advertising campaigns to say to its customers "we understand it can be a hassle running a business or being part of a business, so we're here to make it easier." Using humor and empathy, the advertising has started to incorporate and highlight the Staples.com component of the message.

"In order to translate your brand, you need to be as smart online as you are offline," Lewis says. "You need to provide good images, good experiences, good information, and an easy shopping experience, along with the right tools." In addition, she adds, a site must have the right tone in the way it speaks to a customer—whether in a product description or an e-mail—because businesspeople don't want a lot of "cute stuff"; they want information.

"We have always followed the principle both offline and online that there is no silver bullet in marketing," Lewis says. "You don't just throw $3 million at a Super Bowl ad and expect they will come—nevermind come to buy." Much of the success in translating the brand comes from a direct marketing mentality, she adds.

From her years at Staples, for example, Lewis understood that the company's bloodline was as a direct marketer. In its earliest days, with a single store in Boston and well before it could afford a national television advertising campaign, Staples launched a direct marketing campaign by giving out Staples membership cards in exchange for names, addresses, and zip codes. Thus was born Staples' first customer database.

Lewis brought a direct marketer's mentality to her new role. Mass media campaigns would be crucial, but direct marketing would remain a key element for the new organization. Indeed, Lewis is such a big believer in direct marketing that when she hired a chief marketing officer for Staples.com, she hired a woman with 20 years of direct marketing experience.

"The true promise of the Internet is the ability to understand a lot about your customers so you can serve them better online in ways that are impossible offline," Lewis says. Having a channel available 24 hours a day, seven days a week, allowing people to shop how they want and when they want, online, offline, by phone, is a powerful equation and translates into sales. "You give me a good way to shop with you and I'm spending more," Lewis says.

Perhaps most important to translating the brand is putting the focus on customer service, something e-business retailers have routinely neglected. Lewis points to a survey of dot.com retailers by Forrester Research in Cambridge, Massachusetts. In terms of strategic priorities for the year 2000, raising customer service ranked fourth, with less than half the retailers surveyed even calling it a priority.

Though Lewis acknowledges that profitability is several years away for Staples.com, she says a more important measure right now is positive gross profit, a measure of how much it costs to sell and deliver a product. Right now, Staples.com is at 20 percent positive gross profit, and viewed in a steady-state moving forward, both Lewis and Stemberg are confident that profitability is inevitable and that the online unit will become a key contributor to the bottom line.

Having the chief executive as an enthusiastic participant is also crucial to success. Stemberg calls Staples.com "an entrepreneur's dream. You can make decisions and see the answer almost within 24 hours and change how you are going to do business," he says. "If you are in the automobile business and design a new car, you aren't sure if you are going to make the thing for five years. Here you get answers pretty quick. This takes it from three- to four-month cycles down to three- or four-day cycles."

Nothing, as the old adage says, succeeds like success. For Staples.com, long-term viability will be measured in profits and in the value proposition for customers. E-business winners, especially in retail, will emerge from those organizations that best marry the attributes of all their channels. Understanding that already gives Staples.com a lead in a long race.

Get Radical Now

With these case studies, our intention was to provide a wealth of examples of how some of the best thinkers are embracing the Internet and e-business. But as with most case studies, the key questions you should be asking are, What does this mean for me and my company? What can I take away and put to use on Monday morning?

Though the companies in our case studies are well into their e-business futures, we believe the curtain has barely risen on the e-business extravaganza. For example, a recent survey of 100 energy companies by Chart-well, Inc., revealed that the majority has only a rudimentary Web presence without sophisticated online customer service. According to the survey, 83 percent of utility companies don't even have a senior manager who oversees e-commerce. This slow-moving approach to e-business is not recommended, and it gives radicals like Enron the opportunity to sprint out ahead. Radicals in every industry are using the Internet to change the rules, and those who continue to hesitate are at risk of becoming new-millennium also-rans.

But the first key message is that there is still time to get in the game. All businesspeople who are sitting in their executive suites wondering whether they've missed their e-business chance need only understand how much at the beginning of the process we truly are. According to *Fortune,* "The dot.com era is over. The Internet era is just getting started. Having failed to overturn the industrial order, the Internet is now looking suspiciously like an enabler of that order."

Or read the words of David Wessel in the *Wall Street Journal,* written not in 1996 but in January 2001: "Until it generates profits as well as page views, the Internet won't realize its potential to improve our lives. No profits, no progress. The potency of the technology is unquestionable. Reorganizing business and society to harness it is hard." According to Oxford University economic historian Paul David, "People underestimate the length of time it takes to discover a new business model."

So much has happened in so short a time that we tend to lose sight of the enormity of the e-business transformation. There are, as the poem goes, miles to go before we sleep. As companies assess their own e-business plans, it is the time to ask, Are you ready to get radical?

Having read the case studies of our radical organizations, you should clearly understand that e-business opportunities are rich and potent, perhaps now more so than ever. In 2000 *BusinessWeek* inaugurated its "Web Smart 50" list to spotlight "real, live, revenue- and profit-producing companies that are changing the way they do business."

Among the Web Smart are Zara, the Spanish clothing design manufacturer that is using the Web to turn out just-in-time fashions every two weeks rather than following the traditional four-season fashion cycle; Miller Brewing Co., which uses the Internet to monitor production lines for breakdowns and quality problems and has reduced the number of defects from 100 per batch to 2 at a bottling line in Eden, North Carolina; and Hallmark Cards, which is using the Web to link mom-and-pop shops with suppliers and anticipates that profits in these stores will rise 10 percent to 15 percent, generating $200 million in annual earnings for Hallmark by 2004.

Another radical in the group is Nestle, the 134-year-old Swiss conglomerate that sells everything from chocolate to Friskies pet food to Perrier. With 230,000 employees in 83 countries, this once-staid $50 billion mega-corporation is changing nearly every aspect of the way it does business—from supplies to marketing—using the Internet. According to *BusinessWeek,* because of new e-commerce initiatives as well as other restructuring efforts, Nestle's net profit rose nearly 35 percent in the first half of 2000 to $1.7 billion. This stodgy giant is now a top stock performer in Europe. "For big companies like us, the Internet is particularly good because it shakes you up," Mario Corti, Nestle's chief financial officer and head of its Internet efforts, told *BusinessWeek.*

Then there is Dell Computer Corporation, which along with Cisco Systems and Amazon.com pioneered the art of doing business online. Speaking at Microsoft's CEO Summit in 2000, Michael Dell said, "The direct model helped reinvent the industry. What we are now calling the *Internet*-direct model has taken this to a new level by increasing speed across our business and reducing friction. It takes our build-to-order process to the next level, removes defects from the process, and overall just delivers a better experience." Dell Computer now completes more than 90 percent of its orders online and has reduced inventories to eyebrow-raising levels—in some cases, factories order just enough supplies to keep production running for the next two hours.

A Radical Checklist

If you are an executive struggling with the e-business quandary, reading success stories may be a double-edged sword. The lessons are invaluable, but it feels bad to read about others succeeding at something that is keeping you awake every night. There is hope however. Because the game is very much still in progress, it is difficult to declare winners. After a long bull market, an economic downturn forced business reality to sink back in. The concept of business cycles has returned and has deflated over-valued companies, both dot.coms and traditional bricks-and-mortar businesses. In any downturn, there is opportunity, especially in e-business, which remains an evolving endeavor, subject not only to mood swings in the market but to changing technologies and emerging customer bases as well.

What we have presented in Radical E are companies that have gotten the basics right, that have established table stakes to the game, and that have met or exceeded those stakes. The lessons they offer are many, but the foundation for every radical e-business player is simply a commitment to move forward and stay focused. Companies that have just begun to build an integrated e-business strategy should assess this basic tenet. In order to bring radical E to your company, you need to ask yourself a few key questions:

- Is your CEO really leading the e-business effort? Is this a top-priority corporate initiative, or is the CEO simply paying lip service to what he or she perceives as the latest business revolution? While we have demonstrated that one resourceful individual, like Louise Kitchen at Enron or Jeanne Lewis at Staples.com, can kickstart the e-business effort, we believe that these companies would remain stuck if not for charismatic CEOs like Jeff Skilling and Tom Stemberg, who not only fully embrace e-business, but fully understand it as well.

- Are you overanalyzing the e-business initiative? Is your organization insisting on a perfect e-business plan before launching it? As we showed with companies like General Motors and Nortel, there is great advantage to getting into the game, albeit with a clear plan, rather than waiting for a perfect solution that is illusive at best. The Internet is a moving target, and those who are hesitating in hopes of finding perfection will only watch the target disappear over the horizon. The most successful radicals understand that you can add and tweak the technology as you move forward. It's better to launch and then learn.

- Is your CIO a savvy business partner in the e-business scheme? Too many Internet initiatives get co-opted into the information technology morass. There is no time for one- or two-year-long technology projects in this landscape. CIOs like Ralph Syzgenda at GM and Jon Ricker at Victoria's Secret have been key catalysts to the emergence of e-business because they understand that the business piece is more important than the e-piece of the equation.

- Is your corporate culture ready for e-business? Technology is important, but industry experts say that entrenched bureaucracies and existing business practices do more to block successful e-business transformations than anything else. Progressive Insurance has to find ways to incorporate the independent agents who sell its auto insurance into its e-business efforts in order to reach a successful e-business solution. Staples set up its own dot.com company within the company but had to settle an angry fight over free coffee, of all things, to move the organization forward. Don't underestimate the cultural ramifications of establishing an e-business unit. They can derail the most clever and well thought out plans.

- Are you using the Internet to build a community? Radicals understand that the real power of the Internet lies in its ability to reach out and communicate across local, national, and international boundaries to bring people in. One of the key factors in e-business success is marketing, and one of the key factors in marketing success is building communities around your brand. GE Plastics has built a community around its GE Polymerland Website by offering far more than transactions. Professionals in the industry can chat with designers or with each other, and can search industry job postings through a partnership with Monster.com. David Bowie not only participates regularly in chatrooms on his Website with members of BowieNet but also offers members exclusive access to recording sessions, archives of his music, and a vast array of other Bowie-related happenings.

- Did you start with a roadmap to profitability? Amazon.com may have changed the world when it comes to e-business, but its business model is not for the faint of heart or light of wallet. Radicals know that online profitability may take time, but they pinpoint where it is on the horizon and aim for it. Victoria's Secret's Website planners designed the site with a path to profitability, which they achieved almost from the outset. For some, the Web simply replaces other means of doing business, and thus the profits will come one way or the other. But for most e-businesses, the goal must be to use the Web to take out costs and add in revenues and profits.

Like other radical endeavors, we fully expect that what we view as radical today will become mainstream within three years. By its very nature, the Internet sprang up and became a living, expanding organism well before most companies were ready for it. In an enlightened age, when we are ridiculed if we don't fully embrace every new technology, the posturing to appear Web savvy has often obscured the difficulties in integrating this powerful yet amorphous new creation.

As David Wessel said, the hard part is reorganizing business and society to harness this creation. The good news is that every one of the companies in our case studies struggled along the way to e-business. Some may still discover that they must rethink parts of their strategies to keep moving forward. The executives portrayed in these pages didn't think of themselves as radical until we showed up and applied the label. Sometimes it is hard to see out of the trenches where much of business is fought and compare your strategic moves to others.

But the more important point here is that none of these companies set out to be radical for its own sake. They all behaved as business pioneers have done for decades: They saw an opportunity and seized it. They were radical because seizing opportunity in this case meant redefining the way they were doing business. They shook up not just their own organizations but their industries as well. As you push forward, remember what Jack Welch of GE said: "Seeing reality today means accepting the fact that e-business is here. It's not coming. It's not a thing of the future. It's here. There is no time for lengthy evaluations of Internet opportunities. We have to pounce—every day!" We agree wholeheartedly. It's time to get radical and pounce.

INDEX

Abeelen, Peit C. van, 38
ADC Inc., 32
Adweek, on Victoria's Secret Valentine's Day 1999 online fashion show, 64
Airline travel:
  and the Internet, 146–147
  Jupiter Research on, 146
Allstate Insurance, 165
Amazon.com:
  and business-to-consumer (B2C) selling, 34
  download time of, 72
  and e-business, 197
  effect of on bookselling, 175
  inability of to turn a profit, 67
  marketing strategy of, 149
  as a Web-only company, 13
America Online, 18, 124
America West Airlines, 147
American Airlines, 147, 148
Autobytel, 124
Automobile insurance:

consumer attitudes toward, 164–165
consumer trends in, 170–171
Automobile purchasing, and the Internet, 122–123

Baan systems, 42
Banks, Tyra, 64
Barnes & Noble, 76
Bath and Body Works, 67
Bauer, Alan, 159, 160, 163, 165, 169, 172
Bay Networks:
  CEO Forum of, 88
  corporate culture of, 22
  merger with Nortel, 21
  Nortel's acquisition of, 87–89
Beach Boys, 103
Bell Labs, 85
Berra, Yogi, 61
Bialosky, William, 162
Bing Group, 133
Blaine, Scott, 32, 37

Blaire, Anne Marie, 68
Bolouri, Chahram, 95
Borg-Warner Chemicals, 27
Bowie, David:
  career of, 101
  Chris Mitchell on, 100
  and consumer empowerment, 19
  and the Diamond Dog Tour, 102
  and e-business, 15
  "Fame," 101
  on the Internet, 99
  as the Internet Music Man, 99
  as an Internet pioneer, 16
  and involvement in e-business,
    103–104
  and involvement in Internet op-
    portunities, 100, 106
  "Let's Dance," 102
  "Modern Love," 102
  reaction of to the Internet, 12
  and the Serious Moonlight Tour, 102
  and son Zowie (Duncan), 102
  "Space Oddity," 101
  "Telling Lies," 103
  as the Thin White Duke, 99
  and transformation of music
    business, 103–104
  and Virgin Records, 104
  "Young Americans," 102
  and Write a Song with David
    Bowie competition, 108–109
  as Ziggy Stardust, 99, 101
Bowie at the Beeb, 107
BowieBanc, 111–112
BowieNet:
  Ask David feature of, 100, 108
  Chris Mitchell on, 16, 108, 110
  continual update of, 112–113
  cost of, Robert Goodale on, 110
  and customer relations, 106–109
  description of, 100
  development of, 104–105
  Karma feature of, 108
  live performances on, 108
  and Lucent Technologies, 109
  Pam Spevak on, 111
  praise of, 106–107
  tools used to assess, 104–105

Broadvision, 43
Brock, Phyllis, 87, 91–92
Bryant, Kobe, 111
Buick, 117
Buick Rendezvous, 137
Burroughs, William, 102
Business 2.0, on General Motors,
  117–118
Business-to-business (B2B) Web-
  sites, 28, 50
Business-to-consumer (B2C) Web-
  sites:
  and Amazon.com, 34
  success of, 66
BusinessWeek, on the General Mo-
  tors Aztek, 135
BuyPower:
  partnerships of with other com-
    panies, 126
  success of, 126

Cable television, 68
Cadillac Evoq, 137
Car insurance. *See* Automobile in-
  surance
Cars.com, 124
Chambers, John, 84
Cheaptickets.com, 146
Chelsea-Paper.com, 189
Cher, 111
Chevrolet Avalanche, 137
Chevrolet Celta, 126
Chevrolet SSR, 137
Chief executive officer (CEO), im-
  portance of leadership, 16
Christensen, Clayton, 22, 85
Christmas 1999, and on-time deliv-
  ery failure, 39
Cisco Systems:
  as an e-business pioneer, 197
  and electronic ordering, 89
  John Chambers and success of, 84
  and Nortel Networks, 81
  and not-invented-here (NIH) syn-
    drome, 21
Clausewitz, Carl von, 4
Clemmons, Lynda, success of at En-
  ron, 59–60

Clickpaper.com, 58
CNF Inc., 136
CommerceOne, 43, 132
Compaq Computer Corporation, 123
Compuserve, 163
Computer reservation systems
    (CRSs), 142, 143, 155
Computerworld, David Bowie in,
    100–101, 104, 105
Conner, Bill, 85, 96
Continental Airlines, 147
Corporate culture:
    and e-business success, 49
    impact on e-business, 40–43
    See also under specific corporations
Corti, Mario, on the e-business suc-
    cess of Nestle, 197
Corvette Z06, 137
Covisint:
    and e-business, 117
    e-business debut of, 7
    formation of, 35, 115–117, 131–134
    impact of on auto industry, 133–134
Cox, David, 57–59
Crosby, Stills, Nash, and Young, 105
Cure, the, and the Internet, 106
Customer loyalty, and online shop-
    ping, 13
Customer relations:
    Bill Conner on, 96
    importance of, 18
Customer.com, 144

DaimlerChrysler, 116, 124
Datek, 111
David, Paul, 196
DavidBowie.com:
    description of, 107
    See also Bowie, David; BowieNet
Dell Computer Corporation:
    as an e-business pioneer, 119, 197
    Michael Dell on, 187
    and transition to e-business, 10, 197
Dell, Michael, 187, 197
Delta Airlines:
    brand identity of, 148
    and customer satisfaction, 146
    and e-business, 147

Deregulation:
    of the electric power industry, 52
    of the natural gas industry, 51–52
Design for Six Sigma (DFSS), 40.
    See also Six Sigma
Digital commerce, Bill Gates on, 14
Direct TV, 128
Disruptive customer, value of, 22
Disruptive technology, 22
DLJ Direct, 111
Dot.coms:
    as conduits for big business, 36
    end of era, 196
    financial crash of, 87, 181
    mania of, 2, 3, 6, 12, 41, 147, 180
    revolution created by, 66, 73
    start-ups and relation to big busi-
        ness, 9, 10, 34
Double entry, as a problem for cus-
    tomers, 37
Dylan, Bob, 111
Dynamic routing, 136

"E Gang," the, 125. *See also* Cham-
    bers, John; Skilling, Jeffrey;
    Welch, John (Jack)
EBay:
    success of, 132
    as a Web-only company, 13
E-business:
    agility in, 20
    and customer service, 93–94
    Dan Garretson on, 123, 137
    and Herb Kelleher, 5, 140
    and Jeffrey Skilling, 5, 15, 104
    and John Roth, 5, 20, 93
    and John (Jack) Welch, 5–7, 104
    Kevin Krone on, 145
    and Leslie Wexner, 1, 5, 6, 67
    and Marcia Stepanek, 7
    as a means of transforming Gen-
        eral Motors, 117–119
    and Peter Foss, 37
    and Peter Lewis, 5
    and Rick Wagoner, 5, 115, 117, 118
    strategies of, 92–93
    and Tom Stemberg, 5, 176
EDS, 119–120, 129

E-GM:
  creation and implementation of,
    117, 122, 124–127
    Mark Hogan on, 125
    Rick Wagoner on, 129
  and customer relations, 128–129
  impact on General Motors, 127–
    129
  lessons learned from, 127–129
80–20 rule, 95
EMI records, 104, 113
Enron Broadband Services:
  history of, 56–57
  and Lucent Technologies, 57
Enron Corporation:
  and Blockbuster, 57
  and business-to-business (B2B)
    Websites, 50
  and career of David Cox, 57–58
  and competitors, 48
  corporate culture of, 49, 58–61
  creation of a telecommunications
    market, Jeffrey Skilling on, 57
  and deregulation of natural gas
    industry, 52
    David Cox on, 59
  e-business debut of, 7, 47
  and e-business opportunities, 5,
    15
  e-business success of, 49, 101
  employee stock option plans
    (ESOP), 60
  employees of, 58–62
  entry into pulp and paper busi-
    ness, 57–58
  financial success of, 48, 53
  first-mover advantage of, 49, 56
  history of, 51–52
  and initial public offerings, 60
  and Jeffrey Skilling, 51, 53
  Jim Walker on, 48, 54, 59
  as a loose/tight organization, 20,
    60, 61
    Jeffrey Skilling on, 60–61
  and Michael Milken, 51
  and new commodity markets, 47
  and the New Economy, 54–55
  online strategy of, 54
  as a radical business, 47, 159, 195
  reaction of to the Internet, 53
  and Richard Kinder, 51
  transition of to e-business, 143
Enron Net Works, 48
EnronOnline:
  corporate creativity of, 56
  debut of, 53
  and internal recruiting, 61
  as part of Enron Net Works, 48
  success of, 50–54
Enterprise resource planning
  (ERP) systems, 42
Ewing, Patrick, 111
Expedia.com, 146, 156
Express, 67
Express Quote, Alan Bauer on, 165

Fast Company, on General Electric,
  28
Finkelman, Dan, 63, 65, 68, 70–71,
  72, 74, 78
Forbes, on General Motors, 125
Forrester Research:
  on Enron, 48
  Internet predictions of, 6
  predictions of for the online mar-
    ketplace, 34
Fortune:
  on Enron, 49, 52, 58
  on the Internet era, 196
  on Peter Lewis, 161
  on Southwest Airlines, 140, 144
Foss, Peter, 16, 27, 28, 31, 37, 45,
Frederick's of Hollywood, 69

Gap, the, 69
Garretson, Dan, 119, 123, 137
Gartner Group, and predictions for
  online market, 34
GE. *See* General Electric
GE Plastics. *See* General Electric
  Plastics
GE Polymerland. *See* General Elec-
  tric Polymerland
General Electric:
  and ADC, Inc., 32
  and Apple Computers, 30

and building an online community, 33–34
business initiatives of:
the buy side, 30
the make side, 30
the sell side, 30
and business-to-business (B2B) commerce, 28
and Chris Groszyck, 32
competition on, 43
and customer SWAT teams, 43–45
and dot.com competitors, 35
double entry, Scott Blaine on, 37
and Dow Chemicals, 34
and Dupont, 34
e-business plan of, 41
and Ford Motors, 30
and GE.com, 41
and Hoover vacuum cleaners, 30
and John (Jack) Welch, 16, 26, 28
mentoring within, 41
and Monster.com, 33
and Motorola, 30, 32
and Nokia, 30
and the Old Economy, 28
online success of, 27
and Pam Wickham, 41
and Peter Foss, 27, 28
and Saturn vehicles, 30
Scott Blaine on, 32
separation of e-business from bricks-and-mortar business, 42
and Sony, 30
technological knowledge of employees, 123
tenets of, 25
and Ticona, 34
transition of to e-business, 10, 26–27
and Gary Podesta, 36
John (Jack) Welch on, 38
and Tupperware, 30
General Electric Plastics:
business initiative of, 30
corporate culture of, 37
and e-business, 27
e-business debut of, 7
Gary Podesta on, 29, 34

and Gary Rogers, 35
innovations of, 35–36
and Jeffrey Immelt, 29
on-time delivery of, 21, 39
and purchase order system, 37
General Electric Polymerland:
attributes of, 33
and competition, 43
and customer education, 43
and customer service, 32, 39
development of, 27–28
and initial public offerings, 45
low cost of, 42
and online assistance wizards, 44
on-time delivery of, 40
revenue of, 33
and Six Sigma, 40
success of, 28
General Motors:
and America Online, 124
approach toward e-business, 17
and Autobytel, 124
and Cars.com, 124
and CNF Inc., 136
and Compaq Computer Corporation, 123
corporate culture of, 127–129
and Covisint deal, 132
Harold Kutner on, 115
creation of technology leadership, 120–124
and culture of the Internet, 137–138
and customer expectations online, 132
and customer relations, 121
Harold Kutner on, 134
and customer relationship to product, 136–138
and DaimlerChrysler, 124
Dan Garretson on, 119
design and production cycles of, 135
and Direct TV, 128
and e-business, 5, 15, 23, 95
Harold Kutner on, 123, 124
and e-business debut of, 7
and EDS, 119–120

General Motors (*continued*)
  first-mover attitude of, 117
  image of, 118–119
  and information technology re-
    structuring, 119–124
  innovation of, Mark Hogan on,
    137
  and Internet training, 123
  and Lear, 133–134
  and the New Economy, 116–119
  old bureaucratic style of, 118–119
  and the Old Economy, 116
  and online automobile purchas-
    ing, 134–135
  and order to delivery, 134
  and process information officers,
    121
  relationship of with suppliers,
    132–133
  and Rick Wagoner on "one-
    company" philosophy, 121
  and Socrates program, 124
  and Sun Microsystems, 124
  transition of to e-business, 10
    Mark Hogan on, 128
    Ralph Syzgenda on, 119–121, 123
  and Vector SCM, 136
  vehicle delivery time of, 136
  and Verizon Wireless, 130
Gibson, Charles, 64
GM. *See* General Motors
GM Aztek:
  commercial failure of, 135
  Mark Hogan on, 137
GM Brazil, and the Internet, 126
GM BuyPower, creation of, 125
GM X-Games, 137
Gomez Advisors, and Progressive
  Corporation, 158
Gomez.com, on Southwest, 149
Goodale, Robert, 105, 110, 112
Goodman, Shira, 185
Gros, Thomas, 56
Groszcyk, Chris, 32
GTE, 111

Hallmark Cards, 196
Hanson, 111

Harvard Business Review, 6
Henri Bendel, 67
Hertz, 146
Hitachi, 95
Hocking, David, 162
Hoffman, Mark, 116
Hogan, Mark, 125, 128, 134–135,
  137
Home Depot, transition of to
  e-business, 10
Horizontal integration, and Enron,
  55
Hotwire, 147
House, David, 88
Hughes Electronics, 129
Human interaction, Alan Bauer on
  the importance of, 172

IBM, 95
Ideal Steel, 133
Immelt, Jeffrey, 29
Initial public offerings:
  and Enron, 60
  and General Electric Polymer-
    land, 45
  Peter Foss on, 45
Innovator's Dilemma, The, 22, 85
Insurance agents, transition of to e-
  business, 170–171
Internet:
  and building customers around a
    brand, 17–18
  as a business opportunity, 13
  and car insurance comparison
    shopping, 165–166
  culture of:
    Dan Garretson on, 137
    and General Motors, 137–138
    Leslie Wexner on, 19, 64, 79
    Ralph Syzgenda on, 137
    Rick Wagoner on, 137
  customer expectations of, 20–21
  and customer experience, 18–19
  and customer relations, 37
  Dan Finkelman on, 65, 70–71, 74
  and Gary Podesta, 31, 33, 35
  Herb Kelleher on, 139
  and Kenneth Lay, 48

as a means to increase profit, 19
and Peter Foss, 31
phases of, 14
reaction of Jeffrey Skilling to, 12
reaction of John (Jack) Welch to,
    12
reaction of Nortel to, 12
reaction of Rick Wagoner to, 12
and Robert Goodale, 105
Robert LaFleur on, 148
and supplier expenses, 133
"suspension of politeness" on,
    166
and Tom Stemberg, 175, 184, 190
Intimate Brands:
    move of to e-business, 69–71
    sales of, 64
    success of, 67
    as a within-company Website
        leader, 77

Jordan, Michael, 111
Jupiter Research, 66, 146, 184

Keiretsu model of business, 132
Kelleher, Herb, 5, 16, 139, 140, 143,
    144,
Kelley, Brian, 116
Kenney, David, 6
Kernkraut, Steve, 65, 69
Keynote Systems, 21, 72
Kinder, Richard, 51
King, Rollin, 140
Kirkelie, Susan, 153
Kitchen, Louise, 49–50
Klum, Heidi, 64
Krone, Kevin, 142, 143, 144, 145,
    149, 150, 153–154
Kunter, Harold, 115, 123, 132, 134

LaFleur, Robert, 146, 148
Lane, Ray, 116
Lane Bryant, 67
Launch and learn:
    as an e-business tactic, 17
    and General Motors, 76, 119, 128,
        129
Lay, Kenneth, 48, 57

Lear, 133–134
Lennon, John, 102
Lerner New York, 67
Lewis, Jeanne, 178–179, 180, 186–
    187, 191
Lewis, Peter, 5, 103, 157, 161, 162,
    164, 167, 168
Limited Technical Services (LTS),
    71, 73
Limited, Inc:
    the success of, 1, 67
    and technology, 68
Loose/tight organization:
    advantages of, 20
    and Enron, 20, 60, 61
Love Field, 139, 141
Lucent Technologies, 57, 81, 109
Lycos, 111

Macys.com, download time of, 72
Marriott, 146
Marrus, Lauren, 189–190
Marshall, John F., 6
Masters, Tom, 169–170
McCartney, Paul, 103
Mentoring, 41
Mercata, 132
Merger, of AOL and Time Warner,
    18
Milken, Michael, 51
Miller Brewing Co., 196
Mitchell, Chris, 16, 100, 108, 110
Moody Blues, 103
Motorola, and General Electric, 32
Murray, Anne, 143

Napster, 103
National Association of Indepen-
    dent Insurers (NAII), 160
Neilsen/Net ratings, 158
Nestle Corporation, 196–197
New Economy:
    and Enron, 54–55
    and General Motors' transition
        to, 116–119
    Jeffrey Skilling on, 55
    and Nortel, 81
    strategies in, 6

New York Times, on Six Sigma, 38
Nichols, Grace, 68, 76
Nicoll, Chris, 84, 89
Nissan, 117
Nortel Networks:
  assets of, 90–94
  and bands, 90
  as a Canadian company, 86–87
  and the challenge of e-business, 96–97
  Chris Nicoll on, 84, 89
  and Cisco Systems, 81, 83
  and "clicks and conversations," 96
  corporate agility of, 84
  and disruptive customers, 94–97
  and e2open, 95
  and e-business, 5, 95
  e-business debut of, 7
  e-business development of, 21
  engineering culture of, 85–88
    John Roth on, 86
  and extranets, 82
  and finding and winning disruptive customers, 94
  and gate reviews, 89
  and Hitachi, 95
  and IBM, 95
  Internet development of, 82
  and Lucent Technologies, 81
  and the New Economy, 81
  and not-invented-here (NIH) syndrome, 85–86
  online customer relations of, 96
  and online sales of merchandise, 95
  and outside contractors and Website development, 91–92
  and outsourcing, 89
  overhaul of old corporate culture, 83
  philosophy of e-business training and development, 91–92
  relation to Bell Labs, 85
  restructuring of, 88–90
  and rumor mill, John Roth on, 90
  and slowing economy, 82
  success of, 81, 82
  John Roth on, 84–85
  Steve Santana on, 83–84
  and Toshiba, 95
  transition of to e-business, 10
    and John Roth, 12, 83
    Phyllis Brock on, 87
  Website of, 87–88
Northwest Airlines, 147
Not-invented-here (NIH) syndrome:
  and big business, 21–22
  Bill Conner on, 85
  and Cisco Systems, 21
  and Nortel Networks, 85–86

Office Depot, 175
Office Max, 175
Office supply stores, and the Internet, 177
Old Economy:
  and General Electric, 28
  and General Motors, 116
Oldsmobile, discontinuation of, 116–117
Omnexus.com, formation of, 35
One-to-one marketing:
  Melissa Shore on, 152
  and Southwest Airlines, 150, 151
Online retail:
  automobile purchasing, Mark Hogan on, 134–135
  experience of, 66–69
  ordering rates of, Ken Weil on, 75
  shopping habits and predictions of Jupiter Research, 184
OnStar program:
  as breakthrough technology, 17
  capability and potential of, 130–131
  creation of, 129–130
  and customer relations, 131
  General Motors' use of, 117
  Mike Peterson on, 130
  and partnership with EDS, 129
  and partnership with Hughes Electronics, 129
  potential of, 130–131
  and Virtual Advisor feature, 130

Optical networks, installation of, 95–96

Orbitz, 147

Outsourcing:
and General Motors, 120
Phyllis Brock on, 91–92

Paine Webber, on Enron, 58

Pearce, Harry, 119–120

Perot, H. Ross, 118

PersonalProgressive, and insurance purchasing, 158

Peterson, Mike, 130

Petty, Tom, 111

Plastics industry, and General Electric, 34

PlasticsNet, 35

Plzak, Tim, on Website design, 72

Podesta, Gerry P., 29, 31, 33–37, 41–43

Pontiac, 117

Predictions for online spending, and Jupiter Research, 66

Presley, Elvis, 105

Priceline.com, 13, 146

PricewaterhouseCoopers, 6, 9, 18

Pricing power, and online shopping, 13

Profit and growth, indicators associated with, 13

Progressive Corporation:
approach to insurance, Glenn Renwick on, 160
attitude of toward technology, 170
attitudes of insurance agents toward Progressive, Alan Bauer on, 169
awards won, 158
business philosophy of, and Peter Lewis, 162
and chief executive officer Peter Lewis, 161
and Claims Workbench, 167
as a "clicks-and-mortar" company, 159
and consumer consideration, 159–160
corporate culture of, 159, 162–163, 172

and creation of Express Quote, 165
customer demographics of, 160
and customer relations, 165
Glenn Renwick on, 168
Peter Lewis on, 167, 168
and e-business, 5
e-mail feedback from customers, 166
and expansion of its Internet services, 171–172
Find an Agent application, 169
first-mover advantage of, 166
For Agents Only feature of, 169
history of, 161–163
and Immediate Response Claims Service, 167
and Immediate Response Vehicles, 167, 168
innovations of, 159
Internet claims tracking of, 171–172
Internet practices of, 158–159
keys to e-business success, 160–161
relationship with insurance agents, 169–170
response to Proposition 103, 164, 167
success of, 157
transformation of claim service, 167–168
transition of to e-business, 10, 168–169
Alan Bauer on, 159, 163
Glenn Renwick on, 159
and Peter Lewis, 157
Website design of, Alan Bauer on, 160

Proposition 103, 164, 167

Purchase exchange model, Harold Kutner on, 132

Purchase order systems, Gary Podesta on, 37

Quill.com, 184

Radical business:
characteristics of companies, 11
definition of, 2

Radical E-business (*continued*)
  John (Jack) Welch on, 200
  lessons for, 15–22
  methods to, 8
Radical E:
  as a business method, 3
  checklist for companies, 197–199
  definition of, 9–12
Radicals:
  corporate heritage of, 57
  decision-making tactics of, 75
  Jeffrey Skilling on, 17, 47, 52
  methods of, 22–23, 110
  as nontraditional business
    thinkers, 17
Ragunas, Michael, 185
Rascoff, Joseph, 105, 106
Raymond, Roy, as founder of Victoria's Secret, 69
Razek, Gary, 63–64, 68
Reiner, Gary, 26, 45
Renault, 117
Renwick, Glenn, 103, 159, 160, 164,
  168
Retailers, and cable television, 68
Reuters, 111
Ricker, John, 21, 68
Rogers, Gary L., 35
Rolling Stone Network, 111
Rolling Stones, 103, 105
Roth, John, 5, 12, 16, 81–86, 90, 92,
  93
Roth's Law, 84

Sahlman, William, and Staples' financial direction, 180
Santana, Steve, 83–84
SAP, 42
Saturn vehicles, and Internet sales,
  126
70–30 inventory model, 40
Seybold, Patricia, 144
SFX Entertainment, 111
Sheriff, John, and Enron's e-business, 50
Shopping experience, as entertainment, 79
Shore, Melissa, 152, 177, 179, 191

Silicon Valley culture, 87
Simon, Paul, 105
Six Sigma:
  customer service, 40
  impact on General Electric, 27,
    38–39
  and John (Jack) Welch, 38
  and Motorola, 38
  Peit C. van Abeelen on, 38
  as a quality management tool, 21
Skilling, Jeffrey, 5, 12, 15, 17, 47–53,
  55, 57, 60–61, 104
Sloan, Alfred, 116
Snap-on Tools, transition to e-business, 10
Southwest Airlines:
  advertisements
    television, 145
    Website, 152
  business philosophy of, 141
  and Click 'n Save specials, 145
  and Computer Reservation Systems (CRSs), 142, 143, 155
  corporate image of projected on
    Website, 153–154
  and customer relations, 150
    Robert LaFleur on, 146
  and e-business, 5
  history of, 140–141
  and Iflyswa.com, 143
  "love" theme of, 141
  mission of, 152–153
  and one-to-one marketing, 150,
    151
  and online competition from
    other airlines, 155–156
  online ticket sales of, 23
    Kevin Krone on, 144
  operating procedure of, 141–142
  philosophy of simplicity of, 148–
    149
  profit of from the Internet, 20
    Herb Kelleher on, 144
  purchasing costs of Internet vs.
    outside agent, 144
  Rapid Rewards Program of, 145,
    149, 151
  and Rollin King, 140

and Sabre system, 142
and success of online ticket sales,
139–140
Susan Kirkelie on, 153
and Top9.com, 140
transition of to e-business, 10,
142–144
Herb Kelleher on, 143
Kevin Krone on, 143
vs. auto travel, 141
and Web economics, 144–146
Website design of, 149–150
Southwest.com:
Kevin Krone on, 149, 150
user friendly format of, 148
SPAN, and on-time delivery, 39
Spevak, Pam, 111
Spike, 16
Standard Oil, as a business model,
56
Staples Inc.:
cannibalization within, 184–186
Tom Stemberg on, 185
catalog sales of, 77
and CNET, 182
and consumer empowerment, 19
creation of Internet division and
Jeanne Lewis, 180
and criticism of e-business transition, 177–178
culture clashes within the company, 186–187
customer retention of, 183, 190
and customer service, 192–193
and customer tracking, 185
as a direct marketer, 192
and dot.com mania, 181
and e-business, 5
and evolving customer relations,
178–184
and financial benefits of the Internet, 182–183
and hiring and retention of employees, 180–181
Internet vs. bricks-and-mortar
company, 184–186
Internet vs. catalog division, 181–
185

leadership teams of, 185–186
and Quill.com, 184
and "share of the wallet," 184–186
and Sprint long-distance services,
190
transition of to e-business, 175–
181
and Jeanne Lewis, 178–179
Meg Whitman on, 176
Melissa Shore on, 177
and Michael Ragunas, 185
Shira Goodman on, 185
translation of brand online, 191–
193
Staples.com:
assets of, 188–191
Melissa Shore on, 191
and attraction of customers, 184
corporate culture of, 186–187
and Jeanne Lewis, 186–187
Meg Whitman on, 186–187
customer service of, Jeanne
Lewis on, 191
design of Website, 188–190
and Internet inventory, 183
and online zipcode request, 189
and Register.com, 191
selling the concept of, 182
services of for small businesses,
192
shopping-basket capability of, 189
success of, 176–177
Lauren Marrus on, 189–190
Tom Stemberg on, 193
StaplesLink.com, 184
State Farm Insurance, 165
Steidtmann, Carl, 18
Stein, Gertrude, 3
Stemberg, Tom, 5, 175–177, 184,
190, 193
Stepanek, Marcia, 7
Sun Microsystems, 124
SWABIZ:
Bob Greenlee on, 155
Cathy Spivey on, 155
and Home Depot, 155
increased efficiency of for busi-
ness travelers, 149, 154–155

SWABIZ (*continued*)
  Kevin Krone on, 155
  and Simply Fashion Stores Ltd.,
    155
Syzgenda, Ralph, 119–121, 123, 137

Telecommunications industry:
  and Enron, 56
  Kenneth Lay on, 57
Tepper, Ken, 111
Ticketmaster, 111
Time, and John Roth, 81
Time Warner, 18
Toshiba, 17
TradeXchange, creation of, 132
Travelocity.com, 146, 156
Turney, Sharen, 77
Twain, Mark, 157

Ultrastar:
  and Bill Gaither, 106
  business model of, 109
  formation of, 105–106
  and Hanson, 106
  and Ken Tepper, 111
  and SFX Entertainment, 111
  and sports teams, 106
  and Website creation, 111
United Air Lines:
  brand indentity of, 148
  and e-business, 147
United NewVentures, 147
US Airways Group, 147
USA Today, and David Bowie, 102,
    104, 107
Utility companies, and the Inter-
    net, 195

Vector SCM, 136
Verizon Wireless, 130
Vertical integration:
  and Enron, 54–58
  and Exxon, 55
  theory of, 55, 93
Victoria's Secret:
  catalog
    Dan Finkelman on, 78
    importance of, 70–71

  Internet effects on, 74
  sales vs. Web sales, 77–79
  commitment of to e-business, 1, 2
  and customer relations, 18
  and eight-second rule, 71
  financial success of, 70
  first-mover advantage of, 68
  and global e-business, 78
  history of, 69–70
  and IBM, 73
  Internet strategy of, 64–66
  lessons learned from the Inter-
    net, 65–66
  and men's online buying, 74
  and online customer satisfaction,
    73–75
  online fashion show 2000, 65
  separation of Website from
    bricks-and-mortar company, 76
  and staying on brand, 75–77
  strategy of cohesion, 77–79
  success on the online channel, 79
  as a successful e-business, 101
  Steve Kernkraut on, 65
  and suitability of Internet to its
    product, 70
  Super Bowl 1999 advertisement,
    63
  transition of to e-business, 71–73
  Leslie Wexner on, 68
  Valentine's Day 1999 online fash-
    ion show, 63–64, 73
  Charles Gibson on, 64
  Dan Finkelman on, 63
  Gary Razek on, 63–64
Website
  Dan Finkelman on, 68, 72
  download time of, 21, 72
  electronic sizing featured on,
    75
  Gary Razek on, 68
  virtual modeling featured on,
    75
  Wish List feature of, 74

Wagoner, Rick, 5, 12, 115, 117–119,
    129, 137
Walker, Jim, 48, 54, 59

Wall Street Journal, on General Motors, 136
Walmart.com, download time of, 21, 72
Warhol, Andy, 162
Welch, John (Jack), 5–7, 12, 16, 21, 25, 26, 28, 38, 41, 104, 200
Wessel, David, on e-business, 196, 200
Wexner, Leslie, 1, 5, 6, 19, 63, 64, 67–69,79
Whitman, Meg, 176, 186–187

Whole Foods, transition to e-business, 10
Wickham, Pam, 41
Wiel, Kenneth, 68, 75
World Link, on Enron, 54

Yahoo Internet Life, and David Bowie, 100, 113
Yahoo.com, 149

Zara, 196
Zysblat, William, 105, 106